THE MIND OF
AN ARCHBISHOP

The Mind of
An Archbishop

*A Study of Man's Essential Relationship
to God, Church, Country, and Fellow
Man as Expressed in the Writings of*

THE MOST REV. KARL J. ALTER, D. D., LL. D.

Archbishop of Cincinnati

Golden Jubilee Edition

Foreword: The Most Rev. Paul F. Leibold, D. D., J. C. D.

Editor: The Rev. Maurice E. Reardon, S. T. D.

PRINTED IN THE UNITED STATES OF AMERICA
BY ST. ANTHONY GUILD PRESS, PATERSON, N. J.

FOREWORD

Fifty years ago, on June 4, 1910, Karl Joseph Alter was ordained a priest for the newly erected Diocese of Toledo, Ohio. Just ten days before, the reigning Pontiff, Pope Pius X, had issued an encyclical letter, *Editae Saepe,* commemorating the canonization of our jubilarian's patron saint, St. Charles Borromeo. The same Holy Father, on the occasion of his own fiftieth anniversary of ordination, wrote that "a genuinely good priest is a treasure beyond compare." Our Eternal High Priest, Christ, likened His priests to salt and light — "You are the salt of the earth. . . . You are the light of the world." In these bold metaphors, He would remind His priests of their world-wide mission of bringing His message to the world.

Pope Pius XI, in whose pontificate our jubilarian was raised to the episcopacy, stated in his encyclical on the priesthood, *Ad Catholici Sacerdotii,* December 20, 1935, that he celebrated his own sacerdotal jubilee "as a dutiful tribute of honor to the dignity of the priestly character." His Holiness, referring to the Church as a beacon of truth amid the awful corruption of human malice, declared: "All the good that Christian civilization has brought into the world is due, at least radically, to the work and words of the Catholic priesthood."

Pope Pius XII, in commemorating his own golden jubilee, issued an encyclical on the priesthood just three days before our jubilarian was installed as Archbishop of Cincinnati, September 26, 1950. Therein, the late Holy Father, mindful of

v

the priest as an "alter Christus," reiterated the solemn words of his commission from Christ: "As the Father has sent Me, I also send you"; "He who hears you, hears Me."

The Most Reverend Karl J. Alter, as a priest, a Bishop, and an Archbishop, has ever been mindful that his priestly office obliges him to proclaim the truth fearlessly, with Christ-like firmness, in the face of all opposition that might arise from purely earthly considerations or lack of appreciation. He recognizes that if men are to act and to live as followers of Christ, both society at large and the individual members of it must come to know Christ and His teaching as it applies to the world of our day. God has given this priest extraordinary powers of perception, both as to the basic causes of the problems that beset our world, and as to their solution on the basis of His unchanging principles. He has endowed him, moreover, with the no less extraordinary power of presenting these truths in an orderly manner, with such clarity as to render them at once a challenge to the intellectuals, and an open vista to the simplest of God's children.

We who are privileged to labor for Christ and His Church under this great prelate join him in his prayers of praise and gratitude to God for a half century as "another Christ" — sanctifier, ruler, and teacher — and, in our gratitude, we thank the provident God for this collection of Archbishop Alter's writings, trusting that, reading and referring to them, we may continue to be guided by the light they give, and savored by the salt they contain.

† PAUL F. LEIBOLD
Auxiliary Bishop of Cincinnati

June 4, 1960

A WORD OF EXPLANATION

The history of a diocese is, to no small degree, recorded in the manuscripts of its Bishops written over the years of their episcopal jurisdiction. The official statements and addresses of the Bishops contain their thinking on the major issues that faced the Church in the days of their episcopacy. It seems fitting that a permanent printed form be given to such writings so that there will be no lack of essential source material when the time comes to compile the complete history of the diocese. It is indeed regrettable when such records are not kept and given permanency; for, lacking them, the historian to come must approximate and improvise. Printed and preserved records are the researcher's delight and the historian's right arm, and it is mainly for this reason that the present volume is being published.

There are, however, other reasons for this publication, which, while secondary, are far from incidental. The questions that are dealt with by the Bishops, even within the limits of their own jurisdiction, most often have far more than a mere local or regional interest. The analyses and distinctions they make and the opinions and solutions they offer can be of practical value in guiding the thinking and acting of the general reading public. And while it is true that the diocesan weekly newspaper, the religious news services, and the limited coverage given by the daily secular press help in bringing the Bishop's words to a wide audience, still a book may find its way into the hands of readers who would not in these other ways be reached.

VII

In the present case, there is still a further reason — and that a joyous one — for publishing at this time *The Mind of an Archbishop*. The year 1960 is a noteworthy date in the priestly life of Archbishop Alter. Fifty years ago, on June 4, 1910, Father Karl J. Alter was ordained in the Cathedral of St. John the Evangelist in Cleveland, Ohio, by Bishop John P. Farrelly. This, then, is His Grace's year of golden jubilee, the year which Leviticus bids us to sanctify. In the words of the Archbishop himself, spoken at the jubilee of a fellow priest: "The celebration of a sacerdotal jubilee can never be an isolated event in the life of any priest. It can never be utterly personal, for the priesthood belongs to no individual; it is not a private possession. By its very nature, the priesthood is a social sacrament destined for the sanctification not only of the recipient but of the whole Mystical Body of Christ. It is with special propriety, therefore, that a priestly jubilee be given the character of a public function and not that of a private devotion. No priest, and certainly no Bishop, can give adequate expression of his gratitude to God unless he be supported by his brother priests and by the Catholic laity. Such a celebration can give rise to mutual thanksgiving and edification."

In addition, on June 17 of 1960 His Grace began his thirtieth year in the episcopacy, having been consecrated in St. Francis de Sales' Cathedral in Toledo in 1931 by Archbishop John T. McNicholas, whom he was later to succeed as Archbishop of Cincinnati. It was on September 26, 1950, that he actually succeeded Archbishop McNicholas, and so 1960 also marks His Grace's tenth year as Metropolitan of the six dioceses of Ohio. To help commemorate fittingly this threefold anniversary, but especially to mark the Archbishop's golden sacerdotal jubilee, this volume is now offered to his fellow priests, to the Religious, and to the laity in general.

A word is in order as to the manner in which His Grace's writings have been presented. After all available manuscripts had been read, it was decided to publish them not merely as an anthology of sermons, addresses, papers, editorials, and the like, with dateline, place, occasion, and complete text as given in the original, but rather to edit out all statements of merely local or passing interest and value, and to retain only the body of each manuscript thus edited; then, to compile all the writings available on a particular subject — say, the ever-recurring question of the proper relationship of Church and state — and by such a synthesis express the complete mind of His Grace on that particular topic. Accordingly, it is not possible to assign an exact date or occasion to the composition of any entire chapter as it appears in this book. In general, the writings represent the mind of His Grace expressed over the thirty years of his episcopacy.

In the composition of manuscripts thus treated, we have attempted to develop and preserve a logical, orderly sequence. Since, however, the content of this volume was not written by the Archbishop at any one time, or at any time with the express purpose of publishing in mind, but over many years and for scores of different occasions, there will of necessity be obvious omissions, some repetition, and an occasional lapse in proper literary continuity. It was, in fact, necessary at times to allow repetition in order to develop with force an original argument. It was judged better to permit these literary inconsistencies than to over-edit the text and thus weaken the original statement or tamper with the original style.

In order to present as easily readable a text as possible, we have deliberately avoided the use of parenthetical annotations, footnotes, and indexes that would give detailed sources in the manner of a scientific thesis. When such a reference is judged necessary, it occurs in the text itself.

The Archbishop's manuscripts are so presented and developed as to form a study of man in his essential religious, social, economic, and cultural relationships. Accordingly, in Part I we read of man in his principal relation to God his Creator, and of the consequent necessary bond of religion in the life of every rational creature.

The relation of man to the God-Man Christ is developed through a series of manuscripts dealing with: first, the nature of the Catholic Church in herself, as a divinely founded visible society of men; then, the Church in relation to the state — the popular "separation of Church and state" issue; thirdly, the Church as a supposed potential threat to the liberty of our fellow Americans; the institution of the Papacy, and the figures of two great Popes of the twentieth century, Pius XI and Pius XII; the nature and office of the episcopacy and of the priesthood; and the place of the Bible in the Church's rule of faith. Some practical observations on the actual planning and building of a great cathedral conclude this section.

In considering man in relation to his country, emphasis is placed on the proper understanding of Christian democracy and of the inroads of totalitarian states or dictatorships upon man's natural rights. The possibility of international peace, the necessary basis of such a peace, and the most powerful means of attaining it, are here considered in turn. The welfare of the nation as it is dependent on the moral vigor of its family life is then discussed, together with the allied subjects of divorce, sterilization, euthanasia, and artificial birth control, with special reference to the current question of an increase in population.

The next nine manuscripts, Chapters XV to XXIII, take up the relationship between the Church, the state, and the individual man in the perfecting of man's intellectual faculties through organized training, that is, through formal education. Here the question of the Church's divinely commissioned right to teach with authority is dealt with; and, growing out of this, such matters as the justification of the Church's separate school system; the intellectual freedom of Catholic colleges and universities, the worth of a liberal education, the obligations arising from a higher education, the vocation of teaching, and the relatively limited contribution of Catholics to the intellectual life of our country.

The broad field of man's social nature — the social order, social justice, social charity, and social service — is next given attention. These manuscripts analyze the Church's efforts toward establishing a better social-economic order through the development of a specific code of social justice, supplemented by the practice of social charity. The inadequacy of social service to replace social charity is effectively shown. As an example of the Church's practical social endeavors, the Catholic hospital is described in its origin, nature, and contribution to society; its mode of operation, ideals, responsibilities, and goals. Another pressing social problem — that of our treatment of the juvenile offender — forms the subject matter of the concluding manuscript of this section.

Next we read of man in his relationship to organized groups and group activities within the framework of the Church, or, more simply, the question of Catholic Action — the official call to the laity to know the mind of the Church and to participate, under episcopal authority, in the Church's work, through such organized societies as the National Councils of Catholic Men and Women, the National Catholic Rural Life

Conference, the Catholic Youth Organization, and the Catholic Students' Mission Crusade.

The religious and devotional life of man within the Church is taken up in a series of manuscripts that deal with the Person of the divine Christ as seen in His birth, life, death, and resurrection; His Blessed Mother Mary; the saints and the Religious life; and with the "pastoral value of promoting a fuller understanding of the sacred liturgy and a more active participation in the public worship of the Church." The fortieth and last manuscript is a meditation on the end of all man's activities on earth, the reality of death — *mors pretiosa.*

The thoughts and the style of the authors that a man reads analytically and extensively are bound to color his own writing. In these manuscripts, the attentive reader will find echoes of at least three of the Archbishop's favorite authors: Christopher Dawson, Luigi Sturzo, and Jacques Maritain. In places the exact words of an author are quoted; in others, the substance of his thoughts are expressed in His Grace's own words. There is this advantage to be derived from such a procedure, that, just as an echo can bring to our ear tones and overtones that we may have missed in the original sound, and thus enrich an already pleasant and profitable experience, so we can often come to a fuller understanding of a truth that was originally expressed in terms above our intellectual range, when that same truth is echoed by another writer in simpler terms. It was this very kind of thing that the poet Browning had in mind when, speaking of the artist's work in "Fra Lippo Lippi," he said: "God uses us to help each other so, *lending our minds out.*" Herein the Archbishop lends his mind out to us.

If it were possible to rerun pictures showing the occasions and the locale of all the Archbishop's addresses that are included in this volume (as the newsreels review the happenings of a half-century for us) we would travel in our own country from the Eastern seaboard to the Far West, from the deep South to the Canadian border. We would be present at a variety of festive occasions: consecrations and installations of Bishops and Archbishops, episcopal jubilees, Eucharistic Congresses, dedications of cathedrals, religious centenaries and anniversaries; we would attend national conventions and conferences met to consider and to help solve the problems of education, social action, hospital administration, family life, missionary endeavors, life on the farm, and modern youth. We would travel also beyond our country's borders to Rio de Janeiro, Brazil, and to Havana to hear His Grace address the Inter-American Catholic Social Action seminars, and to Lima, Peru, where the Archbishop addressed the Inter-American Hospital Association on the elements of a community health program; finally, we would go beyond the Atlantic to Budapest and to Dublin for addresses at the Eucharistic Congresses in those cities. In the thirty years of his episcopal life His Grace has spoken in scores of cities. The substance of most of those addresses is the subject matter of *The Mind of an Archbishop*.

In an anthology, which by its very nature is selective, there must needs be some omissions, and, in this respect, the present anthology proves no exception. Other manuscripts might have been included, since what the reader will find here does not represent the total output of His Grace's pen. A limit, however, had to be set. For although there may be no end to the making of books, there had to be an end to the making of this particular book; just as there should be an end to the making of every type of introduction, and that as close as possible to its beginning.

— *M. E. R.*

ACKNOWLEDGMENTS

It is fitting that due acknowledgment be made to those who, at the sacrifice of their leisure time, and under the press of heavy personal schedules of work, gladly lent their talents to the compilation, typing, editing, and proofreading of the manuscripts for *The Mind of an Archbishop*. Grateful appreciation is extended to:

Father George J. Berwanger, S. T. D., head of the English department of St. Gregory's Seminary, Cincinnati;

Father Eugene H. Maly, S. T. D., SS. D., professor of Sacred Scripture at Mount St. Mary of the West Seminary, Norwood;

Monsignor Edward A. McCarthy, S. T. D., J. C. D., and Father Donald A. Tenoever, M. A., secretaries to Archbishop Alter;

Father Alfred G. Stritch, M. A., professor of History at St. Gregory's Seminary, Cincinnati;

Father Robert J. Buschmiller, S. T. D., Ph. L., professor of Theology at Mount St. Mary of the West Seminary, Norwood;

Father Charles H. Hollencamp, S. T. D., Ph. D., professor of Philosophy at Mount St. Mary of the West Seminary, Norwood;

Father Henry J. Klocker, S. T. D., assistant director of the Archdiocesan Mission Office;

Monsignor Edward J. Graham, Litt. D., Father Lawrence C. Walter, Litt. D., and Mr. James Shea, Litt. D., of the *Catholic Telegraph-Register* staff;

Monsignor Donald A. McGowan, head of Hospitals and Health, NCWC, Washington, D. C.;

Sister Mary Christopher, C. PP. S., Sister secretary to Archbishop Alter;

The secretarial staff of Sister Mary Virginia's office at Our Lady of Cincinnati College, Edgecliff, especially Sister Mary Honora, R. S. M., and Sister Mary Annrita, R. S. M.;

Sister Jane de Chantal, O. P., superintendent of The St. George Hospital, Cincinnati;

The lay secretaries who helped prepare various drafts of the manuscripts: Miss Virginia Hamilton, Miss Mary McDermott, and Mrs. Mary Lou Wegman.

Every editor, of course, is grateful for the patience of the one who brings his work to production. In this respect we are thrice blest, for Father John Forest, O. F. M., director of St. Anthony's Guild, has always patiently borne with literary lags, and generously overlooked past-due deadlines.

— *M. E. R.*

CONTENTS

The editor wishes to thank the following publishers for permission to quote short excerpts from the works cited below: The Macmillan Company, New York, N. Y., *The Spirit of Catholicism,* by Karl Adam; Sheed and Ward, New York, N. Y., *Enquiries into Religion and Culture, Religion and the Modern State,* and *Progress and Religion,* all by Christopher Dawson; Liveright Corporation, New York, N. Y., *Henry the Eighth,* by Francis Hackett.

The Sacred Scriptures have been quoted in the Confraternity of Christian Doctrine revision except in a few cases where the meaning is better served by the Douay version or the Knox translation.

THE MIND OF
AN ARCHBISHOP

Part I

<u>MAN IN RELATION</u>

<u>TO GOD HIS CREATOR</u>

*"God created man in His image. In the
image of God He created him."*

I

THE ROOT OF EVERY LIVING CREATURE

"IF OUR civilization is to recover its vitality or even to survive, it must cease to neglect its spiritual roots and must realize that religion is not a matter of personal sentiment which has nothing to do with the objective realities of society, but is, on the contrary, the very heart of social life and the root of every living creature." Despite the truth of this pointed warning by Christopher Dawson, the most penetrating of contemporary critics and a historian whose special field is the correlation of religion, sociology, and culture, the general attitude of society continues to be that "really nice people" do not publicly discuss questions of religion. It is in bad taste, we are led to believe, to bring the all-important subject of religion out into the open; to pay it the public tribute of intelligent discussion. Religion, according to this view, should be restricted to the bounds of private life, or perhaps even banished to a sort of underground.

Against such a narrow view of man's relationship to his Creator, we express a solemn protest. As a social being, man has not only individual but also social obligations. One of them, the one in fact which God Himself puts first in His list of commands, is to give uncompromising recognition to the Creator: "I am the Lord thy God; . . . thou shalt not have strange gods before Me." The strange gods of today are not graven images of wood or stone but excessive and exclusive devotion to selfish interests, personal ambition, and social pres-

5

tige. When such aims take precedence over the recognition and honor due to God, there is sinful disorder. Religion is not merely a personal virtue but a social responsibility. It must be not merely private in its expression but also public. If it is to be vital and effective, religion must reveal itself not merely in the privacy of the mind and heart but also visibly and publicly in the outward recognition and acknowledgment of the Creator; not solely in actions but also in words. We should be ready to discuss the subject intelligently and to declare our dependence upon God. Far from being a negligible element in our civilization, as the modern secular world is inclined to think, religion is an indispensable factor which can be ignored only at the cost of the complete subversion of our social order and the widespread collapse of our historical culture. Religion is, in short, the very basis of our culture and civilization.

At the very beginning, let us make clear the meaning of three terms: religion, culture, and civilization. These terms will recur again and again throughout the chapters of this book and should be clearly grasped for an intelligent understanding of our general theme.

We use the word "religion" in its broadest significance. By it we understand that spiritual bond which unites man to the invisible, supernatural world in an attitude of reverence and dependence. We do not exclude from the meaning of the term those forms of religion current in the pagan world or in pre-Christian times, even though they contained many false and fantastic ideas about the spirit world, and filled the heavens with spurious divinities. Confucius in China, Zoroaster in Persia, Buddha in India, and Mohammed in Arabia may be regarded, in this sense, as religious teachers, even though their systems of religion contained some truth with a great admixture of error. We are speaking here of religion in a generic sense. We are speaking not merely of the one true religion revealed by God on Mount Sinai and in its fullness on the Mount of the New Testament, but rather of the universal concept of man in relation to divinity.

The second term which needs clarification is "culture" — a word which has many implications. Let us say at once that we are not talking primarily about refinement and good taste, nor about education and travel and broad human contacts, which are the means of their attainment. For our purpose we use the term in its social significance. By culture we understand not only the customs and the habits of the people: their language, dress, songs, games, and style of architecture; but more particularly their ideas, attitudes, and principles of conduct, which reveal themselves in their social institutions: their governmental structure, their educational system, their economic organization, their domestic life, and their public worship.

This word "culture" is a sociological term which may be better understood by means of a simple comparison. Human nature may be likened to a field or a plot of ground. If left in its primitive state, untended by the hand of man, it produces a rank growth of vegetation. But let human thought apply itself to its cultivation and let human skill and energy plow the land, harrow it, and sow in its soil fertile seed, then there springs up a uniform and vigorous growth of grain and fruit and useful herbs that satisfies the needs of man. In this latter case we say that the field is cultivated. We speak of the process as a culture — namely, agriculture or horticulture.

So too with human nature. In its primitive state it is fallow ground; untended, it will produce barbarism and savagery. It needs the application of the rational process and of virtue.

It needs the plow of human energy and the seed of human thought; it needs the application of human will and intellect if it is to pass from its state of primitive nature to a state of culture and civilization.

Our third term, "civilization," is a word derived from the Latin "civitas," which, of course, means city or state. Civilization, therefore, implies that form of culture or human development which is found associated with the state; which reveals itself in connection with political organization or government. Civilization, although often used as synonymous with culture, generally implies advanced progress or a high degree of culture. Civilization denotes the conquest of nature. It means that man has attained such a degree of control over the elementary forces of nature that he can be definitely differentiated from the primitive man, the savage.

The savage is a mere child of nature and largely the victim of elementary, natural forces. He has not learned to provide food, clothing, and shelter for himself, either with adequacy or with security. He lives a precarious existence. He dwells in a cave, a wigwam, or an igloo because he has not learned to refine metal from the ore of the mines, to fashion stone from the rock of the quarry, or to build his house with wood from the trees of the forest. A savage, he either fasts or feasts because he has not learned to store his food in the day of abundance against famine in the day of scarcity. He invokes magic against disease because he has not learned the source of infection nor the remedy of medicines. He clothes himself with the skin of animals because he has not learned to weave and to sew. The savage learns only from oral tradition and personal experience because he has not learned to make written records nor to treasure his discoveries in books. In his progress toward a better life, he is always starting from scratch. He is bounded narrowly in his physical movements because he knows nothing of speedy transportation or distant communication. And what is most important, he is bound even more narrowly in his intellectual life. The horizon of his mind is as limited as his natural vision. He measures life with a yardstick.

Civilized man, in contrast, has conquered the forces of nature and subjected them to his will. The outward marks of his culture are many. Not only does he conquer external nature, but he builds for himself social institutions perfecting the relations between man and man. He explores the infinity of the heavens and he seeks the answer to the greatest questions of the human mind — whence he came, whither he is going, and what is his relationship to the divine power that rules the world.

There are two theories current today respecting the origin and the cause of both ancient and modern civilizations. One is that offered by Communism, which states that man is a mere creature of circumstance; that he reflects in his inner life merely the environment in which he lives. Marx, Lenin, Stalin, and their host of followers tell us that man's outlook upon the world — his political, his social, and his religious life — is determined by his economic environment. The material circumstances of his existence determine his ideas, his attitudes, and his principles of conduct. All this is summed up in the theory which they call "economic determinism," or, in a different phrase which has the same meaning, "the materialistic conception of history." In other words, man does not make his world in which he lives; the world and its external material conditions make the man.

There are many variations of this general theme. In Hitler's Germany we had the theory that race or blood was the important factor in man's development. Goering and

Goebbels were constantly expatiating on the need of maintaining the purity of the Aryan race; hence their anti-Semitism. For them it counted much more what kind of blood coursed through the human veins than what kind of ideas flowed through the human mind. We have, in addition, the notion or theory of some sociologists that civilization or culture is merely the result — or at least primarily the result — of a favorable climate or particular geographic conditions. No matter what influence one might attribute to such factors, certainly today we must reject the notion that such limited forces can constitute the ultimate explanation of human progress or cultural development.

The second theory is diametrically opposed to that which has been described. It attributes the rise and fall of culture and civilization not to our outward environment, not to material conditions, not to economic circumstances, but to the inner world of man, to his ideas, his attitudes, his principles of conduct.

Among these ideas and attitudes there are none so forceful, so penetrating, so creative as religious ideas and beliefs. What a man thinks of his own nature, whether matter or spirit; what he thinks of his origin, his destiny, the purpose and the value of his life on earth; what he thinks of God, of the future life, and the means to attain it — all these constitute essential elements in any particular pattern of culture. They are the warp and woof in the structure of civilization, and they are of the very essence of religion.

The Western world prides itself on its progress in culture and civilization. We look upon the culture of China and Japan, of India and the far-flung territory of Islam with a sense of our own superiority. We of Europe and of America consider, and rightly so, that our civilization is something pre-eminent and unique in the history of the human race. What many, however, do not realize is the source and origin of that peculiar distinction.

Our civilization is not something that just happened. It is not a result of spontaneous generation. It is not a mere accident, an effect without a cause. Even if we were not possessed of an inquiring turn of mind, our attention should at least be arrested by the fact that this culture of ours is historically associated with Christianity and that it is everywhere conterminous with its boundaries. Wherever the Christian Gospel has been preached and its principles put into practice in the lives of the people, great social improvements have taken place. This was true in the ancient world and it is true today. As Christian truth advances, society improves. As Christian truth retreats, society falls first into confusion and then into decay. The inner spirit, the driving force, and the outstanding characteristics of our culture and civilization are the outgrowth of a specific body of truths and practices which in its last analysis has no other foundation than the Christian Gospel. Tell us what the attitudes of a people are toward human life, toward property, toward labor, toward marriage and the family, and toward government, and we will tell you the degree of civilization that those people have attained.

Let us develop each of these points.

First, is human life the property of God or is it the property of man? Upon the answer given to this question depend the sacredness, the dignity, and even the security of human life. If human life is from God, then it cannot be declared forfeited, it cannot even be curtailed in any way by the authority of man. If it is from God, and He alone has dominion over it, then suicide and homicide in any form are an attack upon the rights of God, and must be reprobated and rejected com-

nomic production, whether by the individual or by groups joined together in corporations, is contrary to Christian teaching. But neither is that all that this phrase may be taken to stand for. While it is impossible to give an exact definition, nevertheless, broadly speaking, finance-capitalism implies an irresponsibility which breaks up the moral organism of society into a chaos of competitive individualism. It denies the sovereignty of the moral law in the economic world and substitutes for it pure self-interest. In the political order it denies the principle of authority and substitutes for it the arbitrary will of the majority. And in religious matters it denies the existence of objective divine truth and substitutes for it merely private opinion as a rule of faith.

While finance-capitalism sins by excess in emphasizing the rights of individual property, Communism goes to the opposite extreme and repudiates the divine commandment "Thou shalt not steal." Communism has ruthlessly confiscated the ownership of both productive and use property; it denies that the individual has any right in property antecedent to, or superior to, that of the state or the community. In robbing men of property, it robs them of true liberty and freedom, and it subjects the citizen or the individual to the community, thereby making him a slave of the state just as certainly as any slave was ever bound to an individual master. We again warn the reader against the easy assumption that theories do not count, or that principles and attitudes in regard to property have no bearing upon practical life.

Here in our own country much of the present social unrest is caused by labor disputes and strikes. Manifestly, the minds of our employers and of our employees fail to meet in regard to the rights of property and the rights of labor. Now, what light do Christian principles throw upon this dispute? At the outset we must have a right understanding of the dignity of labor. The Church teaches us that labor is honorable; it is divinely ordered; it is worthy of its hire. Most certainly it is not a commodity to be purchased in the open market. God has decreed that all men must work: "In the sweat of your brow you shall eat bread." The Son of God, when He came into this world, chose to be known as the son of Joseph the carpenter. He took the role of a workingman in order to teach us the abiding lesson that the work of the laboring man is worthy of reverence and respect.

What important consequences flow from an understanding of these truths? If we look to ancient times, we find everywhere that the hard and disagreeable work of the world was done by slaves. In all ancient civilizations manual labor was treated with contempt. Wars were engineered often with the direct purpose of capturing human beings to serve their masters as slaves. That is the way the pyramids of Egypt were built. In Athens there were twenty thousand free men, but two hundred thousand slaves. With the advent of Christ's teaching, slavery slowly disappeared from the face of Christian Europe. At first there was no forceful prohibition by law; slavery was simply incompatible with the new concept of the dignity of man. Man, a creature of God, redeemed by Christ, a brother in grace — could such a one be treated as a slave?

In our modern social organization, under the influence of competitive individualism, a new doctrine took the place of Christianity. Men were no longer regarded as brothers in Christ but merely as so many hands. Labor was a commodity to be purchased. Wages were not determined by the amount of wealth produced, but by the old slave principle of minimum subsistence. The principles that regulated relations between employers and employees for all too long a time were: "Might makes right"; "Fortune smiles upon the strong"; "Every man for himself and the devil take the hindmost." What was the result? Long hours for labor; hard work; minimum wages. No wonder Leo XIII, as early as 1891, was forced to write an encyclical deploring the condition of the working classes, and recalling the attention of the Christian world to the fundamental principles of Christ's Gospel. The rights of labor were once more vindicated: namely, the right to a decent wage, the right to humane working conditions in keeping with the dignity of man, the right of collective bargaining, the right of working-men's associations, and the right of workingmen to choose freely their own representatives.

These Christian moral principles are so important to the whole labor program that without them the problems will never be solved. That is why the Popes have preached unceasingly in their encyclicals that we must restore Christian principles to their rightful place in the rule of our economic life.

Turn your mind now to the question of marriage and the family. From the time that Christianity first made its presence felt in the ancient world, the sanctity of the family has been safeguarded by a definite code of domestic ethics. When Christ began His public life, He worked His first miracle at the marriage feast of Cana, as if to show His deep concern with the family as the fundamental social unit. He reminded His disciples that marriage is one and indissoluble. He raised this natural bond, this most solemn contract among men, to the dignity of a sacrament. What happens when this teaching is disregarded? When marriage is completely secularized and amounts to nothing more than a civil contract or a companionship of temporary duration or convenience, we deny the very essence of the Christian concept of the family. To break its unity, therefore, with wanton divorce is to let loose a host of evils upon the world. To frustrate its purpose by artificial birth control is to foster death and not life. The family is *the* social unit. Change it in essence or destroy its character, and civilization as we have known it for more than one thousand years, will be inevitably changed or destroyed.

Finally, in analyzing the origin of our social principles and our social attitudes, we turn our attention to government itself. Today all thoughtful students of public affairs are watching with keen anxiety the steady drift toward state dictatorship. We have dictatorships of the right and of the left. In Russia, there is the dictatorship of the proletariat; and here and there throughout Europe there are a half-dozen other brands, in each of which we have a new concept of government. The citizen no longer has any inherent rights as a man, antecedent and prior to all government. Instead, he is made the creature of the state.

In America we still point proudly to our Declaration of Independence and to our Constitution, in which is set forth the doctrine that there are certain inalienable rights given to man by the Creator: namely, the right to life, liberty, property, and the pursuit of happiness. Since the emergence of the totalitarian state, these rights are no longer recognized in a large part of the world. The state encompasses within itself now the whole of man; it tells him not merely what he can do in public, but also what he must think in private. In consequence, there is no freedom of conscience, no freedom of worship, no freedom of assembly, no freedom of the press.

If you seek the explanation of this new phenomenon you will find it in the gradual departure from Christian truth which has been taking place in the intellectual life of the world for the past several centuries. Only now is it reaching its

climax and final fruition. Christianity teaches that the citizen precedes the state. It teaches that man has a value and a dignity all his own; that he has rights that are inseparable from his existence as a man; rights given to him by his Creator which no state can steal. The Church does not impose any particular form of secular government upon her members. They may choose a republic or a kingdom, a democracy or an empire, but the Church does teach that whatever be the form of government it is limited in its powers. Even though its authority is from God, the rulers who exercise this authority are not divinely appointed but are designated by the citizens themselves by human means.

The state, therefore, must subordinate its plan of human welfare to the prior rights of the plan that God Himself fashioned. The state, in other words, must carry out its work within the moral order that God Himself established. If you accept these principles, then no matter what you may call your government, it never becomes an absolute dictatorship or a comprehensive totalitarian state.

We have repeatedly called attention to the fact that we must not look upon these principles as mere academic theories. They are theories loaded with dynamite. What people write in one generation is popularized in the thought of the second, and then reduced to practice in the third. How different would have been the history of the past two hundred years if the intellectual leadership of the world had remained in Christian hands, instead of passing to men who had little sympathy with and less understanding of the Christian philosophy of life. In politics, in sociology, in science, and in economics the secularist point of view and the ultraliberal spirit have predominated. We can illustrate this fact by citing the names and the works of four men who were in the forefront of these respective fields of thought and activity during this period.

In political science, Jean Jacques Rousseau has exercised more influence than any other writer of the past two hundred years. His *Social Contract* gave direction and impetus to the liberal democratic movement, but it did so by repudiating, not merely the divine right of kings but also the divine right of the Lord Himself. The principle of divine authority was shattered. The will of the majority was made the supreme law of society. Thus minorities were left defenseless in the face of attack on those inalienable rights with which they had been endowed by their Creator.

In social science, Auguste Comte, who coined the word "sociology," easily assumed the leadership, and gave this so-called science a definitely anti-Christian bias. Comte denied the validity of any objective standard of morality and substituted in its place the shifting norm of human tradition, custom, and fashion. Morality became mere conventionality. As a result, men felt free to tinker with the sacred institutions of society, such as marriage and the family. Experiments in sterilization, birth control, and euthanasia supplanted the right to life and personal integrity.

In the field of experimental science no name is more significant than that of Charles Darwin. Even though he did not originate the theory of evolution, yet his book *On the Origin of Species* did create an entirely new spiritual mood or temper of mind in which to pursue experimental knowledge. If the theory of evolution carried over disastrously from biology into metaphysics, psychology, and religion, it was largely due to his book *The Descent of Man*. Science, after Darwin, became irreligious in tone and purpose.

In social economics Karl Marx became the new evangelist, and his work *Das Kapital* became the new gospel from which millions of people were to seek, in our generation, the inspiration of their economic and political activity. When Red revolution flames fearfully in many countries of the world, do not forget that the one who lit the torch was Marx, the author of the *Communist Manifesto*.

These four great secular evangelists of the past century gave a definitely anti-Christian tone to the main current of thought. Nothing can be more false than to assume that theories do not count. St. Paul understood well the mischief that can be done by intellectual error, and it was no idle warning he gave to his disciples at Colossae when he said: "See to it that no one deceives you by philosophy or vain deceit, according to human traditions, according to the elements of the world, and not according to Christ."

Ever since the days of the Renaissance we have been moving toward a complete secularization of society. It was the great misfortune of our world that the leaders of that movement, otherwise so beneficial, erred egregiously in their appraisal of human values and fumbled the relation and distinction between nature and grace. They grossly exaggerated man's perfectibility by merely human means. They placed a false estimate on man's ability to achieve unrestricted progress by dominion over his merely physical environment, without that mastery of his inner self whereby a divine synthesis is established between nature and grace. The train of events set in motion by the Renaissance is only now reaching its ultimate conclusions. Such always is the course of false philosophy.

Karl Adam states that "The sixteenth century revolt from the Church led inevitably to the revolt from Christ of the eighteenth century, and thence to the revolt from God of the nineteenth. . . . And thus life has lost its great meaning, its vital strength and high purpose, its strong pervading love, that can be enkindled only by the divine."

Christopher Dawson says practically the same thing: "Protestantism, Liberalism, and Communism are the three successive stages by which our civilization has passed from Catholicism to complete secularism. The first eliminated the Church, the second eliminated Christianity, and the third eliminates the human soul. We cannot have a Christian society or a Christian economic life until our civilization has recovered its moral conscience, its faith in God, and its membership of the Church."

During the past four hundred years the Church has not been able to lead a normal life. She has been forced to stand upon the defensive. She has been like a country that is invaded, like a city that is besieged. Her energies have been absorbed in fighting for her very life, and hence whole provinces of human life and cultural activity have been lost to her beneficent influence. Philosophy, literature, art, politics, economics — all these have repudiated their alma mater and have become prodigal sons wandering in a wilderness of doubt, confusion, and despair.

For a long time the battle was fought in the field of dogma. The Church had to vindicate the fundamental truths concerning her own divine establishment, the divinity of Christ, the authenticity of the Sacred Scriptures, and the very fact of revelation. But the old battle line is changing. We are no longer defending the ancient doctrines of Christian revelation. Now we are face to face with a general attack upon the entire code of Christian conduct. The very commandments of God are under fire. The traditional standards of Christian ethics, on the basis of which our civilization was built, are being subjected to a heavy barrage of higher criticism.

The wise words of Christopher Dawson pointedly sum up our own thought in this regard: "The central conviction which has dominated my mind ever since I began to write and which has increased in intensity during the last twenty years, is the conviction that the society or culture which has lost its spiritual roots is a dying culture, however prosperous it may appear externally. Consequently, the problem of social survival is not only a political or economic one; it is above all things religious, since it is in religion that the ultimate spiritual roots both of society and of the individual are to be found."

Religion, then, far from being a negligible element in our civilization, as the modern secular world is inclined to think, is, we repeat, an indispensable factor which can be ignored only at the cost of the complete subversion of our social order and the widespread collapse of our historical culture.

Religion shapes the destiny of nations, governments, families, and individuals. Man, whether singly or in organized groups, can never, without disaster, deny or ignore the obligations that spring from his very nature as a rational creature of an all-wise Creator. Man's conscience will not let him escape from an awareness of these duties. And yet, unaided, man cannot successfully meet this challenge. He needs divine help. God, however, has not abandoned man to a dilemma. Through His Incarnate Son, the God-Man Christ, He has established in the world, to last to the end of time, a visible Church, invested with the power and the authority to help man in the very name of God. And thus it is that man, painfully aware of his needs and his frailty, turns to this Church, divinely founded by Christ, for help in his struggle toward salvation.

Part II

<u>MAN IN RELATION TO</u>

<u>THE GOD-MAN CHRIST</u>

"God, who at sundry times and in divers manners spoke in times past to the fathers by the prophets, last of all in these days has spoken to us by His Son."

II

AN INSTITUTION TRULY UNIQUE

THE Church, as the kingdom of God among men, is not a thing of yesterday. It has a long history of growth and development. From all eternity God planned a universal kingdom here on earth in the beginning of time, made up of loyal sons, attached to Himself by bonds of love and destined ultimately to share with Him eternal happiness. Adam's sin deprived man of this inestimable privilege. The consequence of that defection in the head of the human race was universal disaster for his descendants. But in the midst of gloom there was a ray of hope. God promised a second Adam, who would restore what was lost. Mankind, however, while waiting for this promise to be fulfilled, steadily drifted further and further into error and corruption. Because of this widespread apostasy God sent the flood to wipe out sinful men. Nevertheless, the Creator was merciful and saved a remnant of the race in Noe and his family. Thus God began a second time to fulfill His design for mankind. Time went on, and again sin conquered the hearts and minds of men, alienating them from their true and final end. Spurned once more by man's perversity, God temporarily abandoned the plan of establishing a universal kingdom of truth and holiness. The Scriptures tell us that He turned to Abraham, a man of faith, in order that in him and in his seed He might set up a chosen people, a new nation under God, one which would be segregated from the rest of mankind and would thus ensure the preservation of truth and

25

virtue, at least in part of the world and in part of mankind. God promised Abraham that he would become the father of a mighty nation, a nation which would preserve in the world the true knowledge of God. God made a covenant with Abraham and his descendants — if they proved faithful, He would bless them; He would be their God and they would be "His people." To this people God sent Moses and the prophets. He surrounded them with special favors. They alone were privileged to have a code of laws that was clear, definite, and authenticated by God Himself. They alone were the beneficiaries of a special revelation of divine truth. They alone had a divinely sanctioned priesthood and acceptable sacrifices. They alone were put in full possession of the divine secret, the promise of a Messias or Saviour who would rise from their own ranks and re-establish a universal kingdom. This new kingdom would have unity and universality based, not on race or language or human factors but on the relationship of sons of God with their Father. This, in brief, is the early history of the Church. It is the history of Israel — the shadow and prefiguration of the Church that was to come.

St. Paul, in his letter to the Hebrews, begins his discourse on the eternal priesthood of Jesus Christ by reminding his hearers of all these things that went before. "God, who at sundry times and in divers manners spoke in times past to the fathers by the prophets," so he writes, "last of all in these days has spoken to us by His Son." The word which the Son has spoken is that which He heard from His Father. It is the word which now re-echoes in the Church — the sacramental word which reveals the secret of God's love hidden from all eternity in the mystery of the Incarnation. In its full meaning it is the Word which was made flesh and dwelt among us; the word which was rejected by the world, but which, when received with faith, makes us in truth sons of God, who are born not of the flesh, nor of blood, nor of the will of man, but of God. It is this word or Gospel message which the Church recalls in her liturgy and which she relives in the Eucharistic Sacrifice.

The early Greek-speaking converts referred to the Christian community at worship as the *Ecclesia* — a calling together. By this they meant that it was an assembly of the faithful called together by lawful authority for a specific purpose — namely, to hear an official message. To this message they were expected to give their response with thanks and fidelity; with their "Amen!" "Alleluia!" and "Deo gratias!" The *Ecclesia,* or the Church, is not, therefore, just any kind of assembly. It is an official assembly; it is the answer to an authoritative summons convoking the faithful, not as individuals but as a community, for the purpose of performing a public religious work in which all take part.

Now there is a right way and a wrong way to look at the Church. The wrong way is to think of the Church as if it were merely another human institution — to see the Church, unconsciously perhaps, through the eyes of most non-Catholics. To them the Church is merely a voluntary association of like-minded people, a mere social organization of those who believe in Christ. The Church in their concept is a generic expression, used to designate a loosely knit body of Christian believers whose only bond of unity is faith in Christ, no matter how radically they differ in their interpretation of His doctrine.

The right notion of the Church, however, implies something quite different. The right view looks upon the Church as a unique institution, utterly unlike any other society known to man. The Church differs notably from such human institutions as the state or the nation; and even more radically from such voluntary societies as the Red Cross or the United Nations.

The Church belongs to the supernatural order. Those outside the true fold speak of the Church as an organization. Those of us within the fold speak of it as an organism. We hold that it is a living thing, pulsating with divine life. We hold that the Church has its own interior principle of life. This principle of life is none other than Christ Himself. He is the vine; we are the branches. He is the Head of the body; we are the members. From Christ, the living Head, there flows into the members that supernatural grace which was merited in superabundance by Christ on the cross and then communicated to us through the sacraments and the Eucharistic Sacrifice. The Church lives and moves and has its being in Christ.

Both in structure and in function the Church is unique. The illustrations which the Scriptures use spell out its distinctive character. The parable of the vine and the branches and the comparison with the human body not only emphasize the essential unity and interrelationship of the faithful with one another, but they make clear that Christ is the vital principle of all spiritual life, both in the individuals and in the corporate group. St. Paul says: "It is now no longer I that live, but Christ lives in me." The vision of the Church, moreover, as a city on the mountaintop emphasizes the fact that the Church is a visible, tangible society which all can recognize. Its identity can never be lost in a mist of confused claims. When Christ describes the Church as a sheepfold or a kingdom, He brings out its hierarchical character. Christ is the good shepherd. The sheep must have a shepherd or they become lost. The kingdom must have a ruler or there is chaos and disruption. Hence Christ spoke to Peter the oft-quoted words: "I say to thee, thou art Peter, and upon this rock I will build My Church, and the gates of hell shall not prevail against it. And I will give thee the keys of the kingdom of heaven; and whatever thou shalt bind on earth shall be bound in heaven, and whatever thou shalt loose on earth shall be loosed in heaven."

St. Luke tells us that in the forty days that followed the resurrection, Christ repeatedly appeared to the apostles, "speaking [to them] of the kingdom of God." In this period, as well as earlier in His earthly life, Christ laid the foundations of the Church, endowing it with those prerogatives which would keep it forever the same. He gave it the right to speak in His name: "As the Father sent Me, so I also send you." "He who hears you, hears Me." He gave it the right to command: "If [any man] refuse to hear . . . the Church, let him be to thee as the heathen and the publican." He gave the Church a guarantee of perpetuity in the promise of the Holy Spirit: "I will ask the Father and He will give you another Advocate to dwell with you forever, the Spirit of truth whom the world cannot receive, because it neither sees Him nor knows Him. But you shall know Him, because He will dwell with you, and be in you." He added the assurance of His own everlasting presence: "Behold, I am with you all days, even to the consummation of the world." No other society known to man has such a unique character; and no other society has equally endured the test of time and maintained its identity both in structure and in function.

The Church, in fact, is Christ. It is Christ continuing His divine mission on earth; not in the flesh, not in the particular human body which He took from the Blessed Virgin Mary, but rather in a mystical body made up of those into whom He has infused His own divine life.

The term "Mystical Body of Christ" is relatively new in the language of theology. We are told by scholars that it made its appearance in formal use no earlier than the twelfth century. The first full-length treatment of the subject in an encyclical letter of the Popes is that of Pius XII in our own time. The idea itself obviously is an old one, being used frequently by St. Paul when he speaks of the Church as the Body of Christ.

In his encyclical letter *Mystici Corporis,* Pius XII clarified this theological concept by pointing out the distinctions between a physical body, a moral body, a juridical body, and the Mystical Body of Christ. In a physical body, such as a human being, the part exists for the benefit of the whole. The eye does not exist for itself; nor the ear, nor the hands, nor the feet; but all exist for the whole man, for the total human personality. In a moral body, by contrast, the whole primarily exists for the benefit of the individual parts. The state, for instance, as a moral and juridical body, does not exist for itself, but for the benefit of its citizens. In a moral body, moreover, the principle of union is not something intrinsic as in a physical body, but rather something extrinsic, such as a common end and common co-operation under proper authority. In a juridical body, the bond of union is the disciplinary code or law enforced by public authority with punitive measures. It has no intrinsic principle of life and can communicate no power to facilitate observance of the law.

In the Mystical Body of Christ there is a supernatural bond of unity between one member and another, and between all the members and Christ, their Head. The parts exist for the whole and the whole exists for the parts in a marvelous interchange of divine life. Nevertheless, as the Holy Father made clear, the individual members, though intimately united with one another and with Christ, are left the complete enjoyment of their own personalities. This unity therefore is distinctive, supernatural — far superior to anything in the natural order. No wonder St. Paul could exclaim in wonderment as he contemplated the mystery of God's goodness: "You are now no longer strangers and foreigners, but you are citizens with the saints and members of God's household; you are built upon the foundation of the apostles and prophets with Christ Jesus Himself as the chief cornerstone. In Him the whole structure is closely fitted together and grows into a temple holy in the Lord; in Him you too are being built together into a dwelling place for God in the Spirit. . . . Oh, the depth of the riches of the wisdom and of the knowledge of God! How incomprehensible are His judgments and how unsearchable His ways!"

If we read the pages of the Sacred Scripture we find that the Gospel of Jesus Christ is one of individual salvation. Every man must save his own soul. There is no such thing as group salvation. To conclude from these premises, however, that the individual can save his soul solely by his own individual efforts, without help from outside himself, without membership in the Christian community, without the Church, would be an egregious error. In the plan of Jesus Christ, the Church is the medium of salvation. It is the Church which dispenses the sacraments; the Church which breaks the bread of truth for the faithful; the Church which has been constituted the guardian of the deposit of faith; the Church which alone possesses the means of sanctification. And in this sense, outside the Church there is no salvation.

The function of the Church is to give continuity to the mission of Christ. In His Mystical Body, Christ continues to exercise His office as prophet, priest, and king. Through the lips of His priests, He continues to preach His Gospel just as He did on the hillsides of Judea or in the porches of the temple; in the holy sacrifice of the Mass, He continues to offer adoration to the heavenly Father and to make atonement for sin, just as He did on His cross on Calvary; in the commands which the Church gives, He continues to act as the good shepherd, guarding and guiding His flock to their ultimate destiny.

It is only when we have this comprehensive concept of the Church; only when we realize our solidarity in Christ; only when we grasp the full meaning of the Mystical Body of Christ that we can appreciate the full meaning of the liturgy and our sublime privilege of participating in it.

What a privilege to be a member of this extraordinary society which bridges the chasm between heaven and earth, which enfolds within her mantle all races and generations of men; which stretches out her spiritual empire to the very end of time; which touches with divinity our mortal nature and lifts it up to God! What a privilege to be a member of this kingdom which knows neither limits of time nor space! The proud Roman might boast of his exclusive citizenship which conferred so many precious rights and privileges; the cultured Greek might glory in the wisdom, art, and beauty of his beloved Athens; but neither of them had one-tenth as much reason to rejoice as the most humble person who holds membership in the Church. He alone is a true cosmopolitan, a citizen of the world, a true nobleman, made such by the grace of God; in very truth, a son of God through Baptism; anointed with the Holy Spirit in Confirmation, and privileged as God's guest to sit at the table of the Lord. In the liturgy of the Church he exercises his right of citizenship; yea, more, he speaks, and acts, and sings in accents of familiar but solemnly reverent intercourse with his heavenly Father in the great and holy sacrifice of the Mass.

III

TWO POWERS, EACH SUPREME

IN ADDITION to the inestimable privilege of being a member of the Church, man, by his very nature, is a social being destined to live in union with other men under some form of lawfully organized government. Accordingly, man owes allegiance both to Church and to state. And therein lies the source of a question that is as current as the rising sun.

The subject of the right relationship between Church and state has, we are well aware, been discussed frequently, but not so frequently has it been clarified as a result of discussion. No other subject, perhaps, is so deeply involved in historical confusion, or so urgently in need of clarification and precise definition as this topic of the right relationship between religion and government. A widespread misunderstanding of the question has given rise to futile controversy and at times has even disrupted the equanimity of our common life. How often do we not see this subject injected into such current questions as the possibility of electing a Catholic president, the appointing of a personal representative of the president at the Vatican, even a formal visit of the president to the Holy Father; or the providing of public bus transportation for Catholic students attending parochial schools? The question, therefore, is eminently practical and current; it is far from being a purely theoretical topic or one of mere historical interest. In view of these facts it is important that we examine carefully the meaning of the much-abused phrase or slogan, "separation of Church

33

and state," in order to clarify our minds on this subject, and to grasp the essential meaning of the provisions of our Constitution in respect to this problem. The question of a right relationship between Church and state has not been satisfactorily answered in any age. To state the problem as one either of outright union or outright separation is a naïve oversimplification. The problem is intricate and the solution needs constant readjustment.

If we wish to understand the historical background of the relations between the spiritual power and the political power, we must take cognizance of the progressive development of Christianity in the social order; and we must, at the same time, have a regard for the complexity of political situations and their ever-changing character.

Going back to the beginning, therefore, we find that the impact of Christianity on the ancient world was unique and unprecedented. Christianity created a profound unity among its members and a transcendent loyalty to Christ, their Lord and Master. Here was a religion which, in contrast to all others, was strictly personal; a religion that was binding on the individual conscience, irrespective of the claims of family, tribal, or national loyalties. Christianity cut asunder the bonds of traditional social cohesion. Call to mind the words of Christ when He was importuned to center His attention on His relatives: "Behold My mother, and My brethren! For whoever does the will of My Father in heaven, he is My brother and sister and mother."

A second characteristic of this new religion was its universality; it was the religion not of one race or nation or class, but a religion intended for all mankind without distinction. Christianity tended to break down the previously existing barriers between these groups and created instead a world-wide brotherhood of man. It tended to minimize between groups the conflict based on diversity of language, customs, color, and political and economic interests.

A third characteristic was the autonomy of this new religion; it derived its authority from a source independent of the state — namely, from God Himself. Christianity tended, therefore, to diminish the absolute sovereignty of the state or the political power. Added to this independent origin there is the fact that from the beginning there existed a separate, even though spiritual, hierarchy within its own organization. We can easily see that Christianity was bound to run afoul of the omnipotent or totalitarian state.

The fourth characteristic of the Christian religion is its unique and exclusive character. For this there was no precedent. The new religion claimed to possess the fullness of spiritual strength in itself alone. It claimed also to administer spiritual means of help without participation by any other agency. It claimed to direct mankind in the way of eternal salvation independently of any other authority. Because of these claims Christianity was bound to excite the opposition of the political power which refused to recognize such claims but asserted, rather, its own omnipotent power.

During the long periods when the nations of the West formed a united Christendom, the idea of a mutual sharing of power and authority by the spiritual and the temporal was accepted with complete unanimity. It was regarded as a normal, logical, and quite satisfactory state of affairs, even though there was a constant struggle both on the part of the state and on the part of the Church to keep their realms of jurisdiction independent and free, one from the other. With the religious upheaval of the sixteenth century things changed radically. The break in Christian unity that occurred at this time gave rise inevitably to a new relationship between Church and state. The Protestant Revolt may not have witnessed the early beginnings of the modern state — for that was a phenomenon already apparent in the period of the Renaissance — but it did definitely accentuate the growth of separatist nationalism in contrast to the earlier concept of a united Christendom.

After the modern state had consolidated its position of authority under the rule of a single monarch whose power tended to become absolute, there developed an intense struggle for national unification. This manifested itself in the creation of various state churches — as for example, in England, Holland, and Germany. On the continent, the wide acceptance of the doctrine "cuius regio, illius religio" — which led to the outbreak of violent religious intolerance — destroyed the historical relations between Church and state.

The secular state made its first appearance with the French Revolution. In the new philosophy of Rousseau and his followers religion was brushed aside as being purely a private matter, if not a postitive hindrance to the conduct of public affairs. The idea of separation between Church and state took a strong hold of the minds of political writers, of statesmen, and even of the masses. The separation of Church and state became really an isolation of the Church in public life. Education was secularized; marriages were regarded as mere civil contracts; divorces were for the first time recognized by public law as legitimate. In the broad field of public politics, the state was supreme, and the voice of religion in political, social, and economic matters was either ignored or treated with contemptuous indifference. We still live within the current of ideas which derive from the French Revolution.

"Union of Church and state" and "separation of Church and state" are not good descriptive phrases. They are in fact slogans or shibboleths, loaded with historical prejudices. Their use should be avoided. When the terms stand alone and without interpretation they breed confusion of thought and needless conflict. As Christians and as Catholics we stand for separation of Church and state provided the terms are rightly understood. It was Christ Himself who laid the foundation for the separation of Church and state when He pronounced the famous injunction, "Render to Caesar the things that are Caesar's, and to God the things that are God's." What Christ stated once was repeated many times by St. Peter, St. Paul, and by the other apostles. Take only that one instance from the Acts of the Apostles when Peter and John, forbidden by the authorities to preach the Gospel, declared emphatically, "We must obey God rather than men."

Before we can make a pronouncement in favor of either separation or union we must know how these terms are interpreted in popular opinion. Douglas Jerrold, the well-known English author, makes a valuable contribution to clear thinking on this subject in his book *The Future of Freedom.* Jerrold emphasizes that neither the state nor the Church is restricted in its authority but rather that both are restricted in their function. This is important. The state is supreme in what concerns the temporal welfare of the community as an aggregate of citizens, and the Church is supreme in what concerns the spiritual welfare of the community as an aggregate of souls. It is the business of the Church to direct men's souls toward their eternal destiny; it is the business of the state to direct citizens toward their temporal welfare. The Church should not interfere in what is strictly the state's business; and the state should not interfere in what is the business of the Church. But we may well ask, what is the business of each?

There are certain postulates which must be considered in determining a right relation between the spiritual and temporal power. Some of these are inherent in the origin, nature, and mission of the Church; others are inherent in the nature, organization, and function of the state. There will of necessity be a common ground of interest since both powers regulate the conduct of the same persons. Human beings, put on earth by God, belong simultaneously to the City of God and to the City of Man. The two societies of which men are conjointly members will differ in function, since the one orders affairs directly for man's spiritual and eternal ends, while the other orders them directly for his temporal and material advantage.

The Church must be free to carry out her divine mission — that is, she must be free to preach openly the doctrine of Christ, free to administer the sacraments, and free to conduct works of education and mercy. Any discrimination such as that contained in the Constitution of the Russian Soviets, whereby atheism has freedom of propaganda but Christianity merely freedom of worship, defeats the mission of the Church. Such discrimination is inconsistent with freedom and utterly unacceptable to any conscientious Christian.

The Church must also be free to establish disciplinary laws within and for her own communion; she must be free and independent of state control in choosing her clergy and her hierarchy; she must be free in her use of the means of communication with her own members; she must be free to use the natural means necessary to accomplish her essential mission, and therefore she must be free to own and use property. The Church cannot exist in a vacuum, and as long as we are creatures of flesh and blood she must have some physical or material means of fulfilling her functions. To deny this is to deny her right to exist.

The Church is a unique institution, different from any purely private association; she is endowed by divine origin with a moral personality. She should be recognized as such by the state and not be forced to seek a juridical existence as a mere creature of civil law. The Church does not ordinarily need state support out of the public treasury either for divine worship or for the living of the clergy. She has indeed a claim in justice to public assistance for her work of education and for her works of charity, especially where public taxes are levied universally on the citizenry for these purposes; but even this claim the Church can forgo without jeopardizing her essential freedom. It is only when the state forbids her to exercise the ministry of teaching and beneficence, that she must refuse her obedience: "We must obey God rather than men."

The Church cannot be tolerant of error nor give equal rights to truth and falsehood; but in any civil order where mixed religion obtains she does not demand sole recognition. She does not tolerate the use of physical force for spiritual purposes. Under no circumstances does she consent to the coercion of the human conscience. Physical force can never be an instrument of intellectual conviction or a means of conversion to the faith; hence a policy of persecution must always be alien to her nature and unworthy of her mission. In the last analysis, it is the primacy of the spiritual which she seeks to safeguard and maintain.

The state, too, enjoys equal freedom and equal authority in carrying out its own proper mission. What concerns temporal affairs and material well-being is entirely within the jurisdiction of the state. The sovereignty of the state, within its proper field, is not limited so far as its authority is concerned; for its authority, like that of the Church, is from God Himself. It is, however, limited in its function. God created man as a social being, and civil society is a necessary expression of this facet of his nature. Leo XIII summed up this doctrine in the celebrated passage found in his encyclical letter on the Constitution of Christian States (*Immortale Dei*): "The Almighty therefore has apportioned the charge of the human race between two powers, the ecclesiastical and the civil, the one being set over divine, the other over human things. Each in its kind is supreme, each has fixed limits within which it is contained, limits which are defined by the nature and special object of the province of each, so that there is, we may say, an orbit traced out within which the action of each is brought into play by its own native right. But inasmuch as each of these two powers has authority over the same subjects, and as it might come to pass that one and the same thing — related differently, but still remaining one and the same thing — might belong to the jurisdiction and determination of both, therefore God, who foresees all things, and who is the author of these two powers, has marked out the course of each in right relationship to the other."

The state has no right in justice either to determine the religious and moral content of education courses or, what is only less objectionable, to rule out altogether the teaching of ethics and religion. In either case the state exceeds its jurisdiction — in the one instance by its positive attack on the rights of religion, and in the other by its negative interference.

The same holds true of marriage, divorce, birth control, euthanasia, or sterilization. The state has indeed certain interests in these questions, but for the state to ignore the divine or natural law and to set up by its own legislation an independent ethic in these fields of social policy is not only a trespass on the rights of God but an assumption of totalitarian power. It is a denial of its own principles of freedom of conscience and freedom of the Church. To admit the right of the state to legislate unrestrictedly in these ethical fields is to open wide the door to a state sectarianism, to promote the establishment of a state-church, and to deny our fundamental doctrine of religious freedom and equality.

A few distinctions will be helpful in further clarifying the meaning of separation as well as of union of Church and state. Separation should never be taken as synonymous with or equivalent to conflict between Church and state. Unfortunately this has been all too frequently the historical reality. Witness the Roman persecutions in the early period of Christianity and the attitudes and policies in modern times of the Nazis and the Communists.

There is one kind of separation to which the Catholic Church will always object. It is the kind which separates the Church from her freedom to fulfill her divine mission. It is the kind which separates her from the temporal means necessary to preach the Gospel, to administer the sacraments, and to conduct her institutions of education and mercy.

The Church is, as we showed earlier, a visible society although spiritual in purpose. She has members, rulers, a code of laws, and disciplinary sanctions. The Church is a social institution just as much as the state. The state is not the whole community; neither is the Church. Neither of the two is synonymous or conterminal with human society. Both of them are agencies of society, the one established by God and the other by man; but both are legitimate since their essential authority is God-given. Any philosophy or theory which gives to the state all-inclusive power or unrestricted authority makes the state a dictator and a tyrant. Against this, we protest. All those who subscribe to the principles of democracy reject the notion of a totalitarian state just as do those who subscribe to the principles of Christianity.

If Catholic theologians and canonists have spoken in times past in favor of union of Church and state, it was not because they favored, in a society of mixed religions, the establishment by law of one Church, with exclusive rights to existence; it was not because they advocated the support of divine worship by public taxes; it certainly was not because they thought that the Church should have a veto power on the actions of the state. Rather, it was because the Catholic Church rejected certain fallacies on the subject of religion. The Church rejected the notion or theory that one religion is as good as another; or that religion is purely a private and personal matter and never a public function or social duty. The Church rejects the notion that the Gospels and the laws of morality are subject to the veto of state authority. The Church rejects the notion that rulers are above the law or unanswerable in the sight of God. These are some of the propositions which were condemned by Pius IX in his famous *Syllabus of Errors*.

Our approach to this problem must take into consideration also the underlying Constitutional concepts and traditions of our American form of government. Certain well-established premises serve as a basis. First, our Federal Constitution states that there shall be no religious test as a qualification for office or for any public trust. Second, the Bill of Rights declares, in the First Amendment, that Congress shall make no law respecting an establishment of religion nor prohibit the free exercise thereof. Third, our Supreme Court has, on two separate occasions, in 1892 and in 1952, solemnly affirmed that we are "a religious people."

From these principles, as well as from the debates in Congress and from the judicial decisions of our Supreme Court, we may validly reach certain conclusions regarding the relations between Church and state. First, our government has clearly indicated that it is not in any way opposed to religion or indifferent to its benefits. Second, it has shown, from the time the First Amendment was debated and ratified, that the government will not favor one religion more than another, nor impose a religious belief or practice upon the people of this nation. Third, it will never permit any legal interference with the rights of conscience nor with the free exercise of religion. Contrary, moreover, to the prevailing attitude and claim current in Europe at the time our Constitution was adopted, our government has consistently taken the position that religion is a field of jurisdiction in which the government has no competence. Our government is one of limited powers. The people have reserved to themselves all powers not specifically granted or at least contained implicitly in the Constitution. In the present instance, a specific limitation was actually written into the Bill of Rights. In Europe, only too often, the Church was looked upon and treated as a mere department of the state.

It might seem strange, in view of these premises and the pronouncement of the U. S. Supreme Court in the McCollum case in 1948, that the same Supreme Court should on two separate occasions officially declare that we are "a religious people." This affirmation is strengthened by significant facts which form an integral part of our national history. For instance, the same Congress which decreed that no law should be made respecting an establishment of religion, actually provided by statute that there should be chaplains to open sessions of Congress. It provided also for chaplains in our military services. Congress furthermore provided, by appropriations of public moneys, that chapels should be built for religious services at the military academy at West Point, at the naval academy at Annapolis and at the air force academy at Colorado Springs. The practice introduced early in our history has been continued in much more widespread fashion by similar establishments of chapels in our various military posts both in our own country and abroad. Congress also appropriated funds for the National Youth Administration to enable students to pay their educational expenses at any school of their choice. The same is true with respect to the G. I. Bill of Rights. Any veteran of the late war can select his own college or university. The government is willing to pay his tuition whether he chooses a private institution under the auspices of a religious body or a public, non-denominational school.

The Declaration of Independence makes specific mention of the fact that our inalienable human rights are a divine endowment given us by the Creator Himself. Our official coinage bears the inscription "In God We Trust." Our courts require an oath from all witnesses proclaiming their intent to make God a partner in their testimony and to call on Him to sanction the truth of their statements. The Founding Fathers who passed the First Amendment wrote, at the same time, the North-West Ordinance (1787), which was the original charter of this territory in which we now live. That ordinance declared: "Religion, morality and knowledge being necessary to good government and the happiness of mankind, schools and the means of education shall forever be encouraged."

Going back farther to the conditions which prevailed in colonial times, we discover that ten states or colonies out of the original thirteen actually had established churches. This means that they provided tax support for public worship in a particular church. During the Revolutionary War all but two of these states disestablished religion, the reason being that they wished to break completely with England, the mother country. When subsequently it came time to adopt a national Constitution for these thirteen original colonies, the question of a sound public policy in the matter of religion was brought up for discussion. Practically all New England, with the exception of Rhode Island, was strongly committed to the Congregational or Puritan religion. Virginia and the South were mainly Episcopalian, Maryland had a large segment of Catholics, Pennsylvania, under William Penn, was predominantly Quaker. As a result, when the representatives of these states gathered in convention, they were determined that no one religion should be given a preference over any other. They wanted absolute equality of all religions and no compulsion to support any church. In this sense only did they prohibit the "establishment of religion." The debates which were held in Congress from June 8 to September 29, 1789, clearly indicate that this was the sole objective of the legislators who adopted the First Amendment.

One of the best commentaries that has ever been written on this relationship between Church and state came from the pen of a distinguished American jurist, Judge Julian P. Alexander, presiding over the Supreme Court of the State of Mississippi. This is what he said: "Useful citizenship is a product and a servant of both the Church and the state; and the citizen's freedom must include the right to acknowledge the rights and benefits of each, and to import into each the ideals and training of the other.

"There is no requirement that the Church should be a liability to those of its citizenship who are at the same time citizens of the state. Nor is there any requirement that the state should be godless or should ignore the privileges and benefits of the Church.

"It is the control of one over the other that our Constitution forbids. The recognition by each of the isolation and influence of the other remains as one of the duties and liberties, respectively, of the individual citizen. It is not amiss to observe that by too many of our citizens the political separation of Church and state is misconstrued as indicating an incompatibility between their respective manifestations, religion and politics. The state has a duty to respect the independent sovereignty of the Church as such; it has also the duty to exercise vigilance to discharge its obligation to those who, although subject to its control, are also objects of its bounty and care and who, regardless of any other affiliation, are primarily wards of the state. The Constitutional barrier which protects each against invasion by the other must not be so high that the state, in discharging its obligation as *parens patria,* cannot surmount distinctions which (viewing the citizens as a component unit of the state) become irrelevant.

"The religion to which children of school age adhere is not subject to control by the state; but the children themselves are subject to its control. If the pupil may fulfill its (*sic*) duty to the state by attending a parochial school, it is difficult to see why the state may not fulfill its duty to the pupil by encouraging it by all suitable means. The state is under duty to ignore the child's creed, but not its need."

It is advantageous to discover how this phrase "separation between Church and state" first entered into our juridical concepts. It appears nowhere in the Declaration of Independence; it appears nowhere in the Federal Constitution; it appears nowhere in the Bill of Rights. The first place we encounter its use is in a letter of Thomas Jefferson written in 1802, thirteen years after the First Amendment was adopted. Jefferson used the phrase in an answer which he gave to a memorial address of the Danbury Baptists' Association. This reply was subsequently quoted and approved by the United States Court in 1879 in its decision against polygamy in the case of the Mormons of Utah. In view of this incidental use of what was at first little more than a figure of speech, it is indeed curious to find that the Supreme Court of the United States should attach so much importance to the phrase and use it as a key to unlock the meaning of the First Amendment. We accept, indeed, the policy enunciated when rightly understood, but we reject completely the notion that it constitutes a rule of law.

We realize quite well that Thomas Jefferson was no friend of organized religion, but Thomas Jefferson was not an enemy of religion itself. He proved that fact clearly when he was rector of the State University of Virginia. In fact, his own official action as rector of the university shows clearly that he did not intend to exclude all religion from the campus of the university. He specifically invited the representatives of religion to make use of the facilities and buildings of the university, not only for the teaching of religion but for divine worship itself. This record can be found readily in the official minutes of the Board of Visitors for October 7, 1822, signed by Jefferson himself. It should be, therefore, a conclusive answer to those who on the authority of Jefferson hold that religion in education is proscribed if taught on public property or with the co-operation of educational institutions supported by tax funds. We ask for nothing more than a benevolent neutrality on the part of our government toward religion. Separation of Church and state applies to the political life of the citizen; it does not imply that the citizen must be separated from religion or that a citizen shall suffer legal discrimination because of his religion.

We might ask whether the Church accepts as satisfactory this interpretation of a right relationship between Church and state, or the spiritual and the temporal, as it is found embedded in our national traditions and fundamental laws. The answer is an unequivocal "Yes." For the benefit of those who might entertain any doubt, we can categorically state that there is no doctrine of the Catholic Church which places upon its members the obligation to work for a change in respect to that religious freedom which is guaranteed to all of us by the Constitution of the United States.

A CATHOLIC PRESIDENT?

Recent discussions in the public press have focused attention on prejudices which still exist in the minds of at least a sizable minority of people here in the United States concerning Catholic candidates for public office. So far as we are able to learn, there has been no pressure from any Catholic source urging the election of a particular individual because of his faith. It would be highly improper if such were to be the case.

Various sampling processes have been undertaken to determine whether the voters are still infected with the animus which sent Governor Alfred E. Smith to defeat in the bitter election contest of 1928. The results of the polls indicate that there has been some improvement in the general attitude; nevertheless, the record reflects little credit on the existing state of public opinion. Suspicion and inveterate prejudice still seem to handicap any Catholic who offers himself as a candidate for the highest public office on the national level. There is no specific argument — much less a valid one — on which this opposition is predicated, but unfortunately it still endures as an aftermath of the religious intolerance which characterized the past century.

There are certain observations which seem to be pertinent to the current discussion. The one which immediately leaps to mind is that the spirit of democracy as enshrined in the Constitution has failed to take root in the consciousness of a large number of the citizens of the United States. They give only lip service to the provisions of the Constitution which declare that there shall be no religious test for public office.

To focus attention upon the issue of religion in politics renders no service to the cause of genuine democracy, nor does it help the cause of good public relations among our citizens. Continuous discussion of the subject in the public press tends to exaggerate the political significance of different religious convictions. There has been too much talk already about the religious preferment of a particular candidate for the highest public office in the gift of the electorate, and more of it is decidedly unwelcome. The persistent reference to only one religion as against all others in evaluating the eligibility of a candidate for office is in itself an incitement to make an issue of the fact. No other candidate is being subjected to such a religious test, and it would be quite improper and unwarranted were this to be done.

Religion is not an unimportant factor in our public life. Due acknowledgment of the sovereignty of God and an attitude of reverence toward the primacy of the moral law have always been regarded by the mass of the American people as the foundation of good government. We are "a religious people," in the words of the United States Supreme Court; but to subject theological principles to public debate in the evaluation of a candidate's eligibility to public office violates both the letter and the spirit of our national Constitution. There are only two questions which rightly should occupy the minds of the voters in their choice of a candidate for public office: Does the candidate have the necessary ability; and does he have genuine integrity of character? Nothing further should be demanded. We have had presidents in the White House professing various religious convictions — Episcopalians, Methodists, Baptists, Presbyterians — and we have never made an issue of the fact.

There is no adequate reason why we should have a president of our own faith, so far as the interests of Catholics are concerned. We have not suffered any serious disadvantage so far. The only interest which we as Catholics have in the question is that no disability be levied against a Catholic because of his religion. It will be disastrous to good public relations in our pluralistic society if this issue is subjected to further debate and to the inevitable contention which would follow. It is time to call a halt to such discussion.

In considering the question of Church and state, it is important also to recall that, historically, union of Church and state existed everywhere in the ancient pagan world. Prior to the advent of Christianity, the head of the state was always regarded as the head of the Church. The temporal and the spiritual order were completely identified, the one with the other. One of the proudest titles of the Roman emperors was "Pontifex Maximus," Chief Pontiff of the Roman people. It was our Lord Jesus Christ who first drew a sharp line of distinction between the function and the authority of government on the one hand, and the function and authority of religion on the other.

The undeviating experience of all history clearly indicates that there resides in the conscience of mankind a moral sovereignty of universal validity outside the dictates or statutes of the political state. This moral sovereignty rests on the law of nature, written by God on the tablets of the human mind and heart, and it finds its most forceful expression by and through the Church. Hitler and Stalin could find a legalistic justification for their brutal tyranny in the positive decrees of their totalitarian dictatorships, but they could find no justification of their conduct in God's law or in the human conscience.

Actually, there are only three possible policies or attitudes which governments can take in respect to religion and the Church. They can adopt a policy of opposition and suppression, as is done in Russia and in the satellite states. Secondly, they can ignore the existence of the Church, as if the problem did not exist, or as if the human conscience did not owe allegiance to God as well as to the state. There are some who may call this neutrality; but no man can be neutral toward God. We are either with Him or against Him. Thirdly, governments can follow a policy of co-operation, which rests upon mutual understanding and respect. This co-operation can be fruitful and beneficial, provided there is no confusion between the respective and distinct functions of Church and state. There will be no confusion and no conflict so long as the state recognizes that it has no authority and no competence in matters of religion, and, by the same token, recognizes that the Church has no competence in temporal and material things. Admitting frankly that there may be debatable ground at times as to which is which, nevertheless this is the only way, in a pluralistic society such as ours, to bring about a reconciliation of the two authorities, human and divine. This is the only way we can reconcile the statement of the United States Supreme Court, that "We are a religious people," with the declaration in the Bill of Rights that "Congress shall make no law respecting an establishment of religion, nor prohibit the free exercise thereof."

For quite some time the slogan "A free Church in a free state" was considered sufficient to express the right relationship between Church and state. Today the most thoughtful scholars and statesmen are none too sure of this simple solution. If mere naked power and stark national interests are not to be the final test of our domestic and foreign policy, then ethics and morality must be reintroduced as the standard of judgment. There is no other alternative. The question, however, persists: whose ethics and whose morality? Shall it be that of the Russian Soviets or of the Western democracies? Besides, what is the ethical standard of the Western democracies? Is it Christianity? If so, who shall teach and define the Christian ethics? Right there we face once more a very old problem.

In the easy assumption of the liberal statesmen of the eighteenth and nineteenth centuries this ancient ghost was supposed to have been effectively laid; but it seems to be very much alive once more. The question of the proper relationship between Church and state will not lie still. Any question of right or wrong, of justice or injustice, of honor or treachery requires of necessity that there be a norm or standard of judgment. More and more it is being recognized that any effective defense of true democracy, of freedom of conscience, of the dignity and rights of human personality requires in its last analysis the affirmation of a moral sovereignty outside the political state. The state cannot consistently assume the office of teacher of morality or Christian ethics. Once the mind admits this fact, then it is impossible to pretend that the Church is not a decisive factor in social relationships.

Obviously, this short statement does not exhaust the subject, but we set it forth as fundamental to a right understanding of the relationship between Church and state. To sum up the basic problem, recall these facts: There are two self-contained societies existing side by side; one spiritual, one political. The Church is a social institution just as much as the state. The state is not the whole community; neither is the Church. Both of them are agencies of society; the one established by God and the other by man; but both are legitimate.

The Church has members, rulers, a code of laws, and disciplinary sanctions, just as does the state. She can never be subordinate to the state in fulfilling her divine mission; neither can the state be subordinate to the Church in fulfilling its temporal mission.

The two are co-ordinate in power but in the hierarchy of values the spiritual and eternal is a higher function than the temporal and material. The two should remain independent of each other in their function. We call this separation. They should be united, however, in pursuit of the common welfare. We call this union. The question, therefore, is not one of "either-or," but rather one of "both-and." We must have both union and separation. The state needs the Church and the Church needs the state, but neither should dominate the other.

This relationship does not need to be expressed by means of a concordat — that is, in juridical terms — but it must at least be expressed in social action by impregnating our public laws and institutions with Christian principles.

The decision rendered by the Supreme Court in the celebrated Trinity Church Case of 1892 pointedly reminds us that:

"If we examine the Constitutions of the various states, we find in them a constant recognition of religious obligations. Every Constitution of every one of the forty-four states contains language which, either directly or by clear implication, recognizes a profound reverence for religion, and an assumption that its influence in all human affairs is essential to the well-being of the community.

"There is no dissonance in these declarations. There is a universal language pervading them all, having one meaning. They affirm and reaffirm that this is a religious nation. These are not individual sayings, declarations of private persons. They are organic utterances. They speak the mind of the entire people."

IV

A THREAT TO AMERICA'S LIBERTY?

THE past fifty years have witnessed a greater growth of
the Catholic Church in the United States, both in numbers and in influence, than any similar period of time in her
recorded history. It is doubtful if half a century ago it would
have been possible to count ten million Catholics in our country, whereas today there are almost four times that number.
There are more priests and Religious, more charitable and
educational institutions in ratio to the Catholic population, and
more effective organization of our resources, than in any other
country in the world. We do not claim pre-eminence in
scholarship or in sanctity, but the Church in America has been
outstanding for its initiative and devotion. God, in His divine
providence, has blessed it in an extraordinary manner. Zealous
and saintly pioneers laid the foundations and deserve the
credit. There is reason also to rejoice that the political institutions and traditions of religious freedom which prevail in this
country have contributed greatly to this magnificent achievement. We would be ungenerous if we did not express our gratitude to our fellow citizens for the liberal attitude of mind
which, in spite of sporadic outbursts of opposition among the
ill-informed, has steadily operated in favor of truth and justice.
The Catholic Church quite generally has been recognized as
a beneficent institution.

Fifty years ago the Church in the United States was just
beginning to emerge from its missionary status. Up to that time

we were still receiving large numbers of Catholic immigrants. We were in large measure dependent on other countries to supply priestly personnel, and to found and staff new Religious communities. Today, by contrast we are sending missionaries into foreign lands in ever-increasing numbers. In terms of financial support we are the mainstay of the Church, not only for the propagation of the faith but for all the great works of international relief and charity. Recently our own American-born Cardinal Stritch was called to Rome to undertake the direction of the important Congregation of the Propagation of the Faith. The fact that, in God's providence, he did not live to fulfill his task does not diminish the significance of this great change in our ecclesiastical status.

Fifty years ago the number of priests in our country laboring for the welfare of souls was less than sixteen thousand; today we count more than fifty thousand — three times as many. What is even more significant is the fact that fifty years ago the proportion of foreign-born priests and foreign-born Catholics was very high, perhaps a third of the total. Today we can claim that the Catholic Church in the United States is an indigenous institution. No longer can our separated brethren assume the attitude that they alone are to the manner born; that Catholics are somehow less American than the early settlers; and that therefore the Catholic's right to influence American policy in public affairs can be discounted as being an alien influence.

In fact, today things seem to have reversed themselves. Yesterday we were told that we did not carry our full share of responsibility in public life. Today our separated brethren express the fear that we have too much influence. Union of Church and state, censorship of movies, magazines, TV, and the possibility that we may attempt to impose our Catholic code of family ethics on the whole nation — these are said to be the chief objects of their so-called fears. Actually, it is nothing more than an ancient prejudice which makes it possible for the opposition to envision such a threat to religious liberty. Even if Catholics should become a majority of the population — which is not likely — there would be no grounds to fear our influence. Again and again we have declared that we stand by the Constitution and would never undertake to change its guarantee of religious freedom. We should like to persuade others to believe as we do, but we have no desire to implement our convictions with any kind of force. Such a procedure would be contrary to all our principles.

Among the many changes in our American mode of life there is one which interests us greatly, because it may have considerable significance in our religious life in the future. Fifty years ago the ratio of the American population which was actually affiliated with one or another of the many Christian denominations was less than half of what it is today. Today there is an unmistakable movement in favor of religion. We must keep in mind that the American people have always been a religious people, even though they were not always a church-going people. The broad statement that we are a religious people surely cannot be interpreted in the sense that there is any unity of belief and worship. As a matter of fact, there is perhaps no other country with such diversity of religious convictions — many of them contradictory in their affirmations. We live in a pluralistic society as far as religion is concerned. What is true, however, is that there is an almost universal respect and reverence for things religious. In spite of this general public attitude, however, there is no doubt that the general tone of society is secularist. The things that men esteem are for the most part the things of this world, such as health, material prosperity, human comforts, and social status. We might, with the celebrated sociologist of religion, Will Herberg, describe the attitude as one of religiosity — that is, a mixture of religious sentiment with secularist tendencies. It would not be wrong to say that the prevailing religious attitude of the majority of the American people is orientated in the direction of man's welfare here on earth rather than toward the honor and glory of God and man's eternal destiny hereafter. It is a religion which is man-centered, not God-centered.

One of the results of this peculiar American development is the danger of accepting doctrinal indifference or toleration of conflicting moral principles as a religious postulate, instead of recognizing it as a political postulate only. Another consequence for us, as Catholics, is that it makes more and more difficult the work of extending the one true Church among our fellow citizens so that they may share its blessings in full. There has developed over the years an attitude of religious complacency among the great mass of people, with the result that there is no longer an eager inquiry into the unique claims of the Catholic Church as the one necessary Church which Christ established for all men. No doubt the work to win converts will become increasingly difficult.

The changes over the past fifty years have been many. We have noted some. But in the midst of these changes there is one thing that has not changed, namely, the Church. Catholics continue to hold the same religious truths as in all the ages past — one Lord, one faith, one baptism, one set of sacraments, one system of doctrine, one hierarchical order. This is the Church which Christ established as the one authentic medium of salvation, the Church which safeguards revelation. It is this same Church which administers the sacraments, which gathers together the prayers of the faithful and offers them with Eucharistic Sacrifice as true worship to God; the Church which gives continuity to the very mission of Christ.

In our own day, however, certain minority voices have been raised questioning the advantage or benefit of a further growth and development of Catholic life. It has been said that the Church and her teaching constitute a threat to the liberties of our nation; and that a dominant majority of Catholics, if there should ever be such, would spell the end of religious freedom, and invalidate the guarantees of our national Constitution in this respect. The argument advanced in support of this thesis rests on a misrepresentation of Catholic teaching and Catholic history.

Pope Pius XII took cognizance of this situation, not so much as it reveals itself here in our national life but rather in its impact on international relations. His Holiness laid down the principles and clarified the policies regarding the problems of religious liberty and tolerance in the growing community of nations. Those principles and policies may well be emphasized again, as we recall the history of religion in our own country during the past fifty years. We consider it a great disservice to our country and a libel on Catholic loyalty and honor to impute to us a political intolerance which is erroneously assumed to be a corollary of our religious convictions. It can be stated categorically that there is no doctrine of the Catholic Church which places upon its members the obligation to work either individually or collectively for a change in respect to that religious freedom which is guaranteed to all of us by the Constitution of the United States. It is true that Pope Leo XIII made the observation "that the Church would bring forth even more abundant fruits if, in addition to liberty, she enjoyed the favor of the laws and the patronage of public authority." But all such requirements can be met by a more liberal interpretation and a more generous application of existing laws.

Pope Pius XII, in a historic pronouncement to the Italian Catholic Jurists on December 6, 1953, had this to say on the subject of religious toleration: *"The affirmation that moral and religious misdirection must always be impeded, when it is possible, because its toleration is in itself immoral, cannot be valid with unconditional absoluteness. Furthermore, God has not given to human authority such an absolute and universal precept, neither in the field of faith or morality. Neither the common conviction of men, nor the Christian conscience, nor the founts of revelation, nor the practice of the Church knows such a precept....Therefore the duty to repress moral and religious deviations cannot be an ultimate norm of action. It must be subordinated to higher and more general norms which, in certain circumstances, permit, and even make it appear the better part not to impede error in order to promote a greater good."*

This statement, coming from the supreme teaching authority of the Church, ought to set at rest any doubts or anxieties concerning the Catholic attitude on the subject of religious toleration.

It is fitting, even imperative, that we make clear our attitude in respect to our growing numbers and influence. Why do we glorify our progress? Is there not perhaps something suspect in our eager desire for conversions? With the utmost sincerity we declare that the Church has no other desire in the extension of her membership than the desire to share with her fellow citizens the full truth of the Gospel of Jesus Christ and to enable them to be partakers with us of all the blessings of the Redemption. Less than this we could not do and be loyal to our own convictions.

As Catholics we have no ulterior motives, no political objectives, no desire to achieve power in a spirit of vainglory or ambition. Our objectives are purely spiritual and our motives dictated solely by the charity of Christ. We love our country and its political and social institutions. We love all our fellow citizens without exception, and we reject every form of hatred, bitterness, or ill-will which might disrupt the sacred bonds of peace and concord. We proclaim in words and we wish to vindicate in action our profound belief in mutual justice, peace, and charity. The Church is not and never will be, no matter how vast she grows numerically, a threat to the liberty of our nation.

THE BISHOPS PROTEST AGAINST BIGOTRY

Recently the Catholic Bishops of the United States joined in protesting against manifestations of anti-Semitism and other forms of religious and racial bigotry. The bigotry which we have been witnessing of late is a strange and disturbing phenomenon. It is strange because it has occurred not only abroad, in European countries, but even here in the United States. It is strange because we in the United States have always entertained the thought that our people were somehow immune from racial or religious hatred. It is disturbing because these exhibitions of ill-will, even though they be sporadic in nature, nevertheless indicate that there are growing tensions in our society, and that the friendly relations which formerly existed among all citizens seem to have deteriorated.

It is good for us to keep a sense of balance, and not exaggerate the extent of this manifestation of bigotry. But, at the same time, it would be unwise for us to ignore it altogether.

The protest of the Bishops was based on certain fundamental postulates which derive their validity and cogency both from our Constitutional law and from the virtues inculcated by religion itself. When the Founding Fathers of our country faced the fact that we have here a pluralistic society in respect to race and religious convictions, they recognized that the only way to achieve peace, justice, and public order was to establish the principle of equality before the law, in favor of all citizens, with preference for none. They adopted, therefore, the First Amendment. Subsequently, after the Civil War, the adoption of the Fourteenth Amendment extended this immunity from discrimination to all people, irrespective of race or color. In keeping with this principle of toleration, the Constitution itself provided that there should be no religious test for public office. The wisdom and effectiveness of these provisions have been demonstrated time and again by the continued existence in this country of the largest measure of peace, freedom, and good order enjoyed by citizens anywhere in this world.

There are certain moral obligations which any sincere religion imposes on its adherents. They must, unless false to their convictions, have respect for truth in their statements of fact; they must practice justice and charity.

When we speak of respect for truth, we have in mind not only objective truth, but also the way in which the human mind arrives at truth. The use of force or compulsion, whether it be by physical violence, by legal discrimination, or by social ostracism, is utterly alien to the concept of freedom of conscience. The mind can be convinced only by persuasion and by rational argument. The use of any other means is an offense against the very nature of religion, for it would lead necessarily to hypocrisy and subterfuge. God has endowed the human person with freedom, and it is only when man takes possession of the truth freely and willingly that he follows the divine dictate of his nature. Toleration, therefore, is not only the wisest policy from a practical viewpoint, but it proceeds from higher and nobler motives.

Religion, moreover, not only emphasizes respect for the way in which we arrive at truth, but it inculcates two other important virtues — namely, justice and charity, both of which have an important part to play in creating a spirit of tolerance. It is a clear violation of justice when people are guilty of false-hood, innuendo, or misrepresentation in regard to their neigh-bor's actions, attitudes, or beliefs. The circulation of unfounded rumors, suspicions, and false interpretations of their beliefs is indefensible.

The virtue of charity demands that we treat our neighbor as we would have him treat us. One of the first duties in keeping with this imperative is that there be not only generosity of the purse, but also generosity of mind. If a man truly loves his neighbor, he will necessarily give him credit for honorable motives and upright purposes, unless the contrary is proved. Charity is not, as some people would have us believe, merely a form of almsgiving. Charity consists, rather, in the giving of oneself in love for one's neighbor.

For all these reasons — patriotic, religious, and social — an attitude of tolerance is the only safeguard of peace and justice in a pluralistic society.

These considerations still leave the main question un-answered, as to the cause of the recent eruption of bigotry and what we can do about it. What has happened, we ask, that might account for this resurgence of ancient prejudice? Frankly, we do not know the answer. We do know that there has been a growing tension generally throughout the world, which re-veals itself in exaggerated nationalisms, class conflict between capital and labor, religious antagonisms which spill over into political life, and in general a state of uneasiness and suspicion. Perhaps the aftermath of World War II has something to do with it. Perhaps the shift of prestige and influence within our population, from the older, well-rooted Americans to the newer groups derived from immigrant stock, accounts for it in part.

Anyone who has gained an acquaintance with sociological studies is aware of the phenomenon that is called xenophobia. This rather formidable word, from the Greek, means "fear of the stranger." We know from experience that whatever is strange, unfamiliar, or unknown is apt to induce a sense of wonderment. This attitude of wonderment passes readily into suspicion, and then often into unreasoning fear. Immigrants to this country have experienced this reaction. The mere fact that they are different from the native-born, whether in language, dress, customs, or religion, arouses a certain opposition, even though it be subtle and unrealized. The more these differences become cumulative, the greater is the degree of withdrawal or exclusion of that group from community life in general.

The remedy for these manifestations of hatred is a quick reaction of protest on the part of the more sane, more thoughtful, and more temperate group of citizens. There must be a joint effort to create a healthy climate of public opinion. Those under attack must stand together in mutual helpfulness; for what is injurious to one group will ultimately be injurious to all other groups and to society itself. Differences of conviction in respect to ethical and religious questions do exist among us, and it will do no good to pretend otherwise. There is no adequate reason, however, for them to become a source of ill-will and intolerance in our civic and social life or in our mutual relations. There are differences of racial origin, and some also of a political nature, such as those between liberals and conservatives, between "America First-ers" and interventionists. These differences constitute the very nature of a pluralistic society. The problem will be solved, not by emphasizing the differences but by emphasizing our mutual interdependence and by exercising the virtues of truth, justice, and charity in achieving the goals of our common welfare.

V

THE PAPACY AND THE POPES

THERE is no institution existing in the world today so well
deserving of our historical research nor any so productive
of lasting benefits to mankind as is the Papacy. No royal dynasty or civil government can claim such antiquity as that of
the Popes. The Papacy flourished in the days of Constantine
and Charlemagne, both of whom gave it honorable recognition.
It was strong and vigorous before any of the modern nations
had witnessed the beginnings of their history. It was the
instrument of the civilization as well as of the Christianization
of all the new countries of Europe. The Papacy called into existence the music and the art associated with the great cathedrals
and monastic foundations. It planted the seeds of ancient learning in practically all the great universities whose names are
famous in the records of art and science.

All these things are true because the Papacy is not merely
a human institution. It was Christ our Lord who established
Peter as the head of His spiritual kingdom, and it was to Peter
that He gave the keys of that kingdom.

The nations of the world have a purely human origin, and
that often steeped in war and bloody conquest. The Church
alone claims true nobility of origin and a divine guarantee of
perpetuity. "I am with you all days, even unto the consummation of the world."

The Papacy began its history in obscurity and impotence.
For three hundred years, to be chosen a successor to St. Peter

constituted an invitation and a consecration to martyrdom. The royal purple which is now the badge of the papal court is no mere insignia of earthly honor, but rather a forceful reminder of that purple cloak of scorn worn by the Master in His passion, and worn also by so many of His disciples in their own bloody death during the days of persecution.

Ever since Christ gave St. Peter the keys of the kingdom of heaven, there has been a struggle between the See of Peter and its antagonists over those keys. Who shall possess them? What is to be believed concerning Christ? What are the nature and the destiny of man? What is the nature of divine truth and what is the norm by which the actions of men shall be declared good or bad? To whom belongs jurisdiction over truth and goodness? These are questions which profoundly agitate the minds of men and cause human wills to clash in high places.

From the first recipient of the keys there has descended, in mystical succession, a dynasty on which rests a divine promise that guarantees its permanence and assures its ultimate victory over the rulers of the world of darkness.

Christ's kingdom can never be anything else but spiritual, except by the accident of history. It is spiritual in the purpose it serves; it is spiritual in the means it uses; it is spiritual in its origin and in its nature. Like Christ, its Founder, the Papacy must be prepared to trample underfoot all perishable grandeur should such prove a hindrance to its divine mission; and time and again in the course of its long history it has done so. But the Church must also be ready to use every human means to advance the interests of Christ's kingdom. Power and wealth, science and culture, art and beauty, all created goods must be pressed into the service of the Most High God and used as sacramentals in the sanctification of souls. Ceremony and sacred pageantry will always be a paradox to those who distort the full meaning of the Scriptures and see a picture of Christ's kingdom only in the stable at Bethlehem or on the desolate hill of Calvary. Such critics affect to see a contradiction between the simplicity and poverty of Bethlehem and the grandeur and dignity of the Vatican Court; they are ready to be shocked by the contrast between Peter, the humble fisherman, washing his nets at the side of the lake, and his successor wearing a triple crown, seated on a resplendent throne and ruling with majesty a spiritual kingdom on which the sun never sets. Those who share these sentiments, either sincerely or out of pretense, seem to forget that Christ surrounded Himself with glory when the occasion called for it. He entered triumphantly into Jerusalem amid the waving of palm branches and the shouts of hosanna, while the people literally paved the streets with the very garments they wore. These critics seem to forget that Christ was anointed at the banquet table with royal spikenard, and that He reproached the false disciple who complained about this "waste." They seem to forget that Christ prophesied that His kingdom is like the mustard seed, which is the smallest indeed of all seeds but which grows into a great tree so that the birds can build their nests in its branches.

There are sovereigns who exercise temporal jurisdiction over vast territories and over the lives and destinies of millions of subjects. The temporal jurisdiction of the Pope is utterly negligible in comparison. His territory is insignificant in its extent, and the number of subjects equals only that of a small village. He has, however, a mighty empire of souls under his spiritual jurisdiction. They reach into every land, and when he speaks on moral and religious themes he has the whole world as an audience. As stated by the celebrated scholar Joseph Bernhart: "The Papacy is a sovereignty of a unique kind, which by its very nature is something different from the secular leadership and administration of human associations. It lives not in reliance upon its skill and wisdom but in the consciousness of its timeless ancestry."

When a Pope dies, the chair of Peter becomes vacant and, for the moment, Christ has no Vicar upon earth. The Church is widowed and the children of the faith are orphaned, but this condition is only passing and does not last for long. The office of Peter is the very foundation of the permanency and the unity of the Church. The Papacy is a spiritual sovereignty in which all the powers of government are united in one person. Legislative power, judicial power, and executive power in all things that concern the kingdom of God on earth were vested by Christ Himself in Peter; and, without any diminution whatsoever, those powers have been handed down to each successor of Peter.

While we mourn, therefore, the loss of a Pope, we are conscious of the fact that it is only the person that dies; the office, being not humanly but divinely instituted, continues forever. It is not a hereditary office but an elective one. To be chosen the Vicar of Christ on earth is not the prerogative of any one class but a privilege open to the humblest member of the Church, who can rise from the ranks of the laity to the priesthood, to the episcopacy, and so to the Papacy itself. The Papacy is an office dependent not so much upon the personal qualities of him who holds it as upon the guidance and inspiration of the Holy Spirit. Friedrich Schiller describes this characteristic of the Popes in a pointed paragraph: "However unlike these Popes may be in temperament, outlook, and ability, their policy remains the same always in so far as steadfastness, uniformity, and unchangeableness are concerned. Their temperaments, their abilities, their outlooks seem never to have flowed over into their office. One might put it this way: their personalities were merged in their dignity, their passions were quenched under the weight of the threefold crown. Though every time a Pope dies the chain of succession is broken and must be linked together again at every new election, and though no secular throne has ever so frequently changed its incumbent, or been so stormily assailed and abandoned, yet this remains the only throne on earth which seems never to have changed its occupant. For only the Popes die; the spirit which informs them is immortal." This fact was impressively exemplified in the pontificates of the two previous Popes of the twentieth century, Pius XI, the Warrior Pope, and Pius XII, the Pope of Peace.

When the news broke that Pope Pius XI was dead, the world witnessed a strange paradox. With a unanimity not experienced for centuries, the whole of mankind acclaimed the memory of a Pope at the moment of his death. Not since the days of Gregory VII had a Sovereign Pontiff been forced to combat so many enemies or fight the battle of Christ on so many fronts. Yet, in spite of these bitter struggles, the entire world was now paying homage to this great Christian Pontiff. He was indeed a warrior Pope; but above all he was the world's chief spiritual leader. The consoling feature of such world-wide manifestation of sympathy was the high esteem which thereby was accorded to truly spiritual values. Evidently there exists in the minds and hearts of men everywhere a profound appreciation of the sublime office exercised by the Holy Father.

Pius XI, in his individual and personal life, manifested those great virtues which his office inherently demands. For that he was loved and revered. His daring courage in speech and in action, his enterprising adaptation of every modern advance in science, his dramatic sense of values in the service of religion; these things, as well as his staunch advocacy of peace, his keen analysis of world problems, his paternal kindness, and his patient suffering in illness had captivated the imagination of the world and won the admiration of both friend and foe. He was the world's greatest teacher in the things that concern the spirit; he was a man of intrepid faith. The world is inspired by noble example, and in Pius XI it had not only a supreme teacher whose lips spoke wisdom, but an inspiring exemplar whose public and private life was always in conformity with the truth he preached.

For almost sixty years he had lived a life of comparative obscurity. His talents seemingly were buried during forty years of his priesthood in the uneventful service of libraries. They were great libraries, however, the Ambrosian in Milan and the Vatican in Rome, and his quiet, scholarly research was ideal training for his future responsibilities. Great wisdom steadily grew in his keenly observant mind as he gazed out peacefully on a rapidly changing social order. Like most great men, he grew up in solitude and contemplation. But he was no recluse or hermit; he kept always abreast of the current of world events.

Even his physical habits were in harmony with his intellectual and spiritual pursuits. The high reaches of the Alpine mountain country were his favorite vacation resort. From Mount Rosa, in solitary ecstasy, he could scan the vast expanse of glacier peaks and snow-clad valleys. Here he held communion with the infinite Source of all beauty and grandeur, the Creator of all truth and goodness.

He was a solitary figure all his life, and at the end of his career he was destined to occupy the most solitary office in all the world. By the very nature of his work, the Pope can have no intimates, and few friends. Nevertheless, he is the Father of a mighty household and the entire world treads the pathways that lead to his door.

When Achille Ratti was appointed Apostolic Nuncio to Poland, he became the dean of the diplomatic corps in that country. He stood apart. When Bolshevist armies overran Poland, threatening the very gates of Warsaw, and when other diplomats retired from the capital, he stood at his post alone, encouraging and inspiring the people.

When the Lateran Treaties were signed, he stood out against the advice of many counselors at that historic moment and freely surrendered the Church's age-old claim to the Papal States and the jurisdiction of the city of Rome. He stood very much alone, saying: "I want no subjects, but independence for the Church." History has so far vindicated the soundness of his judgment and the wisdom of his action.

During the reign of Pius XI, the world was in a ferment not only in political and economic fields, but also with respect to social ideals and cultural values. The traditional Christian attitudes on the subjects of religion, the family, marriage, education, and the social and economic structure of the state had undergone vital changes. The Pope recognized the dangers in this upheaval, not only to spiritual values and religion, but also to human welfare and the integrity of civilization. With clarity and conviction, he wrote his great encyclical letters diagnosing our troubles and prescribing wisely the remedies which must be applied. These documents, addressed to the Catholic Bishops, quickly became part of the great tradition of papal letters.

Pius XI was our Father in Christ. It was in this capacity that he loved best to characterize himself. In 1932, when we journeyed to Rome from the International Eucharistic Congress at Dublin, to pay our respects in person for the first time to the Holy Father, it was with this sentiment that he greeted us. "It is fitting and proper," he declared, "that having shown your reverence to the Eucharistic Christ, you should now visit His Vicar here upon earth, who is also the common Father of all the faithful. You are welcome in your Father's house."

We are thankful to God for the understanding and appreciation shown the achievements of this great Pontiff. During his pontificate, Pius XI had seemed to be waging a losing battle against the forces of error and wickedness, but in the moment of his death the whole world saluted his courage and the nobility of the principles he defended. In like manner, long centuries before, Gregory VII, after heroic labors in defense of the Church, died in what seemed to be defeat. "I have loved justice," he spoke with his dying lips, "and I have hated iniquity, and therefore I die in exile." In both cases what seemed to be defeat developed subsequently into a glorious victory.

And so it goes from Pope to Pope. Pius XI was now dead, and a new link in the chain of papal succession had to be forged. Our memory still can easily go back to that day in 1939 when the announcement re-echoed through St. Peter's Square in Rome: "We have a Pope"; and the news was flashed to the world that it was none other than Eugenio Pacelli, our friend and recent visitor here in the United States. Our hearts thrilled at the good news and our minds leaped forward in expectation. We were not disappointed, for throughout the pontificate of Pius XII we had continuous evidence of the Pope's lively interest in everything that concerned the Church in America. Like a true father, he had to be mindful of the interests of all his children, but as chief shepherd he also appreciated, with fine historical perception, that the United States had reached national maturity and would henceforth lead the world either for good or for evil in its attitudes and policies. The ideals which our country would follow and the international pattern which it would create were bound to be determinative for many years to come.

The Pope knew our country, its people, its traditions. Hence his love, his devotion, and his absorbing interest in seeing to it that the Church here should be possessed of those qualities which would enable it to share actively in the destiny of the nation. No other historical figure of this generation so vitally influenced the world for good; no other had such an intimate and comprehensive grasp of the problems which weigh heavily on all mankind. Pius XII brought to bear on the solution of these problems not only the significant intellectual and moral guidance necessary for a clear interpretation of the natural and divine law, but also the prestige of his high office, in order to implement, as far as possible, his teaching through concrete social institutions. His own gracious personality radiated such kindness, such sincerity, and such an unmistakable spiritual aura, that all those who were privileged to meet him were captivated by these qualities and left his presence enriched by their contact with an unforgettable personality.

Seldom are such varied and such admirable qualities found united in a single person. We who are of the household of the faith have every reason to be profoundly grateful to Divine Providence for granting us such a resourceful and inspired leader in a time of great peril. What serenity, what clarity of mind, and what an invincible determination of purpose was his. Pius XII had to be forthright in the conflict with intellectual error and moral aberration, but withal he was gentle in his admonitions and eager for conciliation, so long as principles were kept inviolate.

The numerous encyclicals and allocutions which characterized his pontificate reveal the many facets of his mind. They give striking evidence of the intimate relationship of theology to the concrete realities of our times. In the fields of international co-operation, social justice, education, charity and relief, in juridical problems and physical science, he showed the same familiarity with fundamental principles and their practical application as he did in the field of divinity itself, with its application to doctrinal and moral problems, liturgy, art, and ecclesiastical discipline.

Pre-eminent among the many duties which are inherent in the Papacy is that of safeguarding the deposit of the faith and keeping alive the supernatural element in a secularist world. Pius XII was always, according to the precept of our divine Master, "in the world, but not of the world." He realized that the Church had to be incarnate in human society, but that its function was always to elevate man's aspirations and sanctify his institutions. Holiness was his vocation, and, until the day he died, man's eternal destiny was his ceaseless preoccupation.

The words and deeds and the holy lives of these two great Popes of the twentieth century stand as an enduring monument to truth, justice, and charity. And there rises now yet another successor of St. Peter in the person of Pope John XXIII, a man imbued with the spirit of his noble predecessors, for "only the Popes die; the spirit which informs them is immortal."

VI

WITH MITRE AND CROZIER

THE Catholic Church is a hierarchical society ruled by the Bishops who are in communion with the Vicar of Christ, the Pope, the Bishop of Rome. Above all other things, a Bishop is a man of God. He is the accredited representative of religion before all the world. Religion is his profession, as law and justice are the profession of the judge; or health and medicine the profession of the doctor. If we hold in honor the representative of religion, it is because the honor which is rightly due to God redounds, at least in part, on him who is His servant. It is the Bishop who, in God's dispensation, bridges the gap between heaven and earth. He is the Pontiff *par excellence.*

Many changes have taken place in the world and in the conditions affecting the mission of the Church since that night at the supper table when Christ Himself consecrated His first Bishops. The mission of the Church itself, however, and the means by which it is to be accomplished remain fundamentally the same. There is the same need to preach the Gospel as it was committed to us by Christ, even though the interpretation of its truths in relation to current problems is somewhat different. There is the same need to sanctify mankind by the divinely established means of sacrifice and the sacraments, even though the discipline of their use has somewhat changed. There is the same need for the exercise of authority, in order to maintain and safeguard the integrity of faith and order, even though the

76

Code of Canon Law under which authority is exercised has been partially modified in the course of time.

Because the spiritual needs of mankind remain substantially the same from age to age, the structure and the function of the Church once determined by Christ do not change. The function of the Church, briefly put, is to teach, to sanctify, and to rule. This is the function whereby continuity is given to the mission of Christ Himself. There are other ways, no doubt, by which God could have provided for the extension and perpetuity of His kingdom here on earth, but the establishment of the apostolic hierarchy was the way He did choose and the chief means He did ordain. Christ's first act in His public ministry was to choose twelve apostles. These He trained for three years by intimate and daily association with Himself. Having trained them in His own school of spiritual formation, He finally identified them with Himself and invested them with His own powers — powers which they were to transmit to their successors. In this way He provided for all future time and built the structure of His Church.

In the divine constitution of the Church the Bishop holds a key position. Just as the axiom "Ubi Petrus, ibi ecclesia" holds universal validity, so, within narrower limits, the dictum of St. Ignatius of Antioch also holds good: "Ubi episcopus, ibi communitas Catholica." The popular concept of a Bishop is unfortunately much less significant than that — at least in the common evaluation of his position these days. Many people look upon a Bishop as a sort of ecclesiastical administrator, a kind of religious superintendent, an official who presides at solemn ceremonies with mitre and crozier. The Sacred Scriptures by contrast take an entirely different view of the matter. So also do the Fathers of the Church and all the great theologians. In the language of the Church, the Bishop is "Sacerdos

Magnus" — the lengthened shadow of the Messias, the great High Priest.

Whenever Christ spoke of the organic nature of His Church, He gave special attention to the function of the apostles. He made them His representatives, His spokesmen, and the legitimate successors to His divine mission. Because they were one body, they had to have one head. Peter was the one chosen by Christ for that sublime office. But the other apostles were his associates; as members of that apostolic body they shared both the authority and the responsibility of Peter, their head; always, however, in a manner subordinate to and dependent upon Peter. That is why Christ spoke to Peter first, and then to all the apostles, when He gave them the keys of heaven, saying: "Whatever thou shalt bind on earth shall be bound in heaven, and whatever thou shalt loose on earth shall be loosed in heaven." For this reason the successors of St. Peter, the Popes, in their encyclical letters, address the Bishops not as mere delegates but rather as associates: "Venerable Brethren."

By virtue of his office, the Bishop has power par excellence both over the Mystical Body of Christ, the Church, and over His real, true, and substantial Body in the Holy Eucharist. St. Thomas teaches that within his diocese the Bishop is the head of the apostolate, so that nothing can be done in relation to it without his initiative or consent. The Bishop is the one charged with the sanctity of all. He is the teacher of truth, and the source of grace under God. His work is to assure the generation, conservation, and growth of this supernatural life of grace.

There is no time when a Bishop is so truly exercising his office as when he stands at the altar. St. Paul, in his letter to the Hebrews, comments on this supreme function of a Bishop: "Every high priest taken from among men is appointed for men in the things pertaining to God, that he may offer gifts and sacrifices for sins." If it is said that the priest also offers sacrifice, and that this function is not, therefore, the special prerogative of the Bishop, nor peculiarly distinctive of his office, then it is well to recall the fact that only the apostles, namely, the first Bishops, were present at the Last Supper when Christ spoke the words of command: "Do this in remembrance of Me." Again, we turn to St. Ignatius of Antioch, who states: *"That* Eucharistic sacrifice alone can be regarded as legitimate which is offered while the Bishop or his delegate presides." St. Thomas Aquinas reminds us that the power of the priest to consecrate the Body and Blood of Christ, although equal to that of the Bishop, still depends on his communion with the Bishop, not only for the reception of that power but also for its licit exercise. If it is thought that this distinction minimizes the dignity of the priesthood, then we should remind ourselves of the ordination ritual wherein certain highly significant words are used in communicating the powers of the priesthood to the *ordinandi.* The ordaining prelate, after the imposition of hands, addresses the new levites as "coöperatores ordinis nostri." They are intimately associated with the Bishop in the exercise of his office. Priests are not glorified deacons, with merely something superadded to the sacred orders which they already possess. Rather, they have a new status, and participate in the episcopal office. In a sense they are "assistant Bishops." Obviously there is an essential difference, as the Council of Trent teaches, between the rank of deacon, priest, and Bishop; but the priest does share in the Bishop's work of teaching, sanctifying, and governing the Church.

The role of Christ as prophet or teacher is also given continuity in the office of the Bishop. To him is confided, in the consecration ceremony, the duty of representing the official

magisterium of divine truth. He is the official teacher in his
diocese. In the Gospel we read the words spoken by Christ to
the apostles: "He who hears you, hears Me"; and "Go, therefore, and make disciples of all nations, ... teaching them to
observe all that I have commanded you." It is an office made
visible by reason of the fact that the Church decrees that only
in the Bishop's church may the cathedra, or chair of truth, be
permanently established. Hence the word "cathedral." It is
only in communion with the Bishop that priests are commissioned to preach the Gospel. In order to preach lawfully they
must receive faculties from the Bishop, just as they must also
receive faculties to absolve from sin and to administer the other
sacraments.

In addition to the responsibility which rests upon the Bishop
to sanctify and to instruct the people of God, there is also the
right and the duty to govern them in the pursuit of their eternal
destiny. In His farewell admonition, Christ transferred to the
apostles and their successors that power to rule, which He Himself had received from the Father: "All power in heaven and
on earth has been given to Me. ... As the Father has sent Me,
I also send you." In the Acts of the Apostles, St. Paul re-
affirms this grant of authority with the words: "Take heed to
yourselves and to the whole flock in which the Holy Spirit has
placed you as Bishops, to rule the Church of God."

In the ceremony of episcopal consecration, the "things that
are of God" are spelled out in an elaborate ritual. There is first
the solemn inquiry concerning the faith, which the Bishop must
hold steadfastly and profess energetically above all others. He
is to be its champion and protector — the spokesman who is to
give it eloquent expression in word and in deed. Being assured
of his staunch devotion, the Church then proceeds to confer
upon him those rights and duties which invest him with the

prerogatives of a Bishop. He is charged with the responsibility of guarding both the Mystical Body of Christ, the Church, and His real, true, and substantial Body, the Holy Eucharist. He is empowered in the name of Christ to preach, to rule, and to offer sacrifice. To emphasize this aspect of the Bishop's office and to make his function resplendent in the eyes of the faithful, he is clothed with certain insignia of office which command attention and veneration — the mitre is placed on his head, and the crozier, or shepherd's staff, is put into his hands. These are the emblems of a Bishop's jurisdiction. Many beautiful and expressive words have been employed in Christian tradition to describe the function of the high priest, but there is no tribute of appreciation which sums up the dignity and responsibility of the office more effectively than the simple phrase, "alter Christus — another Christ."

A Bishop of the Church must keep safe the deposit of faith committed by the divine Master to His apostles. He must safeguard it at all costs and keep it free from the encroachment of error. It is the Bishop who exercises the official magisterium in the Church committed to his care. He is the official teacher of religion within his jurisdiction. Unswerving faith, therefore, is the authentic mark of the episcopacy. The Bishop must be "urgent in season, out of season, reprove, entreat, rebuke," but always with all patience and sound doctrine.

It is impossible to differentiate among the articles of faith in regard to their inherent truth; but if there be any doctrines which are of greater significance than others, they are the truths concerning the great mystery of the Incarnation. The doctrines regarding the divinity of Christ and His Real Presence in the Holy Eucharist are the touchstones of the faith. It was these truths which Christ committed to the hierarchy of His Church for special protection, and He made their immediate defense the prerogative of episcopacy. At Caesarea, Christ put the question which overshadows all others: "Who do men say the Son of Man is?" It was the chief Bishop, St. Peter, who spoke up in the name of the apostles, saying: "Thou art the Christ, the Son of the living God."

It was in the synagogue at Capharnaum that Christ for the first time in explicit language laid down the doctrine of the Holy Eucharist. "I am the living bread that has come down from heaven. If anyone eat of this bread he shall live forever; and the bread that I will give is My flesh for the life of the world." When some of His disciples deserted Him, exclaiming, "This is a hard saying — who can listen to it?" Jesus turned to the apostles and asked them, "Do you also wish to go away?" It was Simon Peter, the first Bishop of the Church, who answered once more in the name of all the apostles: "Lord, to whom shall we go? Thou hast words of everlasting life." Ever since that historic moment, the champions of the Real Presence of Christ in the Holy Eucharist have been the Bishops of the Church.

Christ came into this world not only as prophet and teacher, but also as priest. On Calvary He made atonement for our sins by shedding His blood upon the cross. But the saving merits of His sacrifice were to be perpetuated for all time through His Church. Not only the Mass but also the sacraments were to be the channels of His grace and the effective means of salvation.

The Bishop is the minister of the sacraments in a more inclusive sense even than he is the minister of the Mass.

It is the Bishop alone who can give continuity to the Mass and to the sacraments, through the exercise of his apostolic power in the Sacrament of Holy Orders. It is the Bishop again who imposes hands in the Sacrament of Confirmation, so that the laity may also receive the gifts of the Holy Spirit according to their state.

Christ came into this world not only as prophet and as priest, but also as king. This kingship of Christ was first proclaimed by the angelic messenger on the very day of the Annunciation. It was reaffirmed by word and deed many times in our Lord's public life, so that the people rose up at times and in mistaken loyalty would have made Him an earthly king. The principal charge made in the indictment brought against Him before Pilate was that He claimed to be a king. The three-fold title which hung above His head upon the cross proclaimed His kingship to the world. It was a primacy of spiritual power and a sovereignty over the minds and hearts of men to which Christ laid claim. It is this claim to authority on the part of the hierarchy which so disturbs the enemies of religion today, as it did in the time of Christ. With magnificent condescension and divine generosity Christ shares His royal prerogative with the apostles and their successors, with the Bishops of the Church who are, as it were, the shadows of their Master, the Messias.

VII

THE PRIEST AND HIS PARISH

IF THERE is any one duty which more than another devolves upon a Bishop, it is the duty of making adequate provision for the continuity of the priesthood. An expanding priesthood is an indispensable condition of an expanding Church. Without the priesthood there is no Mass, no preaching of the Gospel, no dispensing of the sacraments, and, in the end, no faith and no salvation. The Canon Law of the Church, therefore, imposes on the Bishop, as the chief responsibility of his office, the duty of recruiting, training, and commissioning for the ministry an adequate number of priests. Without vocations there will be no future priesthood.

The history of a priestly vocation and its fulfillment is always a dramatic chronicle of God's providence. No one can chart exactly the movements of God's grace in any individual soul nor determine the precise moment when effective response is made to the special promptings of the Holy Spirit. This much, however, we do know — there are no two priestly vocations exactly alike — "The Spirit breatheth where He will."

Sometimes God's call comes in the morning of life, in childhood itself, as in the case of Samuel the prophet. At other times the call to enter the service of religion comes late in life, as in the case of Matthew the publican. Sometimes God calls a Nathanael, a man in whom there is no guile. At other times He calls a Saul of Tarsus, a persecutor of the Church. No matter when the call comes, or how, the important thing is that the answer be given generously, as both Samuel and Saul gave it: "Lord, here am I," or "Lord, what wilt Thou have me do?"

One of two great fields of activity lies open to the young man who finds himself drawn to the service of the Church: the diocesan clergy, which is engaged in the routine but essential work of caring for souls as organized in parish units; or some Religious Order, with its specialized service in education or social work, either at home or in the foreign missions. Some aspirants to the priesthood have a predilection for community life under vows and for being subject to the immediate direction of superiors. Thus their striving for perfection is reinforced by good example and constant supervision. Others prefer the more isolated life of the diocesan priesthood in obedience to the command of the local Bishop and subject only to the general laws of the Church. All priests alike are dedicated to that life of perfection which finds its highest expression, according to St. Thomas, in the priesthood itself.

The preaching of the Gospel or missionary work is of the greatest importance. In the early Church the apostles delegated the work of charity or almsgiving to the deacons, but reserved to themselves the preaching of the word of God. St. Paul himself says, "Woe to me if I do not preach the Gospel." To the Romans he writes, "Faith then depends on hearing." Again, quoting the prophets Joel and Isaias to the Romans, he said: " 'Whoever calls upon the name of the Lord shall be saved.' How then are they to call upon Him in whom they have not believed? But how are they to believe Him whom they have not heard? And how are they to hear, if no one preaches? And how are men to preach unless they be sent? As it is written, 'How beautiful are the feet of those who preach the gospel of peace; of those who bring glad tidings of good things!' " Missionaries, as the very word itself indicates, are those especially sent to preach the Gospel. They have always been held in highest reverence; but, once their work is done, who shall keep alive the faith and who shall nourish it and bring it to fruition?

The Sacred Canons of the Church lay upon every Bishop the solemn obligation of dividing his diocese into parishes. These parishes are to have fixed territorial limits and their own priests, in order to provide for their spiritual welfare. Canon Law devotes more space to a description of the rights and duties of a parish priest than to any other single office in the Church, except that of the Bishop himself. The parish is indeed the fundamental unit of Catholic life. As the parish stands, so does the Church. If the parish flourishes, Catholic life is strong and robust; if the parish grows weak and anemic, so does Catholic life. If anyone wishes to have proof of this fact, let him visit foreign lands where the faith was once strong but where religious indifference has infected the life of a Catholic people. There they will see the operation of cause and effect in the disintegration of parish life. To keep the faith alive and vigorous there must be a constant ministry of the word and a faithful ministry of the sacraments. Without parish organization this cannot be done.

The parish exists not only for the maintenance of divine worship, the exemplification of the liturgy, and the administration of the sacraments, but also for every good work which is inspired by religion. No parish is properly organized unless provision is made for the Christian education of the young. Therefore schools have always been established within the shadow of the church. It has been well said that the enemies of Christ understand the value and importance of the school even better than some who lay claim to be His followers. Witness the direction of their attacks. Is not the Catholic school singled out as the nursery and bulwark of the faith, and thus made the object of persecution in every country behind the Iron Curtain? Is not the same procedure followed even here in our own midst?

At the very beginning of the Church, the care of the poor and afflicted was a special charge laid upon those who followed the Gospel. "Religion pure and undefiled before God the Father," says St. James, "is this: to give aid to orphans and widows in their tribulation." Our divine Saviour made the service of the hungry, the naked, the sick, and the afflicted the very standard and criterion by which He will pronounce final judgment on our lives. Where is there a parish without its St. Vincent de Paul Society or its equivalent organization for the purpose of bringing relief to the poor? If the charity of Christ is not exemplified in a parish, then the parish is derelict in its duty and false to the teaching of the Gospel.

Not everyone can leave father and mother, home and kindred in order to carry the message of salvation into foreign lands. But every parish has its mission program. The faithful are taught by their parish priests to offer prayers and alms to sustain the missionary at his post in distant lands.

Whenever there is a good work to be performed, the appeal for help will find its way sooner or later to the parish. Catholic action in all its varied phases is rooted in the parish. With St. Paul the parish priest must say: "Who is weak, and I am not weak? Who is made to stumble and I am not inflamed?" The parish priest who wishes to walk worthily in the footsteps of his Master must do today what Christ did in the long ago. He must summon the crowds to listen to his word, whether in the temple, on the seashore, or on the mountain slopes; he must call the children to receive Christ's blessing, whether in the classroom, on the playground, or in the church; when good fortune smiles, he must rejoice; when sorrow and suffering lay their burden on his people, his words must bring sympathy and comfort. He must stand at the bedside of the sick and of the dying; he must seek out the sheep that are lost and welcome the prodigal son who returns to his Father's house; he must break the bread of life in the spoken word from the pulpit, and distribute the living bread in the Sacrament at the altar rail. Although it is not an essential part of the divine constitution of the Church, nevertheless the parish unit is an integral part of the divine plan for the attainment of man's salvation. But without the priesthood there would be no spiritual life in a parish.

The priesthood of the New Testament exists whole and entire in Christ alone; it exists only by participation in all others who share that happy privilege. Religion and the priesthood are historically inseparable.

Religion is the oldest and most universal instinct of the human race. Cicero bears testimony to this fact when he states, "There is no nation existing so barbarous that it does not acknowledge the existence of a God, so much so that men will rather have a false god than no God at all." Now religion without a priesthood is sterile and ineffective. Sacrifice and priesthood are correlative. The heathen philosopher Plutarch writes: "If thou wanderest through the earth thou mayest easily find cities without walls, without kings, without palaces, without money, and without science; but no one has ever yet found, nor ever will find, a people without the knowledge of a God, without prayers, without vows, without religious ceremonies, and without sacrifices whereby to obtain benefits, or to avert evil."

Religion is a profession more ancient than law or medicine. As the lawyer promotes justice; as the doctor protects health;

so the priest proclaims God. The priest by the very nature of his office is a public figure; he is the mediator between God and man; he is the deputy of his people in the things of God. The Scriptures proclaim that the lips of the priest shall keep wisdom. Christ Himself says: "He who hears you, hears Me"; "Whose sins you shall forgive, they are forgiven them." At the altar the priest puts aside his own identity and, bowing low over the bread and wine, impersonates Christ, saying the awful words, "This is My Body. . . . This is My Blood." If value, dignity, and importance are attached to any office, then as surely as there is a God in heaven, the office of the priesthood is worthy of honor and respect. To say these things is not to offer an occasion for pride or vanity, but rather to remind ourselves of the urgent need of cultivating reverence and deep humility.

The proof that there can be no effective religion without a priesthood can be found in the progressive deterioration of religion since the days of the Reformation. The sixteenth-century reformers denied the existence of a priesthood and rejected its need in the divine economy. Not only has divine worship suffered an irreparable loss as a result, but doctrine and morals among our separated brethren have themselves been fragmentized to a point where they can no longer be defined with clearness and certainty. History vouches for the fact that the priesthood established by Christ is the best guarantee of the unity, sanctity, and catholicity of the Church. It is indeed one of the marks of the Church.

Four hundred years ago the seamless robe of Christ was rent asunder by the revolutionary doctrine of private judgment. As a rule of faith it was inadequate and disruptive. Schism had been experienced in the Church before that time, but nothing in Church history had worked so effectively to destroy

consecrate him with solemn ceremony in order that he might
serve the Lord in the office of the priesthood. That office there-
after was made hereditary in the family of Aaron and in the
tribe of Levi. But when the coming of the Messias was foretold, the psalmist declared that there would be a new priesthood predicated not on ancestry but on free vocation. Christ
therefore was to be a "priest forever, according to the order of
Melchisedec." And so is every man who is validly ordained
by a Bishop in communion with the See of Rome. The priest
of the twentieth century is a link with the priests ordained
by Christ Himself. The priesthood is surely one of God's
noblest gifts.

VIII

THE CHURCH OLDER THAN THE BIBLE

IT IS fitting that we should at times publicly reaffirm our faith in the divine origin of the Sacred Scriptures, and encourage the salutary practice of reading them devoutly. It can truly be said that the Bible is the word of God, since it was the Holy Spirit who prompted the authors to write, inspired them as to what they should write, and protected them from error in what they wrote, while leaving intact all the human characteristics which are normally attached to authorship. It was the divinely established Church, however, which gathered together, between the first and second centuries of Christianity, those writings that make up the New Testament. The Church carefully separated the genuine and authentic Scriptures from what was apocryphal and spurious, and formulated the official list of books which constitute the New Testament and which Christian people ever since have accepted as God's inspired word.

Some five hundred years ago Johann Gutenberg of Mainz in Germany discovered the process of printing by movable type. Being a devout Catholic, he decided almost automatically that the first book to be printed should be the Bible, since it was the word of God and therefore the most significant record in the history and experience of mankind. Prior to the year 1452, the Bible existed only in manuscript form and constituted a rare possession, within the reach only of wealthy patrons of learning, or held as common property by churches or monastic corporations. Once the multiplication of copies of the Bible was made possible by the invention of Gutenberg, not only the Latin Vulgate version of the Scriptures began to circulate freely among the cultured, but translations in various vernacular languages such as English and German promptly appeared in print for the use of the masses. All this, it should be remembered, took place before Luther was born.

The invention of printing is second in importance only to the invention of the alphabet itself. Printing was a necessary prerequisite for popular education. Without printing there could be no adequate supply of textbooks; and without textbooks no universal education, no common schools, and no general knowledge of reading and writing. This does not mean that prior to printing people were ignorant of the Bible. Before it was printed, the Bible was taught to the people in a number of ways: by the liturgy, by art, by dramatic performances, and, above all, by sermons. The absence of books did mean, however, that reading and writing were confined to a minority of the people.

For many centuries the Catholic Church has jealously guarded the integrity of the Bible, so that its divine text might not be corrupted by human error. In the libraries of convents and monasteries the word of God was laboriously and meticulously copied by hand, and the Church certified its accuracy. When the full text of the Bible was completed in manuscript form, it represented the work of a skilled craftsman for one entire year. Its cost, therefore, was far beyond the slender means of the individual Catholic. In terms of the present value of money, a single copy of the Sacred Scriptures meant an investment of four to five thousand dollars. Naturally a copy of the Bible was a valuable possession. Hence arose the practice of displaying the Bible for the use of the public at the rear of the churches, on a reading stand, with a strong chain attached, so that the book might not be carried away in the pilfering hands of some dishonest person. The phrase "chained Bible" is sometimes used as a term of opprobrium by ignorant people who do not have the faintest idea of the history and meaning of this custom. To such as these, the "chained Bible" means a prohibition of its use or no access to the word of God, whereas it should be obvious to anyone that we do not chain a cup to a drinking fountain so that people cannot drink, but rather that no one, by stealing the cup, can prevent the rest from drinking.

There are two tragic errors concerning the Bible which have been the cause of much confusion and sad divisions in the history of the Christian Church. The first of these two errors presumes that the Bible is the original source of our knowledge of God's revealed truth. The second error, equally grave and disruptive of Christian unity, is that the Bible is self-explanatory and needs no official interpreter. Both of these errors are intimately associated with that period of history which witnessed the great invention of printing.

It is absolutely necessary for a correct understanding of the history of the Church that we recall the significant fact that Christ Himself never wrote a single word which has come down to us. Christ preached His Gospel; He did not write a book. He gave us instead the living Church. Furthermore, Christ did not instruct His apostles to write books, but rather to go out into the whole world and preach His Gospel to every creature. As a matter of fact, the Christian religion was well established in most parts of the ancient Roman empire long before the Bible of the New Testament was assembled as a uniform record of Christ's teaching. Of the apostles themselves only St. Matthew and St. John left a written record of the life of Christ; and St. John, at the conclusion of his Gospel, states emphatically that the Scriptures do not contain all of Christ's teaching. "There are, however," says St. John, "many other things that Jesus did; but if every one of these should be written, not even the world itself, I think, could hold the books that would have to be written." It is true that St. Peter and St. Jude, who were among the eyewitnesses of Christ's public life, also wrote some brief letters, but St. Peter tells us that "There are certain things difficult to understand, which the unlearned and the unstable distort, just as they do the rest of the Scriptures also, to their own destruction." Throughout the formative period of Christianity — the first hundred years — it was the preaching of the word and not the reading of a book which constituted the means of propagating the new religion. There was as yet no book to be read.

The important fact we must bear in mind is that Christ established a Church as the authorized teacher of His doctrine. "Thou art Peter and upon this rock I will build My Church." So declared our Lord, and again: "He [who] refuses to hear . . . the Church, let him be to thee as the heathen and the publican." The Church came first; the Sacred Scriptures came later. The latter were an additional source of divine truth. We do not minimize their importance. They were a precious and great gift of the Holy Spirit, in order to confirm our faith and expand our understanding of its mysteries.

It was the Church which selected from the many early Christian writings the records that tell with authentic and inspired truth the story of our Blessed Lord's words and actions. It was the Church which guaranteed to the faithful the divine character of the Scriptures under the inspiration of the Holy Spirit. It was the Church which safeguarded the substantial integrity of the text in its various translations and in its multiple reproductions. It was the Church which during the first fifteen hundred years of the Christian religion, when the people for the most part could not read or write, made known to the faithful the contents of the Bible. It was the Church which illustrated the contents of the Scriptures in her cathedrals and monasteries by means of painting, sculpture, stained glass, and sacred psalmody. The simple and irrefutable fact is that there would have been no Bible if there had not been a Church to see to its formation, to ensure its authenticity, to preserve it in existence, and to interpret its authentic meaning.

We recall these facts so as to set the record straight. We do so because unfortunately there has been much public misunderstanding about the Bible. We do not wish to belabor the question of the true origins of the Christian religion, nor stir up ancient controversies about the rule of faith; but we are reluctant to allow misunderstandings to continue and to have repeated the errors of an ignorant past. We wish to focus attention on the divine character of the Sacred Scriptures, to point out their invaluable contribution to an understanding of the teaching of Christ, and to stimulate a renewed interest among our faithful people in the frequent reading of the Bible as a salutary means of sanctification. As St. Jerome points out, the Bible is like a letter of God sent from heaven. In his Commentaries, written in the fourth century, he says: "Ignorance of the Bible means ignorance of Christ." To help dispel such ignorance, an official revised edition of the English translation of the New Testament from the Vulgate Latin of St. Jerome, was published in 1941, after the lapse of almost two hundred years. This literary incident constituted a memorable moment in the Church history of our country. It is important to keep clearly in mind the implications of such an action. This was not an effort to introduce changes into God's holy word. No one would dare tamper with God's revelation. It was not an effort to add anything to or subtract anything from what the sacred authors originally wrote under the inspiration of the Holy Spirit. Rather, it was an effort to present with greater exactitude and greater clarity of expression the precise meaning of the Sacred Scriptures as first delivered by God to the Church.

The advances made in recent times by biblical scholars in interpreting obscure Semitic or Greek passages, as well as the obsolescence of certain English words and usages, made such a revision of the existing text highly desirable. The present Douay-Rheims English Bible was published for the Catholic faithful who lived at the end of the sixteenth century; it was subsequently revised by Bishop Challoner about a century and a half later. Manifestly there had been changes in the use of the English language during the interval. To make the reading of the text more intelligible to the faithful of the present day, the Bishops of the United States invited the Scripture scholars to prepare, under their auspices, an improved text. After five years of study and work, they produced the exact, readable text of the New Testament that it is our privilege to own and study. In the same spirit, a revision of the Old Testament is under way, and those parts that have been completed are incorporated into many Bibles now being published.

It is important to recall that the Scriptures were written not merely for the purpose of historical research but for the edification of the faithful in general. To serve this purpose they must be read, and read frequently. They must not merely be read but also meditated upon thoughtfully and reverently. To this we exhort with earnestness, recalling the prayer of Benedict XV "for all the children of the Church that, penetrated and strengthened by the sweetness of Holy Writ, they may attain to the surpassing knowledge of Jesus Christ." For as Paul tells Timothy, "All Scripture is inspired by God and useful for teaching, for reproving, for correcting, for instructing in justice; that the man of God may be perfect, equipped for every good work."

IX

A VISION OF GREATNESS

THE building of a cathedral church is an historic event, a high spiritual enterprise calling for the best effort of an entire community. The cathedral church belongs, by its very nature, not to one generation nor to one locality. It transcends the limits of time and place and belongs of necessity to all the people. It is a monument to our faith, an expression of our highest spiritual ideals and a fruitful source of blessings for men of every type and condition. A cathedral stands in our midst as a beacon of immortality, a sentinel of ordered peace, a refuge from the storms of life. It is the witness and the prophecy of a better hope.

The comprehensive function of a cathedral in the ages of faith has been well stated by Francis Hackett: "In medieval time the cathedral fringed out into the university, and every road ran through it. It stood in the center of man's city, open to everyone always, catholically conceived, custodian of birth and death and marriage, as broad as its nave and as exalted as its spire. It did not oppose human nature. It marshaled human nature behind it, seeking the good of common humanity as perceived by reasoned common sense, and merely subordinating the tendencies and the variations that gleamed with strange desire. It answered need, extended charity, served and counseled and fathered, and consulted nothing so much as the will of the tribe. It clothed itself in beauty. The roof that shed the Northern snow, and the cool gulf of shade that gave escape from the Southern sun, were equally popular and equally religious. The miracle and the mystery were in every case the burning heart of the cathedral, and authority consoled and subdued the widow, the murderer, the burdened captain, the child. By sanctuary, if not by justice, the church declared its potence, and the lawless came to it in crime as the artist in creation, the king in majesty and the churl in sin. It was a focus of the will, docile yet presumably universal. Energy rushed from it in crusade, in sainthood, in scholasticism, in empire, like free radiants of a fixed and central star. This double movement, out into adventure and home to fidelity, seemed to complete the most perfect of disciplines with the widest of excursions. Outside this there was only exile and desolation, the defiance of the Word, the pride of Lucifer, the iniquity of Apollyon."

Three virtues are intimately associated with the building of a cathedral: the virtues of magnanimity, munificence, and magnificence. The very etymology of the words indicates their aptitude and propriety in bringing to completion a project which taps the resources of mind and heart and purse. Magnificence must be the virtue of the architect and the artists who work in stone and marble, in wood, metal, and glass. There must be greatness in their skillful use of God's created gifts in order that earthly beauty may salute the author of all beauty. Munificence is pre-eminently the virtue of the laity, who must provide the gift of material means with generous and largehearted liberality if a cathedral worthy of its function is to be built. Magnanimity must be the virtue of the spiritual leaders who conceive the plan and project in a great-souled endeavor.

Let us take as an example our own Cathedral of St. Peter in Chains. In the days when Cincinnati ranked next to Baltimore and New York in ecclesiastical eminence, Archbishop Purcell conceived the vision of a cathedral church which would be authentic in the simplicity of its classical lines, majestic in its colonnaded porch and spire, and worthy in its interior appointments to enshrine the glorious liturgy of the Eucharistic Sacrifice. The horologium of Andronikos Cyrrhestes in Athens and the tomb of Lysicrates furnished the inspiration to the architect, but there was no slavish imitation of the models whose elements he incorporated in a new Christian adaptation. It can be truthfully said that our forefathers were great-souled men. The architect of the restoration has been faithful in keeping the early design and has added significantly to the unity and beauty of the original.

A cathedral church worthy of the name will never come into existence without the exercise of the virtue of munificence. There must be benefactors who are not only endowed with the goods of this world but who are endowed also with love for the beauty of God's house and the place where His glory dwelleth. The giving of gifts for any useful or worthy purpose is not a purely spontaneous act, but one that is elicited by cogent argument and by sharing the inspired vision of a dynamic leader. Since the Diocese of Cincinnati in 1845 comprised within its jurisdiction all of Ohio, it was quite fitting that the response to Archbishop Purcell's appeal for support in the building of the cathedral should come from every section of the state. This was true in large measure; but benefactors responded also from distant lands. The memory of generous friends in France, Germany, and Austria is enshrined in the traditions of our cathedral church. Here at home the name of Reuben Springer of Cincinnati, a merchant prince, civic leader, and convert to the Church, will be held forever in grateful remembrance.

The virtue of magnificence may be defined in popular language as the doing of things in a "big" way. Bigness is not a virtue, but neither is littleness, especially if it approaches the spirit of miserliness. Once a vision of greatness has been conceived, it should be carried out in a manner proportionate to the magnitude of the project envisioned. Strict economy may be a virtue at times, but it can be a fatal error in certain circumstances. A cathedral church is not, or at least should not be, restricted to the same dimensions as a parish church, whether in point of expenditure, durability of construction, or the dignity of its appointments and decoration. A cathedral church exists to serve the needs of many generations, and its structure should reflect in a sense its ageless character.

There may have been grave misgiving in the minds of some with respect to the soundness of our judgment in returning to the original site of the old Cathedral of St. Peter in Chains in downtown Cincinnati, especially in view of the evident deterioration of the surrounding area. The neighborhood is not altogether prepossessing. It may not be inappropriate, therefore, to offer an apologia for our decision in making a considerable investment in the rehabilitation of the cathedral in its present location. The first and most weighty consideration was the historical character of the old cathedral. St. Peter in Chains was the first notable church edifice in the Middle West — the only cathedral in that area which has seen continuing service. It was consecrated well over a hundred years ago by Archbishop Eccleston, then the only Metropolitan in the United States. Bishop John McCloskey, who was to become the first Cardinal of the Church in the United States, preached at its dedication. More than thirty Bishops have been consecrated within its walls and hundreds of priests have received in its sanctuary the imposition of hands in sacred orders.

As an architectural achievement it ranks with the outstanding churches of the country — not perhaps in its monumental proportions but in the distinctive character of its style. It grew out of the vision of Archbishop Purcell into reality under the guiding genius of Henry Walter and his associates during the days of the Greek Revival. In support of its unique excellence the celebrated authority Talbot Hamlin has described it as the "largest and handsomest church of that particular style in the United States."

There were other reasons which influenced our decision. A cathedral church is by its very nature the common church of all the faithful. It is the seat of the episcopal magisterium and the center of the liturgical life and worship of the entire diocese. As such it can never be identified with a particular parish. It stands by preference in the center of man's city as an abiding witness to the City of God. It should be accessible to all the faithful; and, as in ancient times all roads led to Rome, so in the modern city all avenues of transportation center in the heart of the city. Moreover, the site of our cathedral within the near future will be the starting point of an elaborate program of urban redevelopment. Not only have plans been made by the public authorities for the rehabilitation of the core area of our city, but the funds have been provided so that vast improvements in the adjoining neighborhood are already under way — improvements which will change the entire face of the West End of Cincinnati where our Cathedral is located.

There will always be some who bemoan the waste of the precious ointment poured out by Mary Magdalene in anointing the feet of our Blessed Lord. We know the scriptural comment on such conduct. Our own sense of propriety, however, would dictate a spirit of magnanimity, munificence, and magnificence when we come to honor the God of infinite might and wisdom, the Creator of all earthly beauty. What could be more fitting than joining together that which is most precious in stone and marble, gold and bronze, carved wood and jeweled glass with the artist's creative talents in form and color in order to celebrate the glory of the Most High God! Thus we make a return to Him of His own generous bounty in our behalf.

A cathedral is dedicated with solemn rites which take us back in memory to a distant past. Almost three thousand years ago, the hymns which are heard re-echoing within the sacred walls of our cathedrals today were first intoned in a solemn ceremony. It was at the dedication of Solomon's temple in Jerusalem that the same words burst forth in song from ten thousand throats. For eleven years a multitude of skilled workmen had labored with zeal and devotion in the construction of Israel's great temple. When the building was finished, it reflected the glory and beauty of God's creation; it was numbered among the wonders of the world.

The Church reaches back into ancient time to find inspiration for the solemn liturgical functions in her cathedrals. She does so in order to emphasize the continuity of the past with the present. The Church of the New Testament is not something radically different from that of the Old; it is, rather, a development and fulfillment of what formerly existed only in type and figure. If the choristers in Solomon's time could sing, "How lovely is Your dwelling place, O Lord of hosts!" with how much greater propriety can we not raise our voices in hymns and canticles to salute Christ in our cathedral church.

In the dedication of the temple at Jerusalem, God placed the stamp of His approval on the grandeur with which Israel did homage to His majesty. The cloud of glory which encompassed the sanctuary at the dedication was a testimony that God was well pleased with the magnificence of the achievement in His honor. If people throughout human history have sensed instinctively that the high functions of civil government should be housed in beautiful and dignified surroundings; if education, finance, and commerce can with propriety pre-empt the services of art to enhance with beauty the buildings they use in carrying out their social functions, how much more should not religion do so, to make resplendent that edifice in which is offered worship to God, the Creator of all beauty! The words of the psalmist re-echo here: "O Lord, I love the House in which You dwell, the tenting-place of Your glory."

It has been said that great monumental and inspiring churches have become outmoded; that they no longer serve a useful purpose. It is claimed by some that they are out of harmony with the spirit of the times and obsolete in their function. One might as well claim that great epic poems like Dante's "Divine Comedy" are outmoded; or that the "Moses" of Michelangelo is outdated; or that the basilica of St. Peter's serves no useful function. There is no reason why we should submit meekly to the utilitarian spirit of the age. If ever there was need of lifting the mind and heart of man above the things of mediocrity and inspiring in him once more a sense of spiritual beauty and grandeur, surely the drab existence of present-day secular life provides adequate justification.

The very buildings in which we offer divine worship should reflect a sense of awe and reverence so as to create a sympathetic atmosphere for the soul's upward flight to God. We reject the puritan austerity of the sixteenth-century reformers who tore down the holy rood or smashed the jeweled windows of cathedral churches, just as in ancient times our forefathers rejected the heresies of the iconoclasts who denounced the sculptured images of Christ and His saints. Instead, we call upon the arts and crafts, upon music, painting, sculpture, and above all on the genius of architecture, to bend their efforts to the soul's search for union with God.

From time immemorial great churches have been built to remind man of the City of God — St. Peter's Basilica on Vatican Hill, Notre Dame in Paris, Westminster Abbey in London, the Cathedral of Cologne, and so on, throughout all the countries where Christ's name and that of His Blessed Mother are held in reverence. Let no one mistake the purpose of our great cathedrals. We know that God does not need a temple fashioned by human hands. We strive to achieve by our efforts a spiritual beauty enshrined in the souls of men. We wish to enlighten their minds with truth and to sanctify their souls with goodness. We hope that our cathedrals, by their very presence in the midst of our cities, will lift up the minds and hearts of all people to heavenly desires. If our cathedrals were to endure merely as architectural monuments; if they were to be nothing more than artists' visions of earthly beauty, they would have failed notably in their purpose. They are intended, rather, to be "sermons in stone," unending hymns of praise to the majesty of God and His goodness to men.

Part III

MAN IN RELATION

TO HIS COUNTRY

"Men who in every nation pray to the same God for peace on earth cannot be at the same time bearers of discord among peoples; men who turn in prayer to the divine Majesty cannot foment that nationalistic imperialism which each people makes its own god."

X

THIS IS TRUE DEMOCRACY

NO PERSON who has kept abreast of public opinion can fail to notice that there has been a growing appreciation of the important place of religion in our public and social life. The daily press, with its news stories, editorials, and commentaries, gives continual evidence that the close relationship between religion and democracy is now generally recognized. We welcome this revival of interest in religion. The relationship of democracy to religion is not something superficial but basic. As the people depend on God, so democracy — a government of the people — depends on that by which a people expresses its dependence on God; namely, religion. Democracy stands to win or lose, to survive or perish, according as we regain our spiritual health or suffer further spiritual deterioration.

To some people the concept of democracy is an extremely nebulous thing. But democracy represents a coherent and systematic philosophy of life resting on clear, precise, and fundamental truths. While in many parts of Europe the word "democracy" is used as a term of opprobrium, in America it is a rallying cry of patriotism. Here it is used as a battle cry of freedom, order, and peace; there it is used as an epithet to indicate the decay of public authority or a decadent form of government which is so weak and inept that it is incapable of deciding fundamental issues. In *Mein Kampf,* Hitler characterized democracy as irresponsible, stupid, and cowardly. Marx,

111

followed by Lenin and Stalin, heaped contempt and abuse upon the democratic concept and upon the political, economic, and cultural systems which derive from it.

Much of the confusion about democracy grows out of the mistaken notion that democracy is identified with the particular political system called "liberal parliamentarianism" or the rule of the majority. Democracy is not synonymous with parliamentary procedure, party politics, majority rule, universal suffrage, and free elections. These are but the corollaries of democratic principles, not the essence. All these political contrivances existed in Italy, Germany, Portugal, and Spain, but they did not constitute true democracy. The thing that these countries experienced was not genuine democracy but a caricature — governments by minority, under the leadership of party cliques, concerned with their own selfish interests and lust for personal power rather than with the common good or the public weal. It is no surprise to us that this kind of democracy was repudiated.

Christian democracy is as broad and comprehensive as the virtues of justice and charity. It penetrates all human relationships and social behavior; it enters into the fields of politics, economics, education, and every form of social life. True democracy is not so much a political system as it is a spiritual philosophy of life.

Democracy, as Christian scholars traditionally interpret its meaning, consists of a series of fundamental propositions concerning man, his individual and social nature, his origin, and his destiny. There is a divine Bill of Rights which Christianity proclaims and reason ratifies, just as there is a civil Bill of Rights which the American Constitution proclaims and the Constitutional Amendments define.

Man is not the creature of the state, but the creature of God. He is endowed with a human personality fashioned to the image and likeness of God Himself, and so shares something of God's own dignity. He is a spiritual being with an immortal soul, and not a pawn in the hands of the political state. He is not merely a unit in a social organization, but an individual with inalienable rights and duties. Precisely because he has these rights and duties as an endowment from his Creator, the state cannot take them away. They are a trusteeship from God and are therefore inviolable by the state and inalienable by man himself.

If life is the property and possession of God, if it is entrusted to the individual man for an eternal purpose, then the state cannot rightfully declare human life in whole or in part forfeited and abridged for political ends. Political bloodpurges, therefore, stand condemned by God as a cruel usurpation of the right to life. If liberty is an endowment granted by the Creator Himself, and not the result of government grant, then there can be no justifiable violation of conscience or invasion of the individual personality by the state. If property is the necessary condition of liberty, then, in justice, it cannot be completely confiscated. If man has the right to pursue happiness, then he cannot lawfully be coerced into a particular social status or deprived of his own personal choice of a vocation, profession, or trade. Now these truths form the fundamental teaching of the Church on the question of democracy, and she rests them on the broad basis that all men are equal in the sight of God; that all men have equal rights by reason of the fact that they are created by God, redeemed by Christ, and destined for the same union with God in eternal happiness. These rights are the postulates of the American Constitution. Each day it is becoming more and more apparent that if people and their governments deny these fundamental truths there is no adequate defense against dictatorship, regardless of whether the dictatorship is exercised in the name of Communism or in the name of a democratic majority.

Contrary to superficial opinion, there can develop a hurtful intolerance, even in a democracy, if we are not alert to discern and quick to repudiate the tendencies partially manifest even today in our national life. The telltale signs of dictatorship follow a uniform pattern. First, there is projected into the national life a public program of universal military conscription, and that not merely in a state of war, but in a state of peace. It was the dictatorship of the French Revolution which first gave us the pattern of total military conscription. The voluntary soldier belongs, we are told, to the past. Today not only do soldiers march in battle, but whole nations are mobilized for war. Surely no one can fail to realize that a large measure of our democratic freedom has disappeared when universal military conscription is made mandatory in peace times. It was not without reason, therefore, that Benedict XV, in his peace program, counseled against conscription as one of the grave causes leading to war. Its elimination constitutes one of the first elements in any sincere disarmament program.

The second step in the process toward dictatorship is taken when the state assumes a monopoly of education. If the government arrogates to itself the complete and exclusive control of the system of education, then the regimentation of the rising generation has begun and the intellectual goose step is in sight. Even if this conscription of the schools by the state is not absolute, nevertheless it is the part of wisdom to resist the very first tendencies in that direction. Partisan discrimination against private schools is a sure sign of such a tendency. Private schools are merely the extension of parental rights over the child and his future destiny. They have a right not only to exist but to be free from penalties or discrimination. To invade the sanctuary of parental rights in this matter of education marks the beginning of a dictatorship.

The third step toward a totalitarian state is the conscription of public opinion. Usually the state begins the process by gaining control over the sources of information, such as the press, the radio, TV, and other means of communication. Then, it develops a program of propaganda in order to implement its policies. If there is to be an effective guarantee of true democracy, the instruments of information and communication must remain within the control of the people themselves.

The fourth in this series of invasions of personal liberty is the conscription of private property. We recognize the need of some public control in the interests of social welfare, but the nationalization or socialization of the instruments of production, excessive taxation, and a state-planned economy are infringements of democratic theory and rights. A managed economy is, of course, always declared to be in the public interest, but it too often turns out to be management by the political state in its own interests. Here we have a confusion of categories. Politics is identified with economics.

Christian democracy, as Leo XIII points out, is not to be identified with a particular political theory or a specific system of government. Christian democracy means that the common good must take precedence over individual advantage. It means that government must promote the public welfare and not merely exercise police power over violations of law. Political democracy has been firmly established for generations here in our country, but economic democracy still lags far behind. Genuine democratic principles cannot be confined to our political life alone. They must have equal application in the all-important sphere of the economic order.

Democratic theory, to be consistent, must provide the same status of equality in economic life that it does in political life. It is bound by its own inherent principles to give to workingmen a share in ownership, management, and profits. This does not mean an equality of wages or of profits or of responsibility, but an equality of opportunity according to individual competence. It is more a question of status in the economic order, comparable to the status which the citizen enjoys in the political order.

In conformity with Christian principles, economic power must be subordinated to human welfare, both individual and social; class conflict must be replaced by corporate unity; ruthless competition must give way to co-operation organized on the basis of a common economic function; greed, whether in the ranks of labor or of capital, must give place to social justice and charity. Only then can the divine plan of human brotherhood, a sufficiency and security for all, become a reality.

The social revolutions of the nineteenth century were fundamentally political in their origin and in their purpose. The French Revolution at the turn of the century, as well as that of 1848 demanded new political rights and the control of government by the citizens. During the twentieth century, however, the demand is for economic rights joined with the desire for a greater cultural and social unity. Democracy, if it is to endure, must meet these demands in a reasonable measure. Workers everywhere are insisting on a right to participate, through their representatives, in the making of policy and to share the benefits of their own economic efforts. Workers have felt themselves isolated and shut out from that sense of community or belonging, which is an essential principle of social stability.

This sense of oneness or community cannot be the result of mass propaganda and mass emotionalism after the pattern of Communism, Nazism, and Fascism. It must be the result of a development of the ideas which are inherent in religion — namely, ideas that promote and safeguard the sanctity of the human personality.

The growth of the Socialist-Labor Party in England and that of its counterpart, social democracy, on the continent of Europe, is the result of a new yeast working in the mass of mankind. The older forms of political organization, such as that of the Liberal or Conservative Parties, have become antiquated since World War II. Today the Social Democrats or Christian Democrats are in power almost everywhere in Europe. If Conservative parties regain control, they will be radically different in character and their public policy greatly modified.

Some time ago a U. S. foreign policy bulletin carried this statement: "The sudden expansion of 'center' opinion in Western countries at the expense of right and left extremism may — provided it does not degenerate into blind reaction — pave the way for a revival of democracy reinterpreted in twentieth-century terms. Such a revival may coincide with a renewed popular interest in religion, accompanied by simultaneous recognition on the part of religious leaders of their responsibility for social and economic welfare."

Let us point out that the Church has never evaded such responsibility. This is not a sudden change of attitude. Nowhere can anyone find a more straightforward recognition of the social problem of the times than in Leo XIII's *Rerum Novarum*. Nowhere can anyone find a more sincere denunciation of social and economic abuses than in the encyclical letters of Pius XI. These letters of the Popes, however, contain not merely a denunciation of abuses; they offer a constructive program for the reorganization of our social order.

The past century witnessed the development of mass industry and the growth of a restless proletariat. It may be difficult for us to realize today that it was not many decades ago that working men labored ten and twelve hours a day, with inadequate wages and under degrading conditions, so that Pius XI could truthfully state that raw material came from the factories ennobled, while men were brutalized and made less human.

Socialistic theory was a logical reaction against this system of "ruthless individualism." This latter economic theory exaggerated the rights of property to the point where there was little or no social responsibility. Ruthless competition was accepted as a matter of fact. It was even held sound economic theory, by the advocates of individualism, that to produce the largest volume of material goods we should follow the policy of "every man for himself and the devil take the hindmost." The result was monopoly by the dictators of economic life, with starvation wages, and neither security nor dignity. When the workers attempted to organize into trade unions for collective bargaining, they were resisted by existing legislation under the specious plea of "freedom of contract" and "no interference in business."

The Socialist parties, which arose in opposition to this state of affairs, went to the other extreme. They advocated public ownership of all productive property. Their proposal was to place all such property in the hands of the state. If there was to be monopoly, they wanted the state to exercise it. They thought — wrongly, of course — that in this way they could substitute social co-operation in the economic order for ruthless competition. They thought that excessive investments at the wrong times and in the wrong places, unemployment, insufficiency, and insecurity would be cured by means of a state-planned economy.

These were the conditions which faced the Popes of modern times when they wrote their encyclicals. To the extreme right there was this theory of rugged individualism with anonymous ownership of large capital and social irresponsibility. On the extreme left was Socialism or Communism with its program of state ownership, state control, and state-planned economy. The letters of Leo XIII and of Pius XI called for a reorganization of the whole structure of the social and economic order. They pointed out that there was a middle way between individualism and socialism. They pointed out that the right of an individual to private property is inalienable — a right inherent in man. But they also pointed out that ownership of property involves social responsibilities and that the first charge against industry, before profits, is to pay a living wage to the worker. They emphasized the fact that the state does not exercise merely a police power over contracts but is charged to promote the common welfare. The Popes unanimously pointed out that the state should not attempt to assume all the responsibility in the re-establishment of social order. To attempt to do so would involve the state in an impossible task. The state would become overwhelmed with a multiplicity of duties, so that it would no longer be able to fulfill its true function of sovereignty.

The Church rejects the idea of a state-planned economy, or the nationalization of industry and business. It proposes instead the principles of subsidiarity and a functional social order. It was Pius XI particularly who insisted that the principle of competition, while good to a limited extent in promoting efficiency, could nonetheless never serve as the organizing principle of economic life. The Christian virtues of social justice and social charity supersede every other consideration. In other words, morality has the first place in the economic order and constitutes the supreme rule in business ethics just as in private conduct.

The Popes were not satisfied with merely stating the need of a moral regeneration; they went further and proposed a clear outline of the principles on which economic life should be based. They proposed that each industry and each profession, even agriculture, should be organized on the principle of a common function. They recognized not merely the principle of collective bargaining between management and labor, but went further, to demand that labor have an equal status in economic life with capital. The two should constitute a partnership; and, in consequence, there should be participation on the part of labor in profits, management, and ownership. To bring this about, a new social and juridical order should be established. Instead of a state-planned economy, as under socialism, and instead of ruthless competition with no plan, as under rugged individualism, the Popes proposed that the plans for economic life in all business, professions, industry, and agriculture be made by those who actually were engaged in these pursuits. This organization should begin on the company- or corporation-level. Then the single corporations of the entire industry should be federated into an Industry Council. Finally, to bring about order, balance, and true progress, regional and national councils of whole industries should be established. Our own government attempted something similar under the ill-fated N. R. A., with its business codes and programs; but that was a lopsided, or one-sided, arrangement, with management solely responsible and labor unrepresented in the Council. Today we have moved much nearer to the principles outlined by the Popes, but there is still room for much improvement and further progress. This progress cannot come about all at once, for, as in all human things, growth is a matter of time. It can be accelerated under favorable conditions, but it cannot be legislated by the state overnight. It cannot be achieved except by sincere co-operation between the owners of the instruments of production and the representatives of labor. The two elements contribute equally to the processes of economic production.

The writings of Popes Leo XIII, Pius XI, and Pius XII should be studied once more, with an open mind and diligent attention. If the principles they advocate were sincerely applied in the organization of our social and economic life, we are confident that we could avoid not merely the dangers which have confronted all the European nations in the social as well as the political order, but we could eliminate most of the conflict which now exists here in our own country between capital and labor, between owners and workers, between employers and employees. As Pius XII wrote: "In the recognition of the royal prerogatives of Christ and in the return of individuals and of society to the law of His truth and of His love lies the only way to salvation."

XI

IS PEACE AMONG NATIONS POSSIBLE?

I T WOULD seem to be self-evident that international peace is universally desirable. We cannot conceive that anyone would willingly or knowingly espouse the cause of strife, conflict, or war as against peace, order, and justice. Theoretically, therefore, there would seem to be no difference of opinion with regard to the value and desirability of international peace. In practice, however, the matter is quite otherwise.

If there are any misgivings on the subject of international peace, or if there is any hesitation in subscribing wholeheartedly to its program, they are due undoubtedly to the following causes: first, to a misinterpretation of the nature and the object of international peace; second to the advocacy of wrong, inept, and inadequate methods by which it is to be advanced; and third, to the adoption of a false philosophy on which international peace is predicated. Let us consider some of these causes, in order that we may clear the ground of misunderstanding and prepare the way for the adoption of a safe and sound attitude toward this vitally important question. We might do well to begin our consideration by approaching the question first from a negative point of view — that is, by explaining what is *not* meant by international peace.

International peace does not consist in the substitution of a vague internationalism for genuine patriotism. We can be wholeheartedly devoted to international peace, and at the same time be truly patriotic to our own country. Pope Pius XI, in

his encyclical *Caritate Christi Compulsi,* on the Sacred Heart
and World Distress, calls attention to the subject of patriotism.
He tells us that the "right order of Christian charity does not
disapprove of lawful love of country and a sentiment of justifiable nationalism; on the contrary, it controls, sanctifies, and
enlivens them." There is, however, an exaggerated form of
nationalism which is directly at variance with charity and
Christian brotherhood. Such a spirit is not synonymous with
patriotism. Patriotism, as the very name itself indicates, denotes that relationship which binds us to our fatherland by
fraternal ties. The relationship between the citizen and his
country is parallel to that which exists between the father and
the child. Just as the child depends upon his parents for his
very existence, so also he depends upon his country in order
that he may continue to live. The bond which exists in both
relationships is of a similar nature, just as the virtues which are
involved in both are of a similar kind — filial devotion to and
reverence for one's origin and source. Patriotism is not merely
a matter of sentiment, not merely a memory of childhood days
and their happy associations; true patriotism has roots which
strike deep into the very soil of human nature. The food which
we eat, and which, by the mysterious alchemy of nature, is
transformed into our own flesh and blood, was once a part
of the very soil on which we live. The bread which we put
upon our tables was once the stalk of wheat growing in the
fields, sinking its roots deep into the earth and drawing up
into its stem the strength of the land to store up in its kernels
the elements which give us life and strength. It is true, therefore, to say that our very life itself depends for its existence,
fertility, and sustaining strength upon the soil on which we live.

Food, clothing, and shelter are essential conditions of life.
Where else in all this world has the Creator scattered His

bounty with such a lavish hand as here in America? We have our fields white with cotton in the South, green with corn and wheat in the North; we have our orchards on the Pacific slopes and along the lake shores, laden with fruit of every kind; we have our plains and timberlands, our mines and our quarries, providing, in the greatest profusion, the raw materials necessary for every type of industry and manufacture. We have mountains and rivers and valleys which, for beauty as well as utility, are surpassed nowhere else on this earth. With justifiable pride we may stand at attention when the old national anthem is sung, and join heartily and gratefully in the words, "We love thy rocks and rills, thy woods and templed hills."

But just as the body is more than the raiment, so the soul is more than the body. Under beneficent political and social institutions, our intellectual, moral, and spiritual life is permitted to develop to its fullest potentialities. The soul is left free and unhampered by political restriction or by social institutions which in many other countries constitute a handicap, or create positive opposition to the exercise of the natural and supernatural rights of men as children of God.

We need only glance at the conditions which presently obtain in Russia to appreciate the favorable circumstances in which our own lot has been cast. Surely there is reason to be grateful to those early pioneers who, inspired by wisdom extraordinary, established a government which respected both the rights of God and of man. The principles, the ideals, and the aspirations which are enshrined in the fundamental doctrine of our Constitution have set forth the rights of citizens and the rights of government in such a way that they are strictly consistent with the Christian code of ethics.

We have every reason to be grateful to our country and its institutions, and every reason to be loyally devoted to its interests. We seek its honor and its glory, but only in a right and proper way. We profess our readiness to advance its interests and to protect it from injury or assault. We do not subscribe, however, to the doctrine or the sentiment expressed by Stephen Decatur when he exclaimed, "Our country! . . . May she always be in the right; but our country, right or wrong." We love our country sufficiently well that we would refuse to defend any wrongful claims which it might assert in a moment of national anger or in a spirit of self-advancement. To put our country above truth and right would be to exalt its claims above the claims of God Himself. This is not patriotism, but a perversion of right order and a denial of the true hierarchy of values. The patriotism which we profess can always be reconciled with justice and truth, and the international peace to which we aspire is but the offspring of the marriage of truth with justice.

To advance any claims of our country either against truth or against justice, to lay claim to territory that is not ours, to demand rights and privileges for ourselves which we are not willing to grant to others, to demand favors in our own behalf, and to refuse to extend equal consideration to others is to fall into the error of exaggerated nationalism. This is the spirit which discriminates against other nations in favor of our own. This is the spirit which makes for violent imperialism. This is the spirit which seeks to dominate the lives and fortunes of others and to subordinate them to our own self-interest. It is nothing else but the spirit of covetousness or cupidity; it is nothing else but pride and vainglory, extended and pushed forward from individual to national dimensions. Patriotism is as much opposed to this exaggerated form of nationalism, which seeks to establish the absolutist state, as is the spirit of international peace itself.

A second misunderstanding is due to the fact that many people think that international peace implies, at least indirectly, an attack upon our military establishment. They seem to think that advocacy of international peace must perforce be a disparagement of our armed forces. On the contrary, we can have the highest regard for the services that are rendered by our army, navy, and air force without in the slightest degree deviating from the requirements of international peace. Those who are best acquainted with the spirit of our military forces can vouch for the fact that there is no imperialistic spirit existing among them. They are not like the bully, proud of his physical strength and superiority, swaggering through a crowd seeking to pick a fight merely to test his powers. It is true that the lovers of international peace are laboring assiduously to bring about a decrease in the armaments of the nations of the world, but none of them are foolish enough to imagine that we can entirely dispense with the services of either army, navy, or air force. The international peace movement deprecates excessive military expenditures and warns against the folly of blind competitive armament. Some of the finest pages in American history have been written by the heroism of our soldiers, our sailors, and our airmen. They have not gloried in brutal bloodshed, but they have gloried in self-sacrifice and devotion to the interests of their fellow citizens, and in devotion to the cause of peace. They have held truth and justice and honor so sacred that they were willing to make the supreme sacrifice of their lives in order to maintain them. Enduring peace can result only from the maintenance of a right order based on truth and justice. We willingly pay a tribute, both to the leaders and to the rank and file in our armed services for their accomplishments, not for the cause of war but rather for the cause of peace. That this is the normal spirit of

American armed forces can be attested by the fact that, even in war, the most powerful motive which could be expressed in a national slogan was the phrase, "The war to end war." Even though we may have been deceived in our objective, yet, when we crossed the seas in 1917, our actuating purpose was to "make the world safe for democracy" — that is, for the rights of the common man.

Let us carry this negative consideration of international peace a step further by naming another thing that it is not. International peace is not synonymous with pacifism. We do not stand for the principle of "peace at any price." We do not for one moment grant that the bad can stand on the same plane with the good. In other words, we do not subscribe to the doctrine that we are to tolerate any and every kind of evil rather than oppose it by force. We profess wholeheartedly that international peace can have no other basis than that of truth and justice. We must therefore be prepared to defend these values against unlawful attack, even though it be at the expense of our own lives and fortunes. There is a certain form of pacifism which has an utterly false foundation. It rests upon a philosophy which holds that physical suffering or loss of material wealth is so great an evil that we must never incur the risk of bringing either upon ourselves. This false philosophy makes physical or material good superior to spiritual or moral good. This we can never subscribe to, and if we should, we would justly incur the opprobrium of sheer cowardice.

International peace, therefore, is not the same as pacifism. Pacifism means peace at any price. It implies that there is nothing so sacred or so precious, nothing so true or so right, that we need to defend it at any cost. No object is supposed to be so worth while that we need to defend it at the expense of our health or at the risk of our lives. It implies that truth and justice are at present unknown quantities, and that they can never be definitely and certainly obtained. Pacifism, in consequence, means that we should yield or compromise whenever there is danger of conflict, even if by doing so we accept what is inherently false and evil. Against this false philosophy we protest, and we condemn it as unchristian and unreasonable.

We do not mean to say that there are not times when we might wisely refuse to offer resistance to physical attack upon our rights. The Church has always given her fullest approval to this attitude on the part of the martyrs, who submitted to unjust attack upon their lives, and who were willing to shed their blood rather than give up their faith in Christ and His teaching. The example of the martyrs is not an example of pacifism, but an example of the staunchest kind of resistance to evil. It is the willingness to shed one's own blood rather than the blood of others in the defense of truth and justice. It is in this sense that Christ preaches against the doctrine of peace at any price. He says, "I have come to bring a sword, not peace." This is the Christian doctrine of passive resistance; *resistance,* mind you, and resistance to *evil.* It is passive only in the sense that the individual who resists suffers the consequences himself, rather than inflicts the consequences upon the unjust aggressor.

When we speak of international peace, moreover, we do not mean that we accept as final and unchangeable the political, economic, and social arrangements which now exist in the world. We do not admit that political boundaries, which now parcel out the world among different nations, are to stand forever as they are and be given a sanctity or permanence which makes them irrevocable. There are many political and economic injustices existing in the world; we do not mean that we condone these injustices, or that we favor a freezing of the world, as it were, into its present *status quo*. We do maintain, however, that there is a better way than war to bring about a redress of grievances. To submit the claims of justice to the arbitrament of war is to assent or to subscribe to the doctrine that "Might makes right." War is a frightfully clumsy as well as brutal, bloody, and wasteful manner of settling international differences.

Briefly, then, let us recapitulate the position of those who espouse the cause of international peace. It is, first of all, not opposed to patriotism; second, it is not synonymous with pacifism; third, it is not a veiled attack upon our army, navy, and air force; and finally, it is not a supine acceptance of the present political and economic organization of the world. It is not an advocate of a *status quo,* with ho hope of change or improvement.

So much for the negative side of the question. Since international peace is none of these things, you might well ask, "What, then, is it?"

The essential claim of the advocates of international peace is that truth, justice, and charity shall dominate our policies and our actions as nations, just as they dominate, or ought to dominate, our attitudes and actions as individuals. We mean to attack the theory of war as a necessary or even satisfactory instrument for settling international disputes. We mean to assert that morality is just as much binding upon nations as it is binding upon individuals. We mean to assert that, just as individuals must not settle their differences by physical combat and by violence, so neither should nations. We mean to assert that, just as the conduct of individual citizens is regulated by civil law — their differences being submitted to the scrutiny and the adjudication of a court of justice; so also the affairs of nations should be regulated by a body of international law — their differences being submitted to its judges. There should be a world court to adjudge the conflicting interests of nations on the basis of truth and justice, and not on the basis of force and violence. It is because we believe that there is a better way to settle the differences among nations, that we advocate a steady diminution in the armed forces of each nation. We favor gradual disarmament, both because competition is a dangerous provocation to war, and because the burden which military establishments impose upon the financial resources of nations becomes in time almost insupportable.

In order to form some estimate of the vast expenditure of money for war and what it might accomplish if devoted to some useful purpose, consider these following facts: with what is spent on armaments each year, we could build a highway twenty-four feet wide and ten thousand miles long. We could, in other words, build three great highways across this country from New York to San Francisco. Or we could build each year one thousand new hospitals at a cost of one million dollars each, and have enough left over to operate them free of charge. Or we could build each year twenty great universities, allotting to each one of them a total sum of one hundred million dollars, to be used for construction and maintenance. Or we could lay out gigantic parks and playgrounds and recreation centers; and over and beyond that, we could provide each year for the complete and proper care of our dependent aged, our dependent children, and our dependent families in this country. With the billions of dollars now going for war purposes, we could provide employment for five or six million of our unemployed. Many of these undertakings would be possible with an expenditure of no more money than is now being spent each year on the world's folly of trying to settle its disputes by means of war rather than by means of peace.

The advocates of international peace are not foolish enough to believe that war can be eliminated by wishful thinking. They realize that peace has been an aspiration of the nations for many centuries. They realize full well that, if the dream is to be realized, they must proceed in a practical way. Two chief objectives are: first, to eliminate the causes of war — namely, the differences and the injustices which now exist among the nations; and, second, to find some practical substitute for war. In other words, they must find some agencies which will be satisfactory and adequate for settling, in an orderly and peaceful way, any disputes that may arise. At no time since the world began has the conviction been so widespread that another great war will not only sound the death knell of Western culture, but will totally destroy all civilization.

It is not entirely an idle dream to think that nations can establish a just peace through the establishment of an orderly procedure for obtaining justice among themselves. There was a time, almost a thousand years ago, when the orderly function of civil government was exceedingly limited or restricted. In those early centuries, individuals who suffered injustice at the hands of their neighbors were left no alternative but to settle the differences among themselves without recourse to law or courts. For example, it was not until the time of William the Conqueror that all England was declared to be at peace. Prior to that time, an individual who suffered personal or property damage at the hands of his neighbor had to seek redress of his grievance through his own personal efforts. Recall the wording of indictments in our present court procedure; they clearly state that any crime committed by a citizen is an attack upon the peace and dignity of the state. This was a totally new idea in eleventh-century England. We have come a long way since then. If it is possible for individuals to settle their differences through courts of law, why can we not hope for a time when nations will do likewise?

Truly touching are the paternal appeals of the great Roman Pontiffs of the past century for justice and peace in the family of nations. To cite only two of them: first, this from Leo XIII: "This Apostolic Chair it was that gathered and held together the crumbling remains of the old order of things; this was the kindly light by whose help the culture of Christian times shone far and wide; this was an anchor of safety in the fierce storms by which the human race has been convulsed; this was the sacred bond of union that linked together nations distant in region and different in character; in short, this was a common center from which was sought instruction in faith and religion, no less than guidance and advice for the maintenance of peace. . . .

"Would that this healing authority had never been slighted or set aside! Assuredly, neither would the civil power have lost that venerable and sacred glory, the lustrous gift of religion, which alone renders the state of subjection noble and worthy of man; nor would so many revolutions and wars have been fomented to ravage the world with desolation and bloodshed."

And could anything be more moving and convincing than these paternal words of Pius XI? "Men who in every nation pray to the same God for peace on earth cannot be at the same time bearers of discord among peoples; men who turn in prayer to the Divine Majesty cannot foment that nationalistic imperialism which each people makes its own god; men who look to the 'God of Peace and of Love' who is 'our Peace,' will know no rest until finally that peace which the world cannot give comes down from the Giver of every good gift on men of good will."

The Catholic philosophy on international peace is well indicated in these few thoughts culled from an address by Anna Dill Gamble: "Reduced to a few words, where the non-Catholic philosophy of peace differs from the Catholic is in its support of secularism in education and syncretism in religion. . . .

"We are at last face to face with what Jacques Maritain calls the two universalities — the authentic universality of Christ, 'the universality of Truth and Faith which excludes error,' and the universality of chaos. I do not see how we can evade the issue. We have either to pledge ourselves to the Peace of Christ in the Reign of Christ — or we are pledged, whether we will or not, to the attempted 'marriage of the yea and nay' — of heaven and hell. . . .

"It seems to me that in emphasizing the unity of mankind we should make a more determined effort to clarify for ourselves, as well as for others, the fundamental Catholic teaching that God has made of one blood all nations and races and that Catholics are all members of Christ, whether we are white or black or yellow or red, American, Irish, English, French, or German. The attempt to base world unity on tolerance of error rather than on the Christian tolerance of blood is one of the authentic marks of anti-Christ."

In other words, international peace ultimately must be predicated on the Christian doctrine, "one Lord, one faith, one baptism." We are one family, through whose veins runs the blood of our first parents, Adam and Eve. There are no differences except such as are accidental. Hence there must be no national or racial discriminations. The world is one human brotherhood, because we are, all of us, children of God.

Finally, one more witness. It is a witness of special value and importance, because it is the testimony of the one-time Protestant president of the American Institute of International

Law, James Brown Scott, who writes: "I would ask your attention now to a state so small as to be lost upon any map with which I am familiar . . . ; and yet, if I mistake not, the State of the Vatican . . . is destined to render services which cannot be foreseen, or measured, or weighed in the ordinary scales of justice. . . .

"A dispute laid before the State of the Vatican for decision would be free from the suggestion of material force to compel its acceptance, would be disconnected from any idea of territorial aggrandizement, would have a presumption of justice in its behalf, because the state itself is a recognition of justice, and the decision, whatever it may be, is bound to be in conformity with the moral code of the centuries and to be dominated by a spiritual conception of things which temporal judges may sometimes be without. Protestant though I be and of the Presbyterian variety, I look forward to the State of the Vatican, barely large enough for the Pontifical throne, an imponderable state, rendering services in the future even greater than the Papacy in the past, because it has neither army nor navy nor territory. It only has a conscience and law under the control of a moral and spiritual conception."

This magnificent tribute honors not only the Pope for whom it is meant, but also the man who uttered it. We quote it because it expresses the attitude, even of the non-Catholic world, regarding the paramount importance of the Church, the Papacy, the figure of the Pope, in a world seeking peace.

XII

NO PEACE WITHOUT PRINCIPLES

BEFORE intelligent persons can effectively discuss the problems of peace and the organization necessary for its possible attainment, there must be a common understanding of the essential terms used, and an affirmation of certain postulates. Peace is not merely the absence of war. It is rather the tranquillity of order. If there is ever to be international peace, there must first be a principle of order accepted by the nations. Such a principle, and indeed the only effective one, is the moral law. There must be a moral sovereignty outside the individual political state to serve as an organizing principle of peace; otherwise there can be no common denominator for a world order. This moral sovereignty rests in the eternal law of God; it is inherent in nature and is expressed in right reason.

We reject as false the distinction between private and public morality, and we assert that nations are obligated by the moral law just as inexorably as individuals are. We reject the notion of race superiority, and we proclaim the solidarity of the human race as one in origin, nature, and destiny. We reject absolutely the principle that "Might makes right."

In order to give validity and effect to a world society or to a commonwealth of nations, there must be intellectual agreement on fundamental values in the moral and spiritual order. This agreement should be made articulate in an international bill of rights to which member states and nations will adhere in order to qualify for membership.

135

In agreement with the American Declaration of Independence: "We hold these truths to be self-evident, that all men are created equal, that they are endowed by their Creator with certain unalienable rights." We herewith submit for the reader's earnest consideration a "Declaration of Rights and Duties" which we believe is essential to the attainment and conservation of international peace.

First of all, as regards human rights of a *religious* nature, we stand for the following:

Freedom from state interference in matters of conscience and worship;

Freedom to impart and to receive instruction in religion without interference from state authority;

Freedom of action in establishing and supporting benevolent institutions or agencies for the spiritual, intellectual, and material welfare of the people; and

Freedom to hold and to use property in so far as it is essential to effect these purposes.

As regards human rights of an *economic* order, we stand for:

The right to private property and to such food, shelter, and clothing as is needed for a decent living;

The right to work and the duty of society or government to provide an opportunity for useful employment in the event that individual effort is unable to secure such opportunity;

The right to social insurance or government assistance in time of sickness, disability, old age, or unemployment;

The right to a free choice of vocation, profession, trade, or state of life;

The right to enter into associations with fellow workers or members of any functional group in order to secure through collective bargaining an adequate family wage, decent working conditions, and reasonable limitations to the hours of work.

As regards human rights of a *political* nature, we stand for:

The right to participate by universal suffrage in determining the kind of government under which each nation shall live;

The right of minorities, either of language, religion, or cultural traditions, to be free from tyranny of the majority;

The right of constitutional guarantees for each individual in respect to life, liberty, and the pursuit of happiness;

The right to equality before the law and freedom from cruel and unusual punishment;

The right to trial by a jury of free citizens;

The right to be free from arrest, seizure of goods, and search of private homes in time of peace without due warrant;

The right to be free from government surveillance or espionage in private life during peacetime;

The right of free speech and free assembly for the redress of grievances; hence the right to free press, free communication or access to adequate information;

The right to modify the structure of government by orderly process, but not by force of arms or violence;

The right to resist aggression against liberties guaranteed by the Constitution and the International Bill of Rights.

In the field of national and international *rights,* we stand for:

Freedom from aggression for every nation, whether large or small, and for the recognition of such by a world society;

The right of access on equal terms with other nations to raw materials of commerce and industry and equal rights in international trade;

The right to be free from military conscription in time of peace and from the intolerable burden of military armament, and to substitute therefor an international police power under the direction of a world society or league of nations.

In the field of national and international *duties,* we stand for the principle that it is the duty of all states:

To observe the sanctity of treaties when freely negotiated and accepted;

To respect the sanctity of the individual person, his freedom to life, liberty, and the choice of a state of life as guaranteed by the national Constitution;

To respect the rights of all minority groups as guaranteed by separate Constitutions and an international bill of rights accepted by all members of the world society or league of nations;

To co-operate with other nations through a world society in effecting disarmament gradually but universally; and in liberalizing international trade through gradual elimination of tariffs, quotas, blocking of exchange of currency, and by establishing a fair rate of exchange between the monetary systems of the respective member nations of a world society;

To modify existing treaties and relinquish legal rights that are detrimental to the equal rights of others in the way of enjoying prosperity and a decent standard of living;

To redistribute responsibility for colonial development among the members of a world society or league of nations according to the needs of the colonies and their preference, and under the decisive supervision of the league or world society.

As corollaries of these principles, rights, and duties:

We stand for collective security through the creation of a world society or commomwealth of nations, to be based on juridical and not merely political principles.

We stand for the creation of a world court competent to arbitrate the grievances of all nations.

We stand for an international code of laws consisting not merely of treaty agreements, but of positive statutes based on natural law (law of nations), governing all international relations.

We stand for the surrender of such sovereign rights on the part of each state as will be necessary for the establishment of the world society and world court operating under an international code of laws.

We stand for the establishment of an adequate international police power, and for its formation by the contribution of men, money, and equipment by each nation in proportion to its resources. We stand likewise for such economic sanctions as may be necessary for the proper functioning of a world society.

We recognize that there is a valid distinction between states and nations. The two are not synonymous. A state is a political sovereign entity from which there can be no higher appeal within its own frontiers. A nation, however, is a community of people, held together by a common bond of ancestry, language, religion, and culture. As such it may or may not be organized under one government. Switzerland, for example, is a state of three nations. We recognize, in consequence of this distinction, that national minorities should be safeguarded in the rights guaranteed by international law, but we recognize also that the right of self-determination of national groups cannot be permitted to become a reason for aggression against the peace of the state in which they dwell.

We demand the substitution of the principle of co-operation and regard for the common good in both national and international economy in place of the principle of cutthroat competition and monopoly. We recognize that in an economy based on private enterprise there must needs be a profit. What we repudiate as the basis of world economy is the notion that profit, computed in dollars and cents alone, is a valid criterion. We advocate instead the organization of domestic and world economy on a basis of full co-operation between owners, managers, workers, and consumers in each industry, and mutually between the various industries under government supervision and regulation. We reject national economic planning by government alone, just as we reject economic planning by owners, managers, or labor alone.

We recognize that the principles, rights, and duties herewith submitted must be implemented by application to concrete problems in order to produce their proper effects. It is not our function to determine precisely what these problems are, but we do hold that whatever these specific problems are, they should be solved in the light of the above-stated principles, rights, and duties.

XIII

PEACE, PROVIDENCE, AND PRAYER

WE LOVE peace and freedom; war and tyranny we hate. There is nothing startling or original in such a statement. Practically everybody subscribes to that proposition. There have been many genuine peace congresses and movements, precisely because most men want peace. The distinctive character of our effort to promote peace lies in the unique way in which we hope to do so. Without disdaining the natural means at our disposal, we place our ultimate hope of attaining peace on something above the purely natural. We base our hope for peace on the providence of God and the power of prayer. We dare to think that if we pray hard enough, and often enough, God will hear us.

This does not mean that we are so naïve or so inept in our choice of means as to believe that we can abolish war by wishful thinking. Existing dangers will not disappear simply because we close our eyes to their existence. War may come in spite of anything we can do. We can control our own actions, but we cannot control the actions of others. If aggressive Communism is bent upon lighting the fires of world revolution; if aggressive nations have no respect for the rights of others and no respect for their own solemn pledges; if they are determined to seize power by violence and subterfuge, then we may not be able to ward off the horrors of another war. But in that deplorable event, we at least, as a nation, must enter upon the struggle with clean hands and a clear conscience. The

141

world must know where we stand. We stand for the sovereignty of God and the supremacy of the moral law. We reject imperialism in every shape and form. We reject domination by dollar diplomacy or by selfish intervention. We reject the notion of White supremacy and declare our abiding faith in the unity of the human race and its brotherhood under God our Father.

Peace is not the fruit of shifting compromise; it is the fruit of justice. Justice demands that we abide by the principles of morality, in public life as well as in private life. Nations may no more break the ten commandments than any individual citizen. Justice demands that we do not trespass on the rights of other nations and that we keep sacred the contracts to which we have freely pledged our word. Peace demands an attitude of patience and restraint, but it does not demand a surrender of inalienable rights, either our own or those of others. We would be recreant to our duty both to God and to ourselves if we ignominiously failed to defend the rights and liberties of other nations whose security is a guarantee of our own.

Peace does not depend upon the strength of our armaments alone, nor upon the sagacity of our statesmen in international conferences. It depends, in the final analysis, on our conformity to the will of God and our trust in His providence. To deserve God's help we must have faith in Him; we must be submissive to His commandments; we must hold steadfast to the conviction that spiritual values transcend material benefits, and that deceit, cunning, and violence are criminal actions for nations just as they are for individuals. Good cannot be achieved through wickedness; the end never justifies the means. And so, when we fight for others, our motives must be pure and unselfish. When we pray, it must not be merely for ourselves, but even for our enemies. We pray not against any nation, but for it. For years our plea has been, "Saviour of the world, save Russia."

Forty-three years ago, when the first World War was raging, an event took place near Fatima in Portugal which was ignored by the world at large, but which in the course of the past four decades has shown itself to be pregnant with meaning. Russia at the time had withdrawn from the battlefront to plunge herself into the Communist revolution. No human mind could have foreseen the sad consequences of that event. The Blessed Mother of God, however, gave us an interpretation of what was to happen. When Mary appeared in Portugal to the three little children, Lucy, Jacinta, and Francisco, she delivered a message to the world which was a prophecy then, but which has come to a tragic fulfillment in our days. The message of the Blessed Virgin to the children was brief but profoundly significant. "God is offended," she stated, "by the sins of men. Do penance and pray. If so, Russia will be converted and peace will reign. If not, Russia will spread evil over the world and the scourge of war will afflict mankind in a worse catastrophe than the one now being experienced." The world did not change its attitude toward God. It gave little credence to the revelations made at Fatima. Since then, however, a second World War has devastated the world. Today the "cold war" still continues. Armies are still ready to be drawn up in battle array. In fact, we face the possibility of a third World War, which, if it should break out, would be vastly worse than anything heretofore experienced. How long, we ask, will the world turn a deaf ear to the divine entreaty: "Be converted . . . and live."

God uses simple means to confound the pride and self-sufficiency of man. With no more formidable weapon than a sling, little David slew the giant Goliath. When on earth,

Christ thanked His heavenly Father that He had hidden the mystery of the Redemption from the proud and revealed it to little ones. When we read the story of the Gospel we cannot help noting how quietly and unobtrusively God works out the mystery of our salvation. At the birth of Christ there was no imperial proclamation; at His resurrection there was no fanfare of trumpets; at His ascension there were only a handful of apostles and a small gathering of faithful followers. The same attitude of indifference characterizes the world today in its relation to God and spiritual values.

At Fatima a most significant event took place; but the leaders of the world press sent no enterprising reporters to investigate the phenomena. If we search the newspapers of that day we shall find indeed that the press of Lisbon carried an account of the strange events in the Cova da Iria, but the rest of the world was utterly indifferent to the story. The startling events were written off as childish phantasy or hysteria. Today even the incredulous cannot shut their eyes to the visible and tangible evidence which has arisen at Fatima to give witness to the truth of our Blessed Lady's appearance. On October 13, 1917, the Blessed Virgin proclaimed herself as Our Lady of the Rosary. Seventy thousand people, made up of all classes of mankind — peasants, artisans, professors, editors — witnessed the phenomenon of the sun whirling in space, suddenly loosed from its anchorage and flooding the countryside with an indescribable rainbow of light. Well, Fatima was a reality; and equally real was the war which our Blessed Lady prophesied.

Our duty is to pray for peace and order. We wish to make amends for our own sins and for the sins of the world. We declare our belief that our Blessed Lady of the Rosary is as potent in her influence today as she was in any of the ages of the past. In her Litany we salute her as the Tower of David, the Refuge of Sinners, the Comforter of the Afflicted, and the Help of Christians. We are mindful of the message delivered to us by Our Lady of Fatima. In keeping with that admonition we acknowledge our sins with contrite hearts. We pray for Russia and all its people — pray that they may be converted to the truth and submit themselves to the law of God.

When the human mind refuses to accept divine truth it creates for itself a mental vacuum into which rush all the phantasies and myths which masquerade as religion. If men reject the kingdom of God, there is nothing left but the vain hope of creating an earthly paradise of material plenty. Communism makes its appeal to this spiritually disenfranchised group. It provides them with a meretricious ideal and supplies them with the dynamic energy which is characteristic of every new revolution. The fact that the whole history of Communism is a record of inhuman misery written in blood has not yet dispelled for some the illusion of a Promised Land in which God is blasphemously made over in the image of man.

For centuries it has been the custom of Christian people to begin the month of May with a tribute to her whom Christ chose as His mother. She is the ideal of maidenhood and motherhood. She sums up in her person all the grace and beauty to which human nature can aspire. She is the Queen of heaven, and also the Mother of mankind, bequeathed to us by the dying Christ to act as our patron and protectress against the powers of evil. To her we turn in our confusion and distress. "O Mary, conceived without sin, pray for us who have recourse to thee."

There are those who disdain such an approach to the settlement of world problems. In many parts of the world May Day has been set aside for a demonstration of hatred toward the Christian social order. Not the banner of Our Lady with its blue and white, but the red banner of revolution, is raised aloft. These enemies of Christ want to tear down and destroy all vestiges of Christianity as a hindrance to human progress. They loudly proclaim that religion is their enemy — the opiate of the people. In their blindness they cannot see that it is not Christianity that has failed the people but rather that the people have failed to practice Christianity. The nations apostatized from Christ, and then wondered why He did not save them. They rejected His teachings and then wondered why His mission in their regard had not been accomplished.

We wish to make amends. We acknowledge the Christ as Saviour of mankind. We confess with Peter that "Thou art the Christ, the Son of the living God." We testify that there is no other name under heaven by which we can be saved. Like David and Judas Machabeus we put our trust in God, not merely in the strength of our arms. We are determined to preserve the traditions of our fathers; not because they are traditions but because they are a heritage with a divine sanction; because they alone give a rational guarantee of human dignity; because they alone constitute a wall of protection for our personal freedom and national security.

No matter how clear our thinking, no matter how forceful the expression of our ideas, no matter how tenacious our convictions, we shall never succeed in establishing a right order or rediscover the tranquillity of peace if we rely on our own puny human efforts. We must put our trust in God and seek His help. Not until mankind retreats from its own proud self-sufficiency and learns the lesson of humble reliance on the strength and the grace of God will it achieve security, peace, and order. There will be no lasting peace without prayer.

XIV

THE LIFE OF A NATION

IT IS obvious to those who consider the subject, that the measure of our national well-being is the well-being of our nation's family life. What is obvious, however, can easily be forgotten. Hence the recurring need to restate and re-emphasize the social axiom that the welfare and stability of a people as a whole suffers as family life disintegrates. The family is the cradle of those virtues which each succeeding generation needs to cultivate in order to keep society sound and wholesome. The family is the nursery of our Christian culture and civilization.

It is not without significance that Christ worked His first miracle at the marriage feast of Cana. It might seem strange to us that Christ did not go up immediately to the temple at Jerusalem and there declare His divine mission. Jerusalem seemed to be the normal setting in which the Messias should reveal Himself to the people. The temple porches might well have been the pulpit for His first sermon, and the backdrop for His first miracle. Even His own brethren indicated as much when they said to Him: "Leave here and go into Judea that Thy disciples also may see the works that Thou dost; for no one does a thing in secret if he wants to be publicly known."

Christ, however, chose a procedure quite contrary to human expectation. He had come to regenerate human society, and in consequence it was fitting that He should begin His ministry where society begins. Because society begins with the family,

147

and the family begins with marriage, His first task was to sanctify the marriage bond. He wished to call attention to the fact that marriage is a religious institution and that upon its divine structure and God-given function depends the welfare of society at large.

At present the Christian tradition as regards marriage and the family is under attack. As faith has declined, a secular attitude toward marriage and the Christian code of domestic ethics has grown. Purely human laws are being substituted for divine law. The unity and indissolubility of marriage are looked upon as a matter of personal convenience. There is a considerable body of public opinion which wishes to emancipate marriage from the protective legislation that has safeguarded it in the past.

Jurists and students of sociology clearly recognize the evils of divorce; they understand that broken homes and multiple parents are the fertile source of juvenile delinquency. Instead of attributing the evils, however, to a departure from Christian tradition regarding the structure and the function of the family, they now talk of a new social approach to divorce. The new approach is to make obsolete the present legal protection. These innovations constitute a challenge which must be met by a reaffirmation of divine truth. People have forgotten that our highly prized civilization is the fruit of a very special body of Christian truths, Christian laws, and Christian attitudes.

The fact stands that wherever Christianity has been preached and its truth accepted into the laws and social institutions of a nation, great social progress has been made. Wherever Christianity retreats, stagnation, then confusion, and finally decay have been the sequel.

To illustrate the point, let us call attention to the Christian attitude toward the sanctity of life, the dignity of the human person, the privileged position of women and children, and the Christian attitude toward wholesome recreation. It is not too much to say that the very nature and quality of any civilization can be determined by the attitudes and convictions that people have on these fundamental subjects. The same is true with regard to the family and the home.

Some years ago the new system of Communism in Russia denounced the family as a bourgeois institution. By this Marx and Lenin meant that the family as a social institution was a mere creature of capitalism; and that it would vanish with the disappearance of capitalism. In fact, they declared that the traditional family concept should be relegated to the scrap heap as a relic of feudal times. Their policy was to disparage the sacred character of the marriage contract in favor of companionate marriage; to emancipate women from the home so that they could work on the assembly line in a factory; and to emancipate children from the loving care of parents in order that they might become wards of the impersonal state. It was not mere theory that they proposed, but actual experiment. They tried it, but it did not work. At one time marriage was permitted in Russia by the mere registration of the names of the interested parties. No ceremony was required and no contract was lasting. Divorce could be obtained by a mere postcard sent to the registration bureau. Russia found from sad experience that this procedure played havoc with social stability. Today there has been a complete reversal of policy: to obtain a divorce in Russia is extremely difficult, and abortion is absolutely proscribed. Bitter experience has led to a return to sanity.

People are apt to forget that in ancient times marriage, the family, and the home were not safeguarded by that ethical code which with the advent of Christianity became universal in the

Western world. In ancient times polygamy was an accepted social institution. Wives and children had very few rights as against the autocratic will of the state, the husband, or the father. Wives could be summarily dismissed in the most arbitrary fashion. Children, if malformed or for some other reason unwanted, could, under the laws of Lycurgus, be exposed to death. This condition obtained even in such an enlightened state as Athens. There were patriarchal societies in which a husband had many wives and all property rights were vested in him alone. There were some matriarchal societies in which one wife had many husbands, and the children never knew the identity of their father. All this is so foreign to our thinking that we can hardly conceive its possibility today. Yet we must remember that similar conditions still flourish in many pagan lands. It was Christianity, with its teaching concerning marriage, the family, and the home, that rescued mankind from that deplorable condition.

The Church taught that marriage was a divinely established institution, consisting of a contract between one man and one woman. This teaching put an end to polygamy. The Church taught that marriage was indissoluble. This put an end to the evil of divorce. The Church taught that marriage imposed rights and duties upon both husband and wife. In the Christian law the husband is indeed recognized as the head of the family, but he is warned by the Sacred Scriptures: "Husbands, love your wives, just as Christ also loved the Church, and delivered Himself up for her." This doctrine put an end to the fallacy of woman's inferiority. The Church taught that both parents have grave responsibilities toward their children; that the parents enjoy primary rights in respect to the health, education, character formation, and vocational guidance of their children. The Church taught that marriage must by its very nature be a free contract between man and woman. Hence parents, while having the responsibility of guiding their children in the choice of their life partners, nevertheless have no right to impose their arbitrary will upon them. The Church became the champion of the freedom of young people to choose their own life partners.

Today, with the diminishing force of Christian influence, the family once more is disintegrating. Let us take a look at the record of our divorce courts. In the year 1887, the earliest for which a record is given in the U. S. Statistical Abstract, there were 27,919 divorces. It is estimated that in the year 1945, about a half century later, there were 300,000 divorces. In fact, the divorce rate has doubled every twenty-five years since our country began to keep records. Counting from the year 1900, there have been more than eight million divorces; and since there are always two people involved in a divorce proceedings, this means that from the turn of the century there have been more than sixteen million divorces created by law. Approximately every seventh person over twenty-five whom you meet on the street today is a partner to a broken marriage. Now, what is the effect of such a situation? What can we expect from broken homes but a mounting wave of juvenile delinquency? J. Edgar Hoover of the F. B. I. has called attention to the fact that juvenile delinquents come in greatest numbers from broken homes. He does not stand alone in this conviction; he is supported by sociologists in every part of the country.

BIRTH CONTROL AND POPULATION

Divorce attacks the very nature of the marriage contract. But there is another evil which attacks the purpose and the function of marriage. In the garden of Eden God said to the first married couple: "Be fruitful and multiply; fill the earth." Today we find this divine injunction nullified by groups which call themselves euphemistically Planned Parenthood Associations. More accurately they should be called Associations of Race Suicide. What is the result? In towns of more than 2500 population in the U. S. A., ten adults were recently rearing only seven children. It does not take a student of higher mathematics to realize that in these towns the population is not reproducing itself. The higher up one goes in the economic scale, the worse is the condition. The more wealth, the fewer children; the higher the education, the lower the birth rate. It should be the exact opposite, according to the theory of the Planned Parenthood. The teaching of birth control has made the practice most destructive precisely among those people who should be rearing the largest families.

This unnatural situation may no longer cause moral concern to some people, but it should cause national concern to every thoughtful American from the economic and social point of view. Social Security is becoming as a consequence social insecurity. The prospect for future America is one of an aging population. The number of old people is constantly increasing in ratio. Every workingman in the future will have to carry on his back an increasing load of dependents, if the birth rate of our citizens declines. There will be fewer hands to work and more mouths to feed. We were once a young people; now we are getting old.

In November, 1959, the Catholic Bishops of the United States issued a joint statement on artificial birth control. Ever since the publication of the Bishops' statement, there has been a running commentary in the press on the question at issue and also on a variety of related subjects.

"Separation of Church and state" came in for consideration and thus helped to further complicate and confuse the precise issues at stake. There have been repeated interviews, letters to the editor, and politically slanted statements by interested parties. Although there has been much discussion in the public press, not much light has been thrown on the specific problem involved.

To keep the record straight, certain facts must be borne in mind. The first of these is that the Catholic Bishops did not take the initiative in precipitating this controversy. Their statement was issued only after a sequence of events that seemed to indicate that an effort was under way to foster the adoption of artificial birth control as part of our national policy in granting foreign aid.

The Draper Report which popularized the term "population explosion," issued in August of 1959, clearly implied, even if it did not say so in specific words, that it favored a program of artificial birth control as a national policy. On November 2, two weeks before the Bishops' statement was issued, Arnold Toynbee spoke in favor of the program in a meeting of the Food Administration Organization of the U. N. in Rome. On the Sunday preceding the Bishops' meeting, the Columbia Broadcasting System presented a full-length program which, because of its treatment, was widely regarded as propaganda for artificial birth control.

That same week in which the Catholic Bishops were meeting in Washington, the Planned Parenthood Association held a national conference in New York City, in the course of which Bishop James A. Pike, of the Episcopal Church, again elaborated his views in favor of artificial birth control. It was also stated that the Catholic Church would no doubt in the course of time modify its own ethical position on artificial birth control. It was in the light of these successive events that the Catholic Bishops, then gathered in Washington for their annual meeting, considered that a statement was mandatory on their part in order to avoid any further doubt about the Church's position.

To form a clear and adequate picture of the entire subject, it is necessary that three totally separate and distinct questions be kept in mind. The first is the ethical or moral question regarding artificial methods of birth control. The second is the economic or sociological question of the nature and extent of the population increase and how its results can be effectively met in the years to come. The third question, a political one, concerns the establishment of a national policy for our country regarding the use of artificial birth-control methods in its foreign-aid program. In any intelligent discussion of the subject, these three questions must be kept rigidly apart or there will be confusion in respect to *who* stands for *what*.

First, the ethical or moral question — whether artificial birth control is, in the sight of God, right or wrong. Here we readily admit that there is a wide difference of conviction. Until the present century, there seemed to be a consensus that the manufacture, sale, and distribution of contraceptives is morally wrong. It was for that reason that prohibitory laws were put on the statute books of some of our states. We wish to emphasize the fact that this action was not the result of any Catholic pressure or initiative. Eighty years ago, when Connecticut and Massachusetts passed laws against artificial means of birth prevention, the influence of Catholics in those states was utterly insignificant. Various Protestant churches at the time were definitely opposed to the dissemination of such information. It was under their influence, or at least with their approval, that the prohibitory laws were placed on the statute books.

Recently the leaders of these churches have changed their minds, and now, seemingly, they want to change the laws. What is more, they want to make their views effective in determining public policy and public legislation. When we as Catholics enter a protest against this effort, by a strange twist of logic we are the ones who are accused of wanting to impose our particular convictions as a norm of conduct on others. Exactly the opposite is true. We are not forcing our convictions on others; but by the same token, they should not force their convictions on us. It is the Planned Parenthood Association and their supporters who want to change the existing order of things. We agree with President Eisenhower that it is not the business of government to enter into the question. It is clearly the responsibility of the individual conscience to determine a course of conduct in accordance with objective standards of morality.

What actually happened in the course of the present century is this: Secular opinion first, and then various Protestant churches, gradually shifted their position so that, one by one, they adopted the view that the nature and meaning of the marriage contract should be adjusted to meet both the personal and economic, as well as the social conditions, of the times.

In 1908 the Lambeth Conference of Anglican Bishops was unequivocally opposed to contraception. In 1920 it reaffirmed this position, but not in such a forthright manner. In 1930 it gave permission for the "conscientious use" of contraception. And in 1958 the same Conference appeared as an advocate of artificial birth control. Other denominations followed a somewhat similar course. Meanwhile the Catholic Church stood firm in its opposition.

The Catholic Church has no desire to see the population increase in some irresponsible manner. It is not in the business of counting heads for its own aggrandizement. Its only purpose is to safeguard the nature and the meaning of the marriage contract and to defend the natural law. It is the natural law, not some ecclesiastical decree, which prohibits the exercise of a human function when its primary purpose is willfully frustrated by artificial means. The Catholic Church holds that marriage rights must be exercised with responsibility, and that to defeat their purpose by unnatural interference is a sin against God, the Author of nature.

There is no intention on the part of the Catholic Church to minimize the problem resulting from a rapid increase of the population. We do not close our eyes to the hunger, disease, and poverty in many areas of the world. We are profoundly sympathetic with those who suffer this distress. It is quite easy to arouse sentiments of pity by graphically portraying the miserable conditions in India and other nations of the East. To assume, however, that artificial birth control is the effective remedy of these evils, constitutes a naïve oversimplification of the problem.

Birth control will not give food and shelter to the many millions of people now living. Children are not a disease like cholera which can be extirpated. Improved methods of agriculture, better seeds, fertilizers, the use of new methods of farming will produce the food that is needed. With good will such a program would not be too difficult to achieve. The food production in India, in fact, could be increased incalculably if the methods of our American farmers were put to use there. If attention were concentrated on this primary objective instead of diverting efforts to foster a program of artificial birth control, India could actually feed its people within ten years.

Mr. Paul Hoffman of the United Nations insists that the problem is urgent now, and that it must be solved within the next ten years or there will be revolution. Even experts, however, admit that it would take many decades of indoctrination by planned parenthood methods before even a discernible dent could be made in the population figures. With a stepped-up program of food production, vastly more good could be accomplished than would be possible with the sterile propaganda of the birth-control advocates. Professor Colin Clark of Oxford University, a noted authority on demographic problems, stakes his reputation on the validity of this conclusion.

Japan during the past century actually increased its standard of living faster than it increased its population. This is only one example of what can be done. In view of the fact that an increase of food production will show positive results, and the other method of birth control by contraception is at best uncertain, we ask why there should be any hesitation in choosing the surest means of providing a solution to the problem.

It is true that artificial birth control would stem somewhat the rapid increase of population for the future, but if the means itself is immoral, we cannot go along with the method. We do not accept the proposition that the end justifies the means.

The third question which has been raised is one which affects the adoption of a public policy in administering our foreign-aid program. There has been sharp controversy in respect to this issue. It has been asserted that we as Catholics now want to impose our moral convictions on the rest of the nation in regard to this question of birth control. As Al Smith used to say: "Let's look at the record." The facts do not support the contention of our opponents. It is they, not we, who want to impose a new national policy on the government in implementing our foreign aid to other nations.

The Catholic Bishops of this country simply stated that they would refuse to support such a program. They did not take the position that the teaching of the Catholic Church should constitute a rule of conduct for those who do not see eye to eye with us on the morality of the procedure. They did not advocate a policy on the part of our government of interfering with the free action of other nations. They simply declared, as President Eisenhower did, that the advocacy or adoption of a program of birth control is none of the government's business.

It is unfortunate that this controversy concerning artificial birth control should be the occasion of still further cleavage between Christian people, and that at a time when we are trying to close ranks against common dangers and promote a greater measure of unity. Our plea, in the first place, is to get rid of suspicion and recrimination in respect to motives and objectives when we disagree among ourselves, whether it be in the field of morals or of doctrine. Let the discussion of difference be carried on in good temper, but first of all let there be a fair and honest statement of our differences. Secondly, let everyone avoid insinuations that our debate on questions of high moral principle is influenced by political considerations or partisan advantages. Sincere differences of conviction can be rightly discussed in public, but only when there is scrupulous regard for factual truth and when the motivating spirit is one of sincere charity.

FALSE IDEALS OF MARRIED HAPPINESS

Besides these outstanding factors which are causing disintegration in our family life, there are the false ideals of

courtship, the false ideals of married happiness, and the false
ideals of feminine independence. These factors bode no good
for the future stability of our nation. We understand full well
that some so-called liberals will regard this statement as reactionary. Quite the contrary! We stand unmistakably as
champions of a sound national eugenic program. We stand
for the protection of women and children. We favor a program
of family allowances. We want to see a reduction of taxes
on family homes and replacement by income taxes. We oppose
the Equal Rights Amendment for women because it is a
misnomer. Such an amendment would wipe out years of protective legislation for women and, far from establishing an
equality, would rather attempt to legislate an identity of function between men and women.

In the face of these disintegrating factors let us consider
some aspects of family life which will help restore the stability
of the family. In the first place, there should be a spiritual
revival within the home. If religion is confined to the Church,
it will soon become a vanishing factor. Its roots lie deep in
family life. One of the most effective means of promoting
unity within the family is the consecrated practice of family
prayers. Such a practice would do more to lift the family
above the boarding-house level and eliminate juvenile delinquency than all the social service which state agencies can
provide. The pictures on the walls, the books in the library,
the conversation in the family circle should each in its own
way conduce to reinforce the spiritual ideals of the home, so
that by word and by example the children will grow up with
reverence and respect for parental authority and genuine virtue.

In times past, before the advent of the factory system, the
home was the economic unit of society. Children learned a
trade or acquired business knowledge by watching their father

carry on his activities within the family circle. Today fathers, of necessity, leave home each morning for the office or work-shop. Hence the economic training of the child is greatly handicapped. Not only is economic training made difficult by social changes but children grow up with the notion that they have no responsibilities toward the economic welfare of the family. Too often they become spenders and not contribu-tors. We might at least teach them to contribute, according to their ability, to the maintenance of the family budget. They should be made to understand that they do not have complete independence or autonomy until they have established their own homes.

Recreation is another aspect of family life which occupies our attention. The family circle should be the normal recrea-tion center for father, mother, and children. Today, unfor-tunately, too many people and far too many children think that they must buy their recreation. They have become so poor in imagination that they cannot create their own amusements and diversions, but must seek instead the commercial ones. Recreations such as the movies, the dance hall, the night clubs have superseded, almost entirely, recreation within the family group. It would be a wholesome contribution to family life if we could recapture some of the inspiring joys of folklore and folk song; of canning bees and sewing circles, with outdoor sports taking precedence over indoor activities.

The prevailing attitude of any society or civilization toward the family and its rights and duties will usually be reflected in the fundamental law of a nation. It is interesting to note that our own Constitutional law provides great safeguards for the liberty, the dignity, and the welfare of individual citizens, but says little or nothing about the family itself. By contrast, some of the newer states have provided in their Constitutions for the specific rights of families as such. The Constitutions of Portugal, of Spain, and of Ireland might be mentioned as illustrating the principle that it is the duty of the state to come to the aid of individual families in matters of education, health, housing, and economic well-being. This is a movement in the right direction, and fully in accord with the natural law and good social order — a recognition of the family rather than the state as the basic social unit. Public law, however, does state that every man is endowed by his Creator with the right to life, liberty, and the pursuit of happiness. While no definition of these terms is given, it must be assumed as a logical sequel that the terms "liberty" and "the pursuit of happiness" imply the right to establish a family and to secure its well-being. Almost a hundred and seventy-five years have passed since our country's Constitution was written. At the time it represented the most advanced thinking of liberal minds in terms of social and political philosophy. Today there is a new orientation of mind reflected in the fundamental law of recently organized states. Neither the Communist nor the Fascist states any longer place major emphasis on the individual; rather, they place it on the community or the collectivity. The welfare of the amorphous mass or the proletariat is their predominant interest. The individual no longer has any claim of security or independence against the state.

Against such thinking, it is important to recall that in the providence of God three distinct societies have been established for the perfecting of the individual: the family, the state, and the Church. These three constitute the God-given environment for the development of the innate talents and capacities of the human person. The family is a necessary society, but an incomplete one. It is incomplete because it needs the assistance of the state and of the Church to supplement its own efforts and fulfill its own responsibilities. It is a necessary society, because without it human life can neither come into existence nor achieve its destiny.

The parental home is not merely the place of birth and the indispensable source of human existence, but it is the best possible environment in which the child can mature and develop. Because the child gives continuity to the life of the parents and because the child is in fact bone of their bone and flesh of their flesh, it follows inevitably that parents will be deeply attached to their offspring. By natural instinct as well as by divine law, the child growing up within the family circle will be fortified with the greatest personal interest, love, and devoted care. The family, as a social institution created by nature, constitutes an environment of security, a seedbed of virtue, and a stimulus for development far superior to that which might be provided under any other conceivable circumstances.

The state is likewise necessary as a society in which the individual grows and develops into a useful citizen. The state is both a complete and a necessary society. By that we mean that it has within its own power and control all the elements necessary to supplement the needs of the individual and the family. It is bound, however, by the principle of "subsidiarity of function." This means that the state is not to assume the responsibilities which can be exercised by the family itself. It must safeguard the health and strength of its citizens, make provision for the education of its members, and organize the economic system so that families can be assured of the physical necessities such as food, clothing, and shelter. It must protect the integrity of the human person. But all these things must be done without interfering with the rights and duties of the family itself.

As the Supreme Court of the United States has declared, the child belongs to the parents and not to the state; hence the parents have both the right and the duty to provide for the physical, social, and spiritual training of their offspring, antecedent to any rights of the state. This principle is of great importance, for it means that the state has no inherent right to interfere with the management of the family, no right to a monopoly of education, and no right to a dictatorial control of the economic life of the family. It is only when the family has been recreant to its duties that the state may justly take over its responsibilities.

There is a third society to which, in the providence of God, all human beings should belong. It is the divinely established Church. The Church is a society which treats of human beings as an aggregate of souls, while the state is a society which treats of human beings as an aggregate of citizens. The Church provides for the spiritual necessities and the eternal destiny of the individual, whereas the state provides for the material needs and the temporal destiny of the citizens.

The Church has the divine commission to teach the message of Christ. As a direct corollary of this responsibility, the Church cannot fail to assume responsibility for the education of the young in all things which concern divine truth and spiritual values. It is the Church which has jurisdiction over the sacraments; therefore, the Church must concern herself with the marriage contract. It is the Church which interprets the commandments of God; therefore, the Church must clarify the laws concerning the function and purpose of marriage. St. Paul tells us that marriage is a great sacrament, but he adds: "This is a great mystery — I mean in reference to Christ and to the Church."

We can give no better illustration of the relationship which should exist between parents and children, husbands and wives, than that which St. Paul himself gave to the Ephesians: "Be subject to one another in the fear of Christ. Let wives be subject to their husbands as to the Lord; because a husband is head of the wife, just as Christ is head of the Church, being Himself Saviour of the Body. But just as the Church is subject to Christ, so also let wives be to their husbands in all things.

"Husbands, love your wives, just as Christ also loved the Church, and delivered Himself up for her, that He might sanctify her, cleansing her in the bath of water by means of the word; in order that He might present to Himself the Church in all her glory, not having spot or wrinkle or any such thing, but that she might be holy and without blemish. Even thus ought husbands also to love their wives as their own bodies. He who loves his own wife, loves himself. For no one ever hated his own flesh; on the contrary he nourishes and cherishes it, as Christ also does the Church (because we are members of His Body, made from His flesh and from His bones).

" 'For this Cause a man shall leave his
    father and mother,
and cleave to his wife;
and the two shall become one flesh.'

"This is a great mystery — I mean in reference to Christ and to the Church."

Time and again Pius XII emphasized the important function of the laity in impregnating our social and civic life with Christian principles. He pointed out that this is a task peculiar to the laity. "The clergy," he states, "must hold itself in reserve for the exercise of the ministry which is properly sacerdotal, in which it cannot be replaced. A balance, furnished by the laymen in the apostolate, is therefore an indispensable necessity."

There are many tasks in the re-establishment of the Christian character of the family which can be performed most effectively by laymen. There are problems of a legal nature for lawyers, problems of an economic and social nature for statesmen, problems of education for parents and teachers, problems of health, family allowances, good housing, and social security for experts in these respective fields; and there is, above all, the spiritual problem which can be solved best when the family becomes a church in miniature.

The position of the Church is fundamentally that of democracy which stands for the rights and liberty of the individual. In defending, therefore, the traditional code of family ethics, we speak as Americans, as true democrats, as well as Christians, in the name of truth.

Part IV

MAN IN RELATION TO CHURCH AND STATE

IN PERFECTING HIS INTELLECTUAL NATURE

"The two pervading errors in our educational system today, errors which vitiate to a great extent otherwise considerable achievements, are secularism and false liberty."

XV

A DIVINE COMMISSION TO TEACH

FROM the very beginning of her history, the Catholic Church has exercised an educational function. When she was commissioned by Christ to continue His work in the world, she was charged with the responsibility not only of teaching and sanctifying the people of His day, but also of bringing to the nations of the world the truth He had taught in all its fullness. Manifestly this teaching function or responsibility concerned itself immediately and directly with the extension and protection of religious truth. Socrates and other Greek philosophers taught, with repeated insistence, that the beginning of all knowledge is: "Know thyself." It is absolutely necessary that we know the origin of man, his nature, his destiny, and his relationship to God, the Author of all being, if we are to be properly orientated toward the world in which we live. Unless a man knows the answer to these questions, he will find himself confused and befuddled in his pursuit of all other forms of knowledge. Hence the educational function of the Church even within its own specific field is of primary importance.

There was a time when this thesis was rejected and treated with indifference or contempt. There was a time not far distant when reason alone was thought to be adequate for all purposes of life. The protagonists of the so-called Enlightenment, especially the rationalists of the eighteenth and nineteenth centuries, rejected the necessity and value of revelation. They drew a small circle around man himself and stated that this constituted his sole area of knowledge. Everything beyond man and his experiences was unknown and unknowable. The disastrous cataclysms of contemporary history, the confusion, unrest, and instability of the intellectual world today have convinced our greatest scholars and statesmen that reason alone is not sufficient to construct even a tolerable earthly order, much less to create hope and happiness for a future existence. If order is to be brought out of the chaotic condition of our educational system, if anything like unity of knowledge is to be established, if order is to be introduced into the intellectual as well as the practical world, it will be necessary to return to the disciplines of the medieval schools and universities. We shall be obliged to restore theology and philosophy to their rightful place as pivotal centers of all knowledge.

When Christ stood before Pilate, the question was put to Him, "What is truth?" Perhaps Pilate put the question in a cynical manner, as if to imply that it was futile to attempt to discover truth. Or perhaps he was honestly expressing his own doubt and uncertainty — expressing a latent desire to reach the truth. Both attitudes have been repeated over and over again in the history of thought. Today there are, once more, faint glimmerings of intellectual humility and a desire, prompted by desperation, to find the truth, the whole truth, and nothing but the truth.

If we study the early history of the Church, we shall find that as soon as she was granted her liberty under the Caesars and emerged from the catacombs, she interested herself in the work of general education. Cathedral and monastery schools grew up on all sides. The fall of Rome and the barbarian invasion blotted out the light of learning, and introduced the beginning of the Dark Ages. As soon as the Christian Church had tamed the wild extravagancies of the barbarian invaders from the north and from the east, she systematically established her institutions of higher learning. There is no need for us to remind the reader of the history of the great universities of Europe. Practically every university whose name is held in honor traces its origin and foundation to a pontifical charter: Oxford, Cambridge, St. Andrew's, Padua, Bologna, Paris, Salamanca, and others.

The Church realizes that all science and all knowledge are merely different facets of one and the same indivisible truth. Truth has many aspects but it cannot be treated in fragmentary fashion. It has its own integrity; if it is wounded in one of its members, the whole organism suffers. If the wound should happen to be in the head — that is, in the field of philosophy or theology — then the whole body of truth is disturbed. To illustrate: How can there be any sound and rational social order until we know the nature, origin, and destiny of man, who is the unit of society? How can we know what is right or wrong for man, whether individually or socially considered, until we know whether God exists, whether Christ is God, whether man has a spiritual nature with an eternal destiny or whether he is merely part of the natural universe without a destiny beyond the grave? All these truths are part of a universal whole. And because the Church realizes this, she considers it to be a necessary part of her mission to establish schools and universities wherein she can exercise her universal magisterium.

In the last analysis, there are only three sources of knowledge: the one is human authority, representing a crystallized experience of past ages; the second is personal observation, sifted by the human mind through analysis and synthesis; and the third, the revelation of God, embodying the truths of divine faith which transcend human experiences and human reason. From Greece and Rome extends the classical experience which represents the finest achievements of human reason. From Jerusalem and Christian Rome extends that divine revelation which, together with the classical tradition, constitutes the foundation of our highest culture and civilization. St. Thomas Aquinas brought together these two streams of knowledge and worked them into a comprehensive whole. Very appropriately, therefore, he has been declared officially by the Church as the heavenly patron not only of theological seminaries but of all Catholic institutions of higher education. He is the "Angelic Doctor," who with something akin to the intuition of the angels, has penetrated the most profound mysteries of our faith and has united in a complete synthesis the knowledge derived from revelation with the sum total of human knowledge derived from observation and the deductions of right reason.

The universal cry of the world today is for peace, order, and stability. There can be no peace, no order, no stability until there is an acceptance once more of those principles on which our civilization was established and on which the whole structure of peace and tranquillity must rest. The two pervading errors in our educational system today, errors which vitiate to a great extent otherwise considerable achievements, are secularism and false liberty. Secularism is the attitude and spirit which denies a place to supernatural truth within the realm of human knowledge. Secularism, or the rejection of revealed truth, is in the background of the whole perverse ideology which dominates Russia and a large part of the world today. It is an ever-present danger in this country and may have serious consequences unless the Christian heritage of our people is reclaimed before it is too late. If those who are to be the intellectual leaders of mankind are taught that they are mere creatures of earth with no eternal destiny, no spiritual nature, no responsibility to God, sooner or later these errors will filter through to the masses and cause them to lead lives marked by class hatred, envy, contention, and revolution.

The second error is the false liberty speciously presented as academic freedom. Behind this false façade of freedom lurk anarchy and disorder. Truth is imperious in its demands. It claims absolute loyalty from every human mind. No one is intellectually free to deny truth or to subscribe to falsehood. Truth, by its very nature, carries authority and is dogmatic within its own domain. When Christ taught in Galilee, the one thing that impressed His hearers was His calm profession of the truth and His affirmation of clear-cut dogmas. The people "were astonished at His teaching; for He was teaching them as one having authority, and not as the Scribes." So, too, must any upright teacher speak, where truth and not mere opinion is concerned. Chesterton said the last word on the controversy concerning dogmatic education when he enunciated the truism: "A teacher who is not dogmatic, is a teacher who does not teach."

When liberty is erected into an end, we are in sight of the death, first, of education; and, second, of the society which has surrendered itself to this grave folly; and, last but not least, of liberty itself. That an unqualified worship of liberty will mean the death of education is obvious, for if the teacher is forbidden in the name of liberty to espouse one view or way of life rather than another, then it is clear that the teacher does not teach. Like Othello, his "occupation's gone." There may be in some court a case for such liberty, but there is certainly no cause for calling it a system of education. It is, to quote Chesterton again, no more a system of education than "sleeping under a hedge is a new form of architecture." Any pretendedly non-dogmatic system of education survives only because, in fact, it is highly dogmatic, and, despite all pretense of impartiality, does impose a definite philosophy of life, even though that philosophy of life be mere agnosticism.

Loss of belief in God has over the ages most logically led to the loss of belief in Man. The Swinburnian halfway house of "Glory to man in the highest; for man is the master of things," was too obviously hollow to satisfy man for any length of time. It has been the happiness and the glory of Europe that the dogmas of her educational system have been those of the Christian religion.

Some years before Hitler came to power, Christopher Dawson wrote in his *Progress and Religion:* "It seems as though a new society is arising which will acknowledge no hierarchy of values, no intellectual authority, and no social or religious tradition, but which will live for the moment in a chaos of pure sensation. . . . It is obvious that a civilization of this kind holds no promise for the future save that of social disintegration." It is not too late to save ourselves by putting the clock back. In education, at any rate, the policy for the future must be one of reaction. And the Church must lead the way, for she has a divine commission to teach the truth to men of all generations.

XVI

A SEPARATE SCHOOL SYSTEM

IT MAY seem strange to some of our fellow citizens that we Catholics should voluntarily accept the burden of supporting a separate school system, particularly when adequate facilities are available in the public schools. Let us assure all those who think along these lines that we as Catholics do not enjoy this unique position. We should much prefer to share the benefits of the tax-supported schools if it were not that deep convictions on our part make it necessary to follow an independent course. A declaration of faith, therefore, in the principles which underlie our educational program seems in order.

We believe in an educational program that develops every aspect and faculty of the human person — body, mind, and heart. This means a balanced program which fits a person for his duties to God, to his fellow man, and to himself. From our very beginnings we have held to the firm conviction that no form of knowledge and no human experience should be withheld from our children or eliminated from the educational process. Education should take into account all knowledge without discrimination. The higher the knowledge, the more urgent its claim on our recognition; the more useful it is in daily life, the more imperative is its inclusion in an educational program. To us it is unthinkable that an educational program can be complete which neglects an essential part of the human personality or a basic area of human knowledge and experience.

175

To us religion is a vital part of education just as is history or literature or science or social relations. Indeed it is more vitally a part of education than any or all of these others because its values are still valid in a life beyond the grave.

We believe that the first right and duty of providing an education for children rests with the parents and therefore we are opposed to any state monopoly or complete nationalization of the educational system just as much as we are opposed to the nationalization of business and industry.

We believe that the state has the right and duty to set minimum standards of education for citizenship; but we believe also that the state is bound to assist parents to fulfill their duties by the use of public subsidy without violating religious freedom or engaging in discriminatory class legislation.

We believe in equal rights and full religious freedom for all citizens irrespective of color, race, and creed; we desire to see all children enjoy the best educational facilities without discrimination. We hold that in the field of education this fundamental requirement of freedom and this postulate of the democratic process are at present being challenged by a prejudice which carries over from the past, and by a failure to understand the danger to liberty and democracy inherent in such attitudes.

We believe in the democratic freedom of all citizens to select that type of education which meets their needs without any legal discrimination lodged against them because they so exercise their constitutional freedom of choice.

We believe in a program of free and universal education, including elementary and high school, for all who are qualified to profit by it. We believe in a system of public-loan scholarships for college and professional training similar to the G. I. program whereby each student can select his own school.

We are definitely in sympathy with the maintenance of the highest standards of professional training and remuneration for all teachers in so far as the tax revenues of our community permit.

We hold firmly that the purpose of education is not merely to prepare men for life here but for life hereafter. We believe that a complete system of education has to do with the will as well as the mind, its purpose being not merely to make men "smart" but to make them good. We are in complete agreement with the philosophy of the Founding Fathers of this country who spoke their mind to us in the words of Washington: "Of all the dispositions and habits which lead to political prosperity, religion and morality are indispensable supports. The mere politician, equally with the pious man, ought to respect and cherish them. And let us with caution indulge the supposition that morality can be maintained without religion. Whatever may be conceded to the influence of refined education on minds of peculiar structure, reason and experience both forbid us to expect that national morality can prevail in exclusion of religious principle."

We take satisfaction in calling to mind the provisions of the North-West Ordinance which was passed by Congress in the year 1787 to regulate the political and cultural life of the territory in which Ohio is now included. In Article III of this early charter the pioneer statesmen and educators laid down the following fundamental policy: "Religion, morality, and knowledge being necessary to good government and the happiness of mankind, schools and the means of education shall forever be encouraged." Please note the order in which these requisites of good government and happiness are enumerated: first comes religion, then morality, and in the third place, knowledge. All three indeed are necessary; all three must be taken together and constitute an indivisible whole. There can be no divorce or separation of these integral elements of education without weakening the latter's influence.

Samuel Lewis, the first state superintendent of schools in Ohio, declares that as late as 1839 a very large number of schools in Ohio were private schools, although publicly supported. Even the present Constitution of the State of Ohio in Article I, Section 7, still reflects this early philosophy. It reads as follows: "It shall be the duty of the assembly to pass suitable laws to protect every religious denomination in the peaceable enjoyment of its own mode of public worship, and to encourage schools and the means of instruction." Morality and religion are inseparable in our conviction. Knowledge apart from morality can never develop character. If there is any one theory that has been completely exploded by practical experience it is the antiquated formula of the French rationalists that "to open a school is to close a jail." The statistics of our modern juvenile courts and the facts of recent world history clearly demonstrate that virtue is not a necessary consequence of intellectual knowledge. The monstrous totalitarian philosophy which precipitated the war did not come from the minds of ignorant men.

Religion furnishes the elements which are essential in the formation of character. These elements are three: first, there must be a clearly defined code of conduct; second, this code of conduct must have some ultimate authority behind it to make it effective; third, there must be adequate sanctions in terms of rewards and penalties. Religion alone creates a court of conscience and a final judgment which gives moral force to the law. Moreover, the most sublime literature as well as the most universal cultural experience which is known to man is found in religious history. Therefore we hold to the conviction that religion and morality must be included in any educational program which aims at the complete development of the mind and the will of man.

There are few today who realize the courage and the foresight required to bring into existence the flourishing Catholic school system. We would not in the least disparage the achievements of zealous priests, devoted religious, and faithful people who have so energetically and generously followed the leadership of their prelates in working for the cause of Catholic education, but we must not forget that it did require a wise foresight to envision the need, and enterprising courage to establish the instruments of popular religious education. This wisdom and energy reposed in the leadership of the Catholic hierarchy of this country.

It is less than a hundred years ago that the American people began their experiment of establishing a universal compulsory system of education. In the beginning there was no clearly defined philosophy of life on which the system was predicated. No matter what tendency toward secularization there might have been in the minds of the chief proponents, nevertheless the American people themselves were concerned mainly with two things: first, that all children should have free access to an education; secondly, that no discrimination should exist in favor of any particular religious group. They little realized that the end result would be a positive discrimination against all religion. They achieved their first objective — namely, universal compulsory education, but they failed flagrantly in maintaining freedom of conscience for those who believe that religion is an essential subject of knowledge and the most constructive element in the process of character formation.

The fathers of the Second and the Third Plenary Councils of Baltimore were the first to recognize the dangers inherent in this system of purely secular education. In spite of unfair competition, and with meager resources at their command, they launched an educational program of their own which is entirely unique in the history of the Church. The essential elements characteristic of this system are: first, it is based on the principle that the child belongs to the parents and not to the state. If the state will not recognize its duty to assist the parents in providing a suitable education in accordance with the rights of conscience, then the parents must assume that responsibility as their own in spite of the unreasonable handicap forced upon them. Second, the system is universal and free, at least on the elementary level, where the essential tools of knowledge are furnished. Third, the system is staffed largely by Religious teachers who by receiving the barest minimum in the way of salaries make possible the financing of this gigantic undertaking. In no other country has anything similar been done.

We remind the reader of these principles and policies, not for polemical purposes but rather to make clear our own position with regard to the policy of conducting separate schools. Unless these reasons be fully appreciated, our attitude in educational matters would necessarily seem strange and unwarranted to the general public. Our isolation in the educational program is not of our choice and certainly does not argue any desire on our part to be an exclusive or an uncongenial element in our respective communities.

The burden which we bear in behalf of our own school program, because of our conviction, is indeed heavy and yet we have never refused to assume likewise our equal share in any community enterprise in behalf of the public schools or in behalf of the common good. "With malice toward none; with charity for all," with frank sincerity we declare our position, confident that in the final analysis it will be recognized as just, reasonable, and conducive to the common good.

XVII

OUR NATION'S SCHOOLS

RECENT pronouncements by recognized authorities in the field of education have focused attention once more on various problems affecting our nation's schools. Among the questions which have been raised there are two which involve difficult decisions in the matter of public policy: first, how shall our country provide adequate educational facilities for the unprecedentedly large increase in the enrollment in both elementary and secondary schools; secondly, how shall the curriculum be organized so as to inculcate more effectively moral and spiritual values in the minds and hearts of youth?

Frequent discussion in the press of the country has made practically everyone familiar with the fact that, following the second World War, marriages multiplied beyond all previous records, and simultaneously the ratio of children per family reached a new high. The resulting child population is now of school age and the pressure on all educational facilities has increased enormously. Throughout our previous history the responsibility for school support and control of schools have been almost completely reserved to local units of government. Some now propose that a departure be made from this traditional policy and that the federal government assume a much greater part of the responsibility. Strangely enough, the pressure of millions of children on the facilities of private and church-related schools has received scant attention in public discussion, and yet their problem is an inescapable part of the total emergency.

Certain policy statements of educational leaders, moreover, illustrate the mounting concern over the appropriate place of religion in the schools of our country. Studies made by the Committee on Religion and Education, under the auspices of the American Council on Education, clearly indicate that the public or tax-supported schools, even under existing legal restrictions, cannot and do not completely avoid religion. This conclusion, we are told, is abundantly substantiated by actual practice and by the judgment of a preponderant majority of those who co-operated in making the studies.

It is encouraging to find that there is a growing recognition of the fact that the schools, including the public, tax-supported schools, cannot remain indifferent to the subject of religion. "Silence," in the words of the Committee, "creates the impression in the minds of the young that religion is unimportant and has nothing to contribute to the solution of the perennial and ultimate problems of human life."

In the report on moral and spiritual values in the public schools, published by the Educational Policies Commission of the National Education Association, we read: "There can be no doubt that American democracy is grounded in a religious tradition"; and again, "To omit from the classroom all references to religion and the institutions of religion is to neglect an important part of American life. Knowledge about religion is essential for a full understanding of our culture, literature, art, history, and current affairs."

The findings of certain exploratory studies indicate that the present policy or attitude in respect to religion in the public schools reveals three sometimes-overlapping and frequently confused patterns, which can be fairly designated as: avoidance of religion; planned religious activities; and factual study of religion. It is recommended by these same educational leaders that further experiments be undertaken to develop a program of factual study of religion, which, if successful, can be widely adopted by tax-supported schools.

Representatives of the Catholic position view with profound sympathy the sincere efforts of many leading educators to solve the problem of religion in education; but much as the former would wish to see religion incorporated into the curriculum of public schools without injustice to anyone, it seems to them that very great difficulties will be encountered in implementing the program if adequate safeguards are to be maintained to protect the rights of conscience for all citizens. Most classrooms will inevitably contain students of various denominations and teachers of widely different religious convictions. It is one thing to recognize the need of religion in education; it is quite another to provide a method and program which would be just and acceptable to the community as a whole. With the purpose, therefore, of clarifying at least in part the position on a national educational policy as seen from a Catholic point of view, we call the reader's attention to the following considerations, some of which have already been mentioned:

Parents are endowed by the Creator with the right and the responsibility to direct the education of their children. This is a primary and inalienable right founded on the very nature of the parent-child relationship. The exercise of this right is, however, subject to the precepts of the natural and divine law. These precepts oblige parents to provide for their children's religious, moral, civic, and physical education in a manner conducive to the purpose for which they were created by Almighty God.

It is an inherent and inalienable right of parents to establish their own schools wherein religious instruction and training according to their convictions can be incorporated into the regular curriculum. "The fundamental theory of liberty upon which all governments in this Union repose excludes any general power of the state to standardize its children by forcing them to accept instruction from public teachers only. The child is not the mere creature of the state." (Pierce vs. Society of Sisters, 268 U. S., 510, 535.) The historical development of the American educational system has, as a result, brought together the public, private, and church-related schools in a common effort to prepare all our citizens for the responsibilities of good citizenship.

The state has a duty to encourage and assist parents in the education of their children. We respect the state's right to oblige parents to educate their children for competent citizenship, in accordance with reasonable standards clearly defined by the state. In order that there may be adequate opportunities for education available to all our citizens, the state should encourage, and, as necessity dictates, establish and maintain schools for such purposes.

In the historical development of education in this country, both public and private schools came into existence; the private and religious school, however, came first. Nevertheless, no conscientious citizen can be indifferent to the welfare of the public schools of this country. Schools are a necessity in a civilized society. If the public schools were not available, there would be no practicable way in which the great majority of the nation's children could receive the necessary education required for good citizenship. It is true that some other kind of school organization could have been adopted in the middle of the past century, when the public school system was being established. Other countries did adopt a different procedure; but the facts of the situation now are such that we must live with what we have.

In view of the circumstances in which we find ourselves, all good citizens must not only be interested in the public schools but must strive to make them as truly effective an agency of education as our resources permit. Contrary to some popular misconception, there is not and there must not be on the part of Catholics any opposition or ill-will toward the public schools. Catholic citizens are vitally interested in the program of the public schools and their achievements. They are eager to see the pupils receive the very best training for life. Any other attitude would be extremely shortsighted and self-defeating, for Catholic citizens must live in the same environment and in the same moral and cultural atmosphere as their neighbors. They must be deeply concerned, therefore, with the product of the public schools.

It would be a dereliction of duty and an offense against both justice and charity if it were to be assumed by representatives of church-related or private schools that their own interests could prosper at the expense of public-school interests. No responsible Catholic authority has ever advocated any such attitude. Whatever criticism has been voiced is predicated on the conscientious conviction that a realistic and effective system of education must include all necessary knowledge, both human and divine.

Instruction in religion should be an integral part of the education of the child, but we realize that there are legal and practical difficulties which exclude religious instruction from the curriculum of our tax-supported schools as presently constituted. Typical of these difficulties are a choice of religious curriculum, teacher-selection, teacher-training, correct interpretation of textbooks, and other problems arising from the deep and wide differences in the religious convictions of our people.

Recommendations of educational leaders with respect to the incorporation of "moral and spiritual values into public school curricula are frequently derived from premises unacceptable to believers in revealed religion and even to those who hold the minimum religious principles concerning the sovereignty of God and the primacy of the moral law. Definitions and sanctions of "moral and spiritual values" which rest solely or even primarily on "public approval in a democratic society" evade the essential teachings of religion and substitute the concepts of conventionality in the place of objective moral principles based on the law of God.

Our public tax-supported schools, through their choice of curriculum, school texts, teacher-attitudes, and other ways traditional in America, should encourage respect and reverence for religion and for spiritual values, even though public law forbids them to give any formal religious instruction or conduct any form of religious worship.

Compulsory religious exercises, even though called "nonsectarian," are improper in a public school's program. Our public-school authorities, therefore, never should compel pupils to participate in such religious exercises. Such compulsion certainly would be a serious infringement on the rights of those pupils whose consciences, or whose parents' consciences, dictate that they cannot in good faith take part in a religious exercise involving tenets contrary to those of their faith.

Legislative programs which conform to the rights of parents to have their children excused from attendance during public-school hours in order to receive religious instruction deserve our approval and support. Such a program of Released

Time is in keeping with our nation's traditional respect for parental rights and the free exercise of religion.

Some recent interpretations of the First Amendment's "establishment of religion" clause are clearly out of harmony with its historical and contextual meaning. The history of the First Amendment as shown in the Annals of Congress clearly indicates that the Founding Fathers intended to safeguard religious liberty; they did not intend to divorce religion from education. Those who want no religion taught to their children on public-school premises are entitled to enjoy the freedom of their convictions, but they should not be permitted to use the first clause of the Amendment to defeat the second. They should not be allowed by judicial interpretation to deprive those who want their children so instructed — namely, on school premises — of what is certainly an equal right under the same Amendment.

When the state undertakes to provide auxiliary services, such as bus transportation to school, health programs, school lunches, and recreational facilities for school children, it has the clear duty of making these services available on an equal basis to children attending all schools. Services established to promote public safety on the highways, health, and welfare are the concern and right of all citizens, and there should be no discrimination against those who choose to send their children to religious schools, since freedom of choice in this matter is an integral part of the religious freedom guaranteed by the First Amendment.

Although the existing system of tax-supported schools was intended by its proponents of the past century to provide both free and adequate education for the entire nation, nevertheless this departure from the voluntary system of earlier years left a large group of children deprived of the educational benefits created by our common tax contribution. These are the children of parents who elect to exercise their Constitutional right of religious freedom by sending their children to schools in which religion constitutes the integrating element of the curriculum. To say that all children have equal access to the tax-supported schools is true, but only on condition that they and their parents conform to a rigid system of education which excludes instruction in those truths derived from divine revelation, and in the specific moral and spiritual values which find their most effective sanctions in religion. To deny to parents the right to have their children so instructed is inconsistent with freedom of religion and freedom of education in a democracy. To refuse them any share in public support violates, at least in fact if not in intent, the principle of distributive justice, creates a sense of unwarranted discrimination, and retards a common effort to improve the educational institutions of our country in the interest of all our children.

Obviously, it will be no easy matter to correct the existing inequities. There are legal and historical obstacles which preclude the adoption of immediate or radical changes in a system of education which has grown up through a period of more than a hundred years. But at least the principles of justice can be frankly acknowledged, even if their implementation may require further study and the gradual adoption of such modifications as experience, good will, and the American sense of fair play may approve. Thus in due time religious freedom in the matter of education may become a fact instead of a penalty for those who now exercise it.

The claim to public aid put forth by many representative spokesmen of church-affiliated or privately controlled schools is based not immediately or directly on any rights of the school as such, but on the inherent rights of parents to direct the education of their children. There are indeed some Catholic authorities who have publicly announced that they would refuse direct public or state aid for their schools. At the same time they defend the right of parents in our pluralistic religious society to receive a share of the common contribution to the compulsory tax fund for educational purposes. There is no compelling need, nor in fact any valid justification, for the public system of education to be monolithic and rigidly uniform for all citizens. A voluntary choice of an educational program for their children could well be allowed to parents, as long as adequate standards are maintained and the amount of public aid given does not exceed the present per capita cost of education in the local school district. The structure and function of our existing educational system, therefore, might well be restudied with a view not to its replacement but rather to its expansion. There are other methods of solving the problem besides a direct subsidy to the schools.

The financing of public elementary and secondary schools is the traditional responsibility of local and state governments. Assistance from the federal government, in view of the danger inherent in federal control, should be justified by incontrovertible evidence that some areas lack sufficient taxable resources to provide for every child educational opportunities which meet the commonly accepted standards of adequacy. When, however, the program of federal aid repeats the same pattern already considered objectionable on the state and local levels, then the advocates of parental rights and freedom of education experience a further sense of grievance. Quite understandably they are reluctant to see a policy of exclusion already embedded in the legislation of our country receive further legislative confirmation. Nevertheless, there has been no concerted effort on their part to impede the passage of federal legislation which would provide adequate educational opportunities for children in the economically depressed areas.

Federal-aid legislation, therefore, if there is proved need, should aim to eliminate inadequacies of educational opportunity rather than standardize the education of the nation's school children. Whether public aid for school construction be derived from federal, state, or local tax resources is a question to be decided by enlightened statesmanship. It is a matter of prudent judgment and does not involve directly a moral or doctrinal principle. There is no religious issue as such which should enter into the debate.

A system of scholarships provided out of public taxes, in accordance with the pattern set by the original G. I. Bill of Rights (Public Law 346, Seventy-eighth Congress), could well be inaugurated as a sound educational policy on the college- and university-level. Such a program of scholarships would relieve the necessity of federal aid for school construction on this level and would promote the national interest by strengthening existing private non-profit colleges and universities.

The statement of these principles does not, of course, exhaust the subject; they are set forth as fundamental in the determination of a sound public policy in regard to our educational needs in this country. Since the studies recently made, as well as others now in progress, have as their purpose a sincere desire to evaluate all elements which enter into the problem of determining a sound educational policy for our country, these principles are here presented as worthy of serious consideration.

XVIII

INTELLECTUAL FREEDOM

THE challenge has been publicly made time and again that no Catholic institution is genuinely free in its teaching. Let us give an example. John H. Hallowell, a distinguished writer, is the author of a book entitled *Main Currents in Modern Political Thought*. In this book he declares that the trend today among intellectuals is back toward religion. The *Saturday Review of Literature* thought sufficiently well of the book to invite Professor H. Stuart Hughes of Harvard University to write a review. In his criticism Mr. Hughes said: "Ten or fifteen years ago no self-respecting 'enlightened' intellectual would have been caught dead with a religious interpretation of anything. Only the Catholics thought in these terms — plus a scattering of Protestants whom we dismissed as harmless eccentrics. We were either 'idealistic' social radicals or skeptical, hard-boiled Freudian Paretans. Any other attitude would have been considered a betrayal of the *avant-garde*. Now Mr. Hallowell confirms the suspicions that have gradually been drifting up to us from the students we confront. The *avant-garde* has become old-fashioned; religion is now the latest thing."

Professor Hughes clearly is not in sympathy with this intellectual trend back toward religion, for he sums up his criticism with the declaration: "Some day we may find ourselves looking for the guarantee of our liberties to the hierarchs of a Church that pours open scorn on the very idea of intel-

191

lectual freedom as we now understand it." The professor evidently does not think well of the Church and its hierarchy as a defender of intellectual freedom. This attitude is not his alone. It is shared by Paul Blanshard and others of like persuasion. It constitutes a real challenge to any Catholic institution of higher education.

The point at issue, then, is this: Where do the higher institutions of education sponsored by the Catholic Church stand in respect to intellectual freedom? In a word, does the Church impose disabling restrictions on its universities and colleges, so as to impede the freedom of their teaching or the validity of their research work?

In order to answer these questions fully, it is necessary to make a clear distinction between various kinds of freedom, namely, religious freedom, political freedom, and academic freedom. All three involve some kind of intellectual freedom in its broad sense.

Religious freedom, in its true sense, is freedom of conscience. Religious freedom means that no person can be coerced by fear or by force to accept any particular religious belief. Truth, recognized as such by the individual, alone can claim the allegiance of the mind. Persecution, threats, punishment, bribes, and favors are therefore utterly alien to the concept and exercise of religious freedom. Their use would contradict the God-given rights of the human personality. The mind was made by God to seek and possess truth. In like manner, the will of man was fashioned to seek and possess what is good. It would be a violation, therefore of the natural functions of both the mind and the will if external pressure were imposed upon the conscience of the individual. This is sound Catholic doctrine; it is also good American practice, to which we readily subscribe.

There is, of course, a distinction between subjective error and objective truth. Man may be deceived through ignorance or through inherited prejudice. He may be biased in his judgments by his social environment. Nevertheless, every man must act in accordance with his own honest judgment, even though his judgment be in error. The Church defends his conscience, but at the same time deplores his error.

Some people think that the Church's doctrine of infallibility directly controverts the doctrine of religious freedom. Unfortunately these people will not take the pains to inform themselves correctly on the precise meaning of infallibility. They entertain disordered notions on the subject, and in consequence become quite confused about its relation to intellectual freedom. When the Supreme Court of the United States renders a decision on the meaning of Constitutional law, no one thinks that our government has interfered with our political freedom. It has, in fact, protected it from abuse. The Church does the same in respect to divine revelation. If God delivered to mankind a definite body of truth, which individuals may interpret differently, there must be some court of final appeal which can tell us clearly and definitely what is the content and the exact meaning of that divine message. To say otherwise is to assert that God commands us to believe His word but does not tell us clearly what it is. The divine guarantee of religious truth is no interference with freedom, but rather a restraint on human error.

If the religious and academic world would once clearly grasp the fact that the infallibility of the Church is concerned only with the message of divine revelation and not with science, art, or culture, then it would find no difficulty in reconciling infallibility with intellectual freedom. To hear, moreover, some of the statements made from the lecture platform or in the public press, one would be led to believe that infallible pronouncements come with monotonous regularity from the Vatican. Such an assumption is sheer nonsense. As a matter of fact, there have been only *two* infallible pronouncements made by the Church in the long period of ninety years which have elapsed since the Vatican Council formally declared the doctrine of papal infallibility. Even at the time of the definition, it was clearly set forth that the Church did not pronounce on questions of political systems, natural science, art, culture, or any other subject of human knowledge which might come within the scope of a college or university curriculum. The Church confines her teaching to matters of faith and morals. She surrounds her pronouncements with such formalities and such strict safeguards that there can be no question in any honest mind as to the limited nature of her claims.

We readily grant that, as a matter of historical fact, there have been some overzealous churchmen, just as there have been careless and irresponsible scientists, who have made pronouncements outside the field of their own competence or far beyond the legitimate conclusions of demonstrated facts. The Vatican Council declared in substance that if at any time there seems to be a conflict or controversy between religion and science, it is due to one or the other of two things: either churchmen have claimed as revealed truth what actually is not and what the Church officially has never sanctioned; or scientists have claimed as established truth what has not been fully demonstrated as such. Science and human research, by their very nature, are not competent to decide the content of revelation. By the same token, the Church has no competence to decide the content of true science. The subject matter of inquiry in each instance is separate and distinct. The methods of investigation are separate and distinct. Hence there is no possibility of conflict.

A Church-affiliated institution of higher learning enjoys as much freedom in its search for knowledge as any other institution, whether private or public, religious or secular. Its right to teach the truth is unrestricted.

The second point of inquiry in our discussion of intellectual freedom is its relationship to political and social life. Let us state categorically that the Catholic Church has never decreed the necessity or obligation of adopting any specific form of government. The Church recognizes that human beings, as members of society, have the right to choose their own type and method of government. In fact, the great defenders of this thesis of political freedom were outstanding saints and scholars of the Church, such as St. Thomas Aquinas and St. Robert Bellarmine. Their writings and their arguments were invoked by the defenders of political freedom in the famous debates between the Whigs and the Tories in England. Many of the fundamental principles enshrined in the Constitution of the United States were developed in those debates.

The question, of course, which constantly recurs in any discussion of political freedom is that of religious tolerance. It is precisely at this point that a great deal of misunderstanding arises. There are two kinds of religious tolerance: the one is political; the other is intellectual. The Church holds the first and rejects the second. The Church maintains that no political government has a right to define any article of faith or religious belief or to impose such a belief on the conscience of its citizens. If a government makes such an attempt, it is usurping the prerogatives of God and violating the divinely ordered plan. Every citizen, no matter what his religion, is equal before the law. This does not mean, as some people have assumed, that the political government must completely ignore religion, or, what would be worse, repudiate religion and discriminate against its adherents. Religious tolerance, in its political interpretation and application, means precisely what our Constitution declared — namely, that the Congress should make no law respecting an establishment of religion, nor prohibit the free exercise thereof. This Constitutional provision is sacred in the eyes of every American Catholic. There is no law of the Catholic Church and no doctrinal pronouncement and no disposition on the part of its hierarchy to nullify or interfere with this sacred political right, guaranteed to us by the fundamental law of the land.

People sometimes confuse tolerance in the political order with tolerance in the intellectual order. The Church does not admit the doctrine that all religions are equally true. Many of them are self-contradictory. Some are patently in error. The Church does not subscribe to the principle of religious indifference. It does not admit that it makes no difference what a man believes. The Church holds that every man must believe what God declares to be divine truth. Man is not free to make up a religion out of his own head. He cannot substitute personal opinions in the place of God's word, nor select out of the divine message only those things which suit his fancy. The utter absurdity of such a position is evident if we analyze any single proposition of religion. Either God exists or He does not. Either Christ is divine, or He is not. Either Christ established a Church, or He did not. We cannot have it both ways. Clearly the Church cannot be indifferent as to whether a man believes one or the other of these things. There must be one consistent body of truths to be believed, and not a contradictory potpourri of personal opinions; either that fact is true, or God's word is unintelligible. We hold that Christ Himself established the Church as the Supreme Court to declare the meaning of His Gospel. Such a claim constitutes no infringement on our political liberty and opens no door to political intolerance in matters of conscience.

Now, what about the claims of academic freedom? In its true sense, academic freedom merely implies that no instructor or professor should be restrained in teaching truth or in his search for knowledge, so long as he follows the discipline and methods of his own particular science or art or form of culture. But this does not mean that a professor has the right to substitute his own theories for facts. To do so would be an abuse of freedom. In a word, every professor must hold rigorously to the logic of demonstrated facts and not exaggerate the validity of his findings beyond the weight of his evidence. The classroom is a privileged forum.

If the term "academic freedom" is taken to mean that the professor has a right to use this privileged forum of the classroom for purposes of propaganda, then we say that such an interpretation is an abuse of freedom. If, for instance, a professor wishes to explain Communism as a theory, surely there can be no objection, so long as he proceeds in an objective, scientific fashion. Should the same professor, however, advocate and defend Communism as a system to be imposed on us, then we say that he is abusing his academic freedom. He should be charged with such an abuse of his privileged position. Therefore, when the authorities of a university dismiss such instructors, they do not violate any legitimate claim of academic freedom; rather are they protecting the public against the fraud of a professor who substitutes propaganda for truth.

The only serious challenge to academic freedom at the present time is found in our tax-supported institutions. The Supreme Court decision denies to these institutions the right to explore the subject of religion. As a result of the McCollum decision, any subject under the sun or any form of human experience can be treated in the lecture halls of a public university except the subject of divine revelation or man's relations with God. This means that religion is put at a distinct disadvantage, is actually given less recognition than the pernicious theory of Communism. Religion at the present time does not enjoy the right of presenting its case with the same cogency in the class-rooms of our public institutions as does its worst enemy. The specious pretext of separation of Church and state is invoked in order to limit and restrict the academic freedom which should prevail in a university. If so comprehensive and so significant a branch of the history of civilization and culture is excluded from the curriculum of a university, then certainly such an institution cannot be said to enjoy complete academic freedom. Surely it must strike even the unthinking man as something of an anomaly that, in the name of freedom, a university may not investigate the very thing from which the university came— namely, religion.

In order to sum up the position of a Catholic university in respect to this matter of intellectual freedom, let us state briefly the following propositions:

A Catholic university has complete freedom to explore the entire field of knowledge and to transmit to the students its findings, unrestricted by the Church, just as any other university in the land.

A Catholic university has complete freedom in the realm of the natural sciences and is limited in its conclusions solely by the rigorous logic of demonstrated facts. Science is not free to make unwarranted excursions into the field of religion; neither is religion free to make unwarranted excursions into the field of science. To permit such a procedure would be bad science and worse theology.

A Catholic university has complete freedom in the entire range of literary criticism and artistic culture. It is bound only by the norms and principles of sound reasoning and good taste.

A Catholic university has the same opportunity and the same responsibility in the field of historical criticism as any other institution which examines the records of the past. It is bound to state the facts without prejudice or distortion and without any partisan interpretation. The great Pope Leo XIII threw wide the doors of the Vatican Library years ago and invited all historians to search its records in order to present in an unbiased manner the history of the Church.

In view of the unwarranted charge that the Catholic Church or its hierarchy interferes with intellectual freedom inside and outside its institutions of higher learning, we consider it necessary to meet this challenge. The main difference in this regard between a Catholic university and our public institutions of higher learning is that the Catholic university possesses a principle of integration that is wanting in the latter. This principle of integration is the perennial philosophy of the Church, which acts as the pivot of the entire program of studies. When there is question of intellectual freedom, we claim that a Catholic university enjoys such freedom in even larger measure than other universities. Because it can synthesize all knowledge, both human and divine, all human experience, whether secular or sacred, the Catholic university possesses a coherent philosophy which excludes inconsistencies and contradictions but places no inhibitions on the sum total of truth.

XIX

A LIBERAL EDUCATION

ANOTHER oft-debated question in academic circles is the value of what is traditionally termed "a liberal education." In discussing the subject, we do well first to consider the characteristics of such an education.

Liberal education, as its name implies and its definition expresses, postulates freedom of the mind from the narrow and constricting influences of prejudice, custom, and tradition. It emphasizes the importance of a correct understanding of man's intrinsic nature, purpose, and destiny; and a realistic evaluation of man's historical experience. Liberal education is an integral part of genuine culture and a practical necessity in any large view of national or international policy.

The scholastic disciplines which set the mind free are generally comprised under the term "humanities." They embrace such studies as philosophy, history, sociology, literature, language, and such educational formation in the physical sciences as will give a broad outlook on life and a right orientation toward the world in which we live. They are essentially the disciplines which cultivate the quality of being human. Championing as we do the cause of liberal education, we subscribe to Terence's dictum: "Nihil humanum a me alienum puto."

Liberal education differs from other forms of education not only in respect to its content but also in respect to its methods. To say that the tendency of modern education has been to favor the physical sciences in contradistinction to the humanities or the social sciences, is to utter a platitude. What has not been equally recognized is the fact that the emphasis placed on the methodology used in the physical sciences has tended to discredit or at least to force into eclipse the equally valid methods used in a program of liberal education. We refer to the notable preference given by some to the methods of scientific induction over those of scientific deduction. We all recognize the validity of the inductive method of reasoning, which proceeds from the observation of phenomena in the fields of physical or material science to their orderly classification. From such data a hypothesis or theory is evolved by which the phenomena can be explained. Finally, the theory or hypothesis is verified by new experiment, and thus a new relationship of cause and effect is discovered and reduced to a scientific formula.

It is not universally recognized, however, that the subject matter of a liberal education is, or at least should be, under an equally rigid discipline, although quite different in character. In religion, in the social sciences, in history, and in the humanities generally, we make use of the deductive method and the juridical process. We depend on the logical sequence from accepted principles or on the testimony of witnesses whose veracity and competence must first be established. But once this has been done, we are entitled to draw conclusions from the facts which constitute legitimate premises as truly as the physical scientist does in his own respective areas and by his own distinctive methods. Unless this procedure is accepted as valid and authentic, there can be no science of human conduct, nor of history, nor of ethics; and, in fact, no social value in a study of humanism. We readily concede that there is a difference between moral certitude in the one case, and physical certainty in the other.

We lay stress on this matter of varying scientific methods because it gives rise to a variety of questions when one is considering the content of a liberal education. Some educators, for instance, on the score of inadequacy of method or uncertainty of conclusions, have ruled out of their curricula the whole matter of religious experience, as if it had no historical significance or no social value. Obviously, religion's chief significance is spiritual. But how anyone can explain the course of history, and the nature of the differing civilizations with their distinctive national institutions and social policies without a comprehensive and accurate knowledge of the pertinent religious beliefs and practices is a profound mystery to us. Our plea, therefore, is that more attention be given to this subject of religion in the curriculum of a liberal education, not only as an important factor in the understanding of social forces, but on its own merits as a necessary study in any significant exploration of truth itself. We recognize that the unmistakable trend in education today lies in that direction.

A liberal education, if true to its name, presumes both a full measure of freedom in the choice of a curriculum and also freedom to implement that choice without penalty or disadvantage. If, therefore, the state sets up a uniform and inflexible system of education with a monopoly of public benefits reserved entirely to itself, it is difficult to see how genuine freedom of education exists. We realize that this question leads into a rather sensitive area, but we see no adequate reason why we should dodge the issue. If the state rules out the private, nonprofit colleges from public support because they are privately managed or because they include in their curricula religious instruction, it restricts, in doing so, the full measure of liberty consistent with *liberal* education.

Any genuine liberal arts college, by its very nature, is a public institution. It renders a public service and cannot do otherwise. Furthermore, the existence of the voluntary non-profit college is in line with our earliest educational traditions. Harvard, Yale, Princeton, and Georgetown are and have been, since their beginnings, private institutions of learning. Washington, Jefferson, Madison, and most of the Founding Fathers were the product of private colleges and a liberal-arts course.

The establishment of liberal-arts colleges organized by private initiative might also be regarded properly as a corollary of our free-enterprise system. We realize that there are certain features of a free-enterprise system which some of us might not wish to endorse; but, in general, it represents the American tradition — namely, that there are certain functions of society which should not be pre-empted entirely by the state. Let us make it unmistakably clear that there will always be need for public tax-supported institutions of education, not only for vocational and professional training, but also on all levels from elementary schools to universities. This will always be necessary if we are to make effective a national program of universal, free education. These schools will not only continue to exist but must be adequately supported; nevertheless, there ought to be room, in a national system of education, for those schools also that do not conform to the theory of a restricted secular curriculum. Difficulties in making the necessary adjustments in national policy will occur, but they can be overcome, provided there is an open mind and good will. There must be a restoration of the conviction that liberal education is an integral part of true culture, and is a practical necessity in any comprehensive view of national and international policy. There must also be a disentanglement of the word "liberal" from certain connotations of a political and economic character. Unless these ends can be gained, it seems to us futile to belabor the subsidiary question of a realistic and effective means of providing financial support for a program of liberal education.

XX

"NOBLESSE OBLIGE"

STUDENTS of history are familiar with the fact that privileged classes have always existed in human society. The special privileges conceded to these groups have varied in character. At times they have consisted of the exclusive right of suffrage; at times, of immunity from arrest, or the exemption from certain legal penalties; at other times, of exclusive eligibility to public office, tax-exemption, or special military status. These privileged classes were organized or established on the basis of ancestry or wealth or some special contribution to the higher interests of the state. In ancient and feudal times, these groups constituted a class apart, generally designated as "the nobility." There was, however, a counterweight to the privileges which they enjoyed; they had special duties to perform. Noblemen were supposed to do noble deeds. Hence arose the popular slogan, "Noblesse oblige" — that is, "Nobility has its obligations."

Today, in our society, we have abolished hereditary privileged classes. We have not, however, entirely abolished all privilege. Today the privileged classes are the college and university graduates. They have enjoyed benefits in the intellectual and social order which have been provided, not by themselves but by society at large. No institution of higher learning can exist today on the tuition fees paid by its students. It must be publicly supported by taxes, by gifts, or by personal service. In consequence, the graduates of our universities constitute an intellectual aristocracy based on privilege; they enjoy a certain patent of nobility granted by society. To them, therefore, the phrase "Noblesse oblige" can aptly be applied. Their privilege carries with it the responsibility of living on a high intellectual plane in contrast to the sterile mediocrity which characterizes the masses of mankind. This should not cause them to cultivate a stuffy pride or smug self-complacency, but rather should be a sobering influence upon them in their evaluation of their social responsibility. Unless society as a whole profits by their intellectual attainments, the investment in their education is without justification and will rightly be regarded as a form of social exploitation. If wealth must serve poverty; if strength must serve weakness, then truth must compensate error, and knowledge counterbalance ignorance.

The particular responsibilities of college graduates might be enumerated under three headings: first, the cultivation of the intellectual virtues and the pursuit of wisdom, not merely knowledge. This world of ours suffers today more from bad thinking than from bad will. Crooked ideas lead to crooked principles, and crooked principles lead to crooked actions. True wisdom is needed in our political, economic, and social life. Those who have had the opportunity of cultivating wisdom should therefore be articulate in public life, and not abdicate their social responsibility.

Second, college graduates should be mindful of the fact that they have enjoyed special opportunities at the hands of the public. Consequently they should make a return by active participation in community life. They should be the outstanding leaders who will promote projects and enterprises which are calculated to serve the common good.

Third, college graduates should, above all things, maintain their own integrity of character. The pattern of behavior which they establish will inevitably be followed by the masses. A virtuous life, marked especially by justice, charity, decency, and purity of conduct, must be their chief goal.

Let us consider these three points at length. Every college or university graduate has given at least four years to a more or less diligent pursuit of knowledge. Knowledge, as has often been observed, is power. What the graduate must remember is that both knowledge and power must be directed to some worth-while purpose if they are to be considered socially useful and spiritually rewarding. Knowledge is a two-edged sword. It can cut both ways. Like power, it can serve either good or evil ends. The knowledge of nuclear fission can promote the cause of human welfare or it can cause death and destruction. Chemical science can alleviate the sufferings of mankind if used to make penicillin; chemical science employed in warfare can devastate a whole countryside.

What we need, therefore, in order to promote true human progress and personal perfection is not mere knowledge but wisdom. Wisdom is the right use of knowledge; it is knowledge used for right ends. Knowledge can be abused; wisdom never. To abuse wisdom is to lose it. Wisdom is a synthesis of knowledge and of virtue. Virtue is a vital element in the cultivation of wisdom and an important factor in the formation of character.

During the four years of college training, the student is occupied not only with increasing his store of knowledge but also with improving his personality. Personality is the sum total of human qualities which distinguish one individual from another. These qualities are physical, mental, moral, and spiritual.

There are no two individuals exactly alike. Each of us differs from his neighbor not only in exterior characteristics but in interior attitudes, habits, and abilities. These differences are the result of three primary factors: heredity, environment, and self-determination.

Heredity accounts not only for such physical characteristics as size and weight, health and strength; it accounts also for certain tendencies or instincts that are related to personal conduct or human behavior. We have, of course, long ago discarded the immature notions solemnly propounded by Cesare Lombroso, to the effect that hereditary characteristics determine moral or criminal conduct. Professor Jennings of Johns Hopkins University, a competent authority in the field of biology, points out that we are the inheritors of a multiplicity of genes in our germ cells; the ones which develop depend to a very great extent on ourselves. Heredity indeed is not to be discounted, but its influence is not to be exaggerated.

Environment is a more important factor than heredity. It is not physical environment, however, as much as social environment which fashions our character or personality. Let us illustrate this fact by calling attention to such ordinary things as our language, our dress, our habits of eating, drinking, playing, and a dozen other routine activities of daily life. These are largely determined by the influences of our social environment. We are creatures of our environment; or, in technical language, we are conditioned by the impact of our social environment.

Self-determination is the third factor. It is the most important of the three. In spite of the influence exercised by heredity and environment, we are nevertheless captains of our own destiny, masters in our own house. Every man is endowed from birth with a mind to know the truth and a will free to choose what is right. If he makes proper use of these endowments, he can determine his own character in its fundamental aspects.

Character is a term ordinarily used in a more restricted sense than personality. Character consists of the attitudes, the dispositions of mind and heart, or the behavior pattern of the individual. For purposes of evaluation, character is normally related to an objective standard of right or wrong. When we speak of a man of character, we usually have in mind integrity of character. Character, however, can be good or bad. A good character is a man of good habits. A bad character is a man of bad habits. Habits, however, are not something innate; they are not the result of spontaneous generation. They are the result of repeated actions. By repetition a groove is worn into our human nature, and along that groove our actions flow with ease.

An old Latin adage invoked frequently in the classroom well describes this impact made upon our human nature by repeated actions: "Gutta cavat lapidem, non vi sed saepe cadendo — The drop of water wears away the stone not by force, but by its frequent falling."

If the question is asked: "Why do men not develop only good habits?" the answer is that the trouble is not in the mind but in the will. The mind of man functions correctly. When our mind is applied to practical questions of right or wrong conduct, we call it conscience. The will, however, functions with difficulty because of the interference of the emotions and the sense appetite. The human passions may be a drag on the will at times, or they may be a spur to action. Sometimes the passions pull us, at other times they push us. There is a new nomenclature for the passions, but the old categories still do duty as explanations of these drives and emotional disturbances. We may call these passions pride or self-assertion; envy or egoism; lust or the race preservative instinct; anger or the aggressive instinct; sloth or the play instinct. Whatever we call them, the fact is that they interfere with the free choice of the will and blind us momentarily to the ultimate good which is the object of the will.

When the passions are aroused, we experience a conflict within us respecting a choice of action. There is a sort of dual personality for the moment. The mind tells us one thing; our feelings, our emotions, tell us the opposite. The will must therefore make its choice under a handicap. Frequently it will follow the dictate of the appetites rather than the calm judgment of the mind. Every student of human nature has recognized this contradiction or dichotomy. Plato describes it in his writings. St. Paul comments on it in his letter to the Romans. He states that he finds a law in his members fighting against the law of his mind; so that the evil which he wills not, that he does, and the good which he wills, that he does not. Then he poses the question: "Who will deliver me from the body of this death?" and he gives the answer: "The grace of God through Jesus Christ our Lord."

Religion has always recognized this conflict in our human nature. It has rejected the idea or theory that man is sufficient unto himself; that by the exercise of reason he can achieve perfection. The Church teaches that no man can always and under all circumstances maintain integrity of character unless he receives superhuman help. The Church also teaches that this superhuman help is always available to those who ask it. In order to maintain steady habits of virtue, or integrity of conduct, three things are necessary:

First, there must be a clear and definite code of conduct. Religion presents such an objective standard in the ten commandments and the Sermon on the Mount.

Secondly, there must be some final authority standing back of the law, giving to it validity and sanctions. It must be an authority, moreover, which is ultimate and from which there can be no appeal.

Thirdly, there must be superhuman ideals, motives, and help. Otherwise we shall succumb to our own innate tendencies. One of the great educators of the past generation, Friedrich Wilhelm Foerster, who for years was the brilliant editor and secretary of the International Ethical Culture Society, learned this truth from his own experience. He writes: "I know very well how far purely human ideals will lead the world of youth, and what a severe blow it will be to those who would replace religion with ethical culture, when I state that my own thoroughgoing experience in this field has proven that it is insufficient; and that it is forced by its own inner psychology to become religious. Ethical culture must be clarified and fortified with superhuman ideals before it can cope with the innate tendencies to evil."

Special responsibilities are carried by all college graduates. But for the graduates of Catholic colleges, there are even additional obligations. If their education under Catholic auspices has not made any difference in their outlook on life or in their mental and spiritual orientation toward the world and its problems, there has been something wrong with our efforts or there has been something wrong with their reactions. To assume that persons educated under secular auspices will have the same convictions as Catholic graduates, the same attitudes, the same solutions for the problems which beset the individual and society is to label our entire Catholic college system a wasted effort. No matter what their future state of life may be and no matter where their activities may lead, Catholic college graduates must always act as intelligent and convinced

Catholics. This means that their standards of judgment must derive validity from the light of God's revelation, and their pattern of conduct from the divine commandments. Knowing that God has established His Church as the pillar and ground of truth, they should make it their constant boast to think as the Church thinks. "Sentire cum ecclesia" should be the mark of every Catholic college student. This does not mean rigid uniformity and loss of initiative; nor does it place hobbles upon legitimate self-expression and originality. Quite the contrary. The Church suffers altogether too much today from lack of initiative and creative effort. What we today need is fresh energy in action combined with surety of direction and certainty of the goal.

The activities of our Catholic college students should be conducted within the framework of the American tradition and Constitution. Foreign ideologies should be avoided not precisely because they are foreign — that indeed would be an exaggerated nationalism and a provincial affectation — but rather because we can honestly hold that no other political organization of society offers us a better opportunity to advance the social well-being of mankind. There are some inequities in our national life and many false social attitudes, but these are not inherent in the political structure of our government but are due, rather, to the false philosophy which infects our national life and its tragic defection from the Christian religion. The American concept of freedom, respect for personal dignity, an innate sense of justice, and even generosity of spirit are still the best hope of man. Youth is perennially idealistic and filled with a crusading spirit; but young people should not be too quick to judge harshly the social institutions of their forefathers. Youth desires change, adventure, novelty. If things must be changed, let it not be the fundamental social system but rather the conditions which they find at variance with the old ideals. America has no shrinking frontiers for the mind; it is still the land of opportunity for adventurous spirits.

XXI

A WORD TO TEACHERS

IT IS fitting, in discussing the broad field of education, that
we direct some word of appreciation, and also of advice, to
our teachers. Priests, Religious sisters and brothers, laywomen
and laymen have done and are continuing to do a truly noble
work in the field of educating our students. Such teachers deserve the commendation of all citizens, for the good effects
of their hard work are felt through all levels of society and
civic life. Our school system could not exist without the serious
sacrifices made by the teachers.

There are two suggestions that we might venture to make
to all of you who are teachers or who aspire to be teachers.
The first is that you have the courage to be conservatives, in
the right sense of the word, rather than mere camp-followers
of novelty in a day of ultraliberalism. The second, that you be
humble enough, and therefore wise enough, to be guided by
lawful authority in your search for truth instead of compla-
cently trusting your own intellectual powers. Do not be misled
by a false or specious independence.

There is a couplet by Alexander Pope which expresses our
first point. You probably have come across it in his *Essay on
Man*. He cautions: "Be not the first by whom the new are
tried, nor yet the last to lay the old aside." Human nature loves
novelty, change, and variety; youth particularly so. Everything,
however, which is new is not therefore bad, and that which is
old is not necessarily superior. Do not reject a new method or

214

a new theory or a new exposition just because it is new; neither accept it for the same reason. You are justified in approaching new things with hesitation, care, and a questioning turn of mind. You are not, however, entitled summarily to reject them without inquiry. Look with interest and reasonable tolerance on all new findings which our busy research laboratories are putting forth. But do not make an act of faith in all the claims of our scientists. This is particularly true in those fields of thought and research which affect the great problems of human conduct. It is comparatively easy to arrive at certitude and sure objective values in the field of the exact sciences, but it is extremely hazardous to assume dogmatic attitudes in the fields of psychology, sociology, education, and political science, wherein the human factors of free will and the more subtle influence of original sin and God's grace complicate the sequence between cause and effect. Not many theories stand up under rigorous criticism. Be prepared to adopt new ideas and new theories only after their objective truth has been established.

In contrast to this attitude, however, be not mere reactionaries or hidebound traditionalists. The old ways, the old customs, the old traditions, are always entitled to reverence and respect, but they are not entitled to an unquestioning acceptance. To take such an attitude would stop all progress. We would have you develop a pioneering and adventurous spirit; an inquiring turn of mind; the readiness to seek out new methods and new ideas, but always with caution, testing their value and their truth before committing yourselves to their adoption.

The Church in her history has been both revolutionary and conservative. The founders of our great Religious orders in a certain sense were revolutionaries, apostles of change. Because they were vehemently dissatisfied with things as they were;

because they recognized that changing social conditions had created new problems, which in turn demanded new solutions, they broke with the past and launched out boldly into new spiritual adventures. Witness the examples of St. Benedict, St. Dominic, St. Francis of Assisi and St. Ignatius; witness the examples of St. Angela Merici, Mother Catherine McAuley, and Mother Elizabeth Seton. Although these great souls set up new institutions to meet new conditions, nevertheless they were conservatives in the sense that they kept their efforts true to Christian principles and always subject to lawful authority. It is precisely this characteristic which distinguishes them from the great heresiarchs who were merely straining after novelties. Be conservative, therefore, but not reactionary.

Our second suggestion has to do with a point we have already touched on, and that is the much-discussed question of liberty or independence of the teacher, the complete freedom of the teacher to expound his own concepts of truth as he sees fit. By this term of liberty or independence the advocates of the theory understand the right to teach any doctrine which their personal opinion favors at the moment. They wish to be free and independent from any authority of parents, of the state, or of the Church. They would seem to arrogate to themselves a kind of divine omniscience or a personal infallibility; they would claim to be independent of any authority other than their own human judgment or opinion.

Now there is something to be said in favor of liberty of teaching, but unfortunately it is frequently said in favor of a one-sided liberty; in favor of a liberty which has been frequently abused and which is sadly at variance with the developments of truth. If any criticism can be justly offered concerning the condition of education in our larger universities and colleges, it is precisely that there has been too much liberty in the sense of irresponsibility.

No one is pleading, least of all the Catholic Church, for an exercise of partisan judgment, for biased propaganda in the classroom, or for the suppression of divergent points of views. There should be freedom in the field of opinion, but there can be no question of liberty of judgment concerning the great verities or certitudes of life.

It happens all too frequently that what the advocates of liberty in teaching have in mind is the privilege of expounding a philosophy of life which contradicts all the fundamental principles of religion. These professors, for instance, want to be free to reject the doctrine of creation in favor of evolution; to reject the idea of miracles in favor of determinism; to reject the supernatural revelation of God in favor of the self-sufficiency of human reasoning; to reject a divinely fixed moral order in favor of a mere changing social convention.

These teachers who clamor for liberty want the right to express their personal opinions in the field of philosophy and religion, and they want this freedom seemingly for themselves alone. They abhor the idea of granting equal freedom to the Church to expound the revelation of God or the Christian philosophy of life. It is not an exaggeration to say that in the past one hundred years Scholastic philosophy and Christian revelation have been treated as a Cinderella in all our great secular universities. In their way of thinking and in their specious defense of liberty, the teaching of Christ's truth is propaganda or mere sectarianism.

To make matters worse, these teachers who clamor for liberty and who reject any form of control over their theories, who rebel against the thought of submitting to authority, nevertheless accept their commission to teach from the civic state while denying any responsibility for their doctrine. They accept the financial support which has been liberally lavished upon them by the citizens of the state, while denying to the citizen any right to determine the subject matter, the content, or the character of their teaching. Hence we have a strange anomaly or paradox; namely, that citizens are compelled to pay out their own hard-earned money in order that their children may be deprived in the classroom of the most sacred convictions that their parents treasure. Liberty of teaching or independence in the classroom which produces such illegal and pernicious results can be regarded only as an abuse, and never as a privilege.

As teachers you are free in the classroom to teach truth, but you are never free to teach falsehood in the guise of truth. You are free to expound any doctrine, any historical fact, any theory, provided you recognize the imperious rights of truth as determined by right reason and by the revelation of God. You are privileged above other teachers because you have the unerring guidance of the Church divinely constituted as the supreme, infallible teacher in all things which affect the standard of right and wrong in human conduct. Greater freedom than this no teacher can have. To ask for more is to ask the privilege of leading human mind into error.

XXII

ARE CATHOLICS INTELLECTUAL LAGGARDS?

THE history of Christianity clearly indicates that education on all levels has been in every age one of the primary interests and objectives of the Church. The fact that education is inevitably associated with principles of religious truth and morality makes it mandatory for the Church to interpret her teaching function in the very widest sense. Wherever the Church has secured a foothold in the life of a nation, she has established schools as an essential instrument in the fulfillment of her divine mission. Of late, however, much attention has been given to the discussion of the failure of American Catholics to exercise a proportionate influence in the intellectual life of the nation. We wish to touch upon certain aspects of this problem. There are three questions to which we should try in all sincerity to give forthright, even though brief, answers. In the first place, is it true that there has been little achievement by Catholics in the intellectual order; second, if this be true, what explains our failure; and third, what can be done to correct the situation?

Recent studies and discussions have led some of our thoughtful scholars to the uncomplimentary judgment that there is little tradition of intellectual leadership on the part of the Catholics of this country. Attention is called to the pronouncements of both Catholic and non-Catholic authorities and to the findings of various surveys indicating that the Catholic body in this nation is contributing far less to creative scholarship than its numbers and resources would warrant. It is pointed out that this is true not only in the field of pure science but in the humanities, the arts, and even in the fields of philosophy and theology, where we would normally be expected to show particular strength. This is the thesis that was elaborated by Monsignor John Tracy Ellis, professor of history at the Catholic University, in an essay in the Jesuit magazine *Thought.* Some years ago Denis W. Brogan, professor of political science in the Cambridge University, stated in a book on the United States: " . . . In no Western society is the intellectual prestige of Catholicism lower than in the country where, in such respects as wealth, numbers, and strength of organization, it is so powerful." Monsignor Ellis, who makes use of this quotation, expresses his own judgment in these words: "No well-informed American Catholic will attempt to challenge that statement." This distinguished scholar then proceeds to offer further evidence in support of his thesis. The evidence which he adduces looks indeed rather formidable.

The first point of our inquiry is whether the facts warrant this severe judgment of the record of our intellectual achievements. We admit frankly that there has not been in the past as great an achievement in creative scholarship as we should desire. We do not have to our credit, as yet, any outstanding contribution to the intellectual life of our nation; but to assert the claim that our Catholic people and their leaders are indifferent to these values, or that there has been a notable failure to stimulate interest in these fields, is to view the history of the Church in this country in a false perspective. We can honestly recognize our limitations without exaggerating their significance. At the same time, we can point to achievements which are absolutely essential as a prerequisite of the higher forms of intellectual life, and for the truly magnificent effort along these

lines we have a right to claim due credit. There are indeed
extenuating circumstances which should in justice modify the
severity of the criticism, but there is nothing to be gained by
engaging in a futile controversy concerning the exact weight of
the evidence. Surely any thoughtful observer of the American
scene must readily admit that the intellectual influence of
American Catholics in formulating our laws, determining public policies, and creating our national cultural and social institutions has been almost non-existent in the past, and is still
relatively insignificant. The importance of intellectual prestige
and influence can be seen in the intimate relation that exists
between the religious and moral well-being of society and the
quality and character of the intellectual leadership of a nation.

Without admitting the full force of the indictment, we
must ask ourselves: What explanation can we discover which
will account for the ostensible facts? The purpose of such an
inquiry is not merely to hunt for excuses of the implied failure,
but rather to find the causes which have produced this lamentable condition and, in the light of that knowledge, to seek to
remove them by honest and intelligent efforts.

Some of these causes are inherent in the historical development of the Catholic Church in this country. We have been,
with few exceptions, an immigrant people — at least up to the
present generation. Our Catholic forefathers came, for the most
part, from European countries where they found themselves
economically impoverished, often politically persecuted, and
culturally underprivileged. Their first task was to achieve an
economic livelihood; the second was to acquire citizenship and
to become assimilated into the body of the American people;
the third was to provide for their children an education better
than that which they themselves had received. All these things
took time as well as effort. The majority of our Catholic citi-

222 . . . . The Mind of an Archbishop

zens, even now, are only two and three generations removed
from an alien status. There has been, in consequence, no adequate opportunity for them to develop a cultural atmosphere
in the home, to acquire habits of serious reading from the
example and precept of parents, and, what is even more important, to secure the advantage of a graduate university education. We think it can be safely maintained that in the age
group of those over forty, from whose ranks alone we have a
right to expect effective leadership, not more than seven per
cent of the college graduates are Catholics. Not more than five
per cent of our people are in the financial category of those
who earn annually ten thousand dollars or better. Those who
earn less are not apt to be substantial contributors to collegiate
endowments. There is taking place, however, a rapid change in
our present generation. We cite these facts, not to evade any
responsibility for putting forth strenuous efforts to better our
record, but rather to point out that the future is not quite so
bleak and hopeless as some would seem to think.

Not only is it true that we have suffered the usual handicap
of an immigrant status, but we have been inclined to adopt a
ghetto mentality by reason of an enforced exclusiveness in safeguarding the Catholic faith of the immigrant. We have also
been forced into a further unfortunate dilemma. Our very
numbers have worked in one sense to our disadvantage. Simultaneously we had to build our churches, our schools, our charitable and social institutions — all of this within a period of a
hundred years, and all this without the public support of tax
money enjoyed by our fellow citizens in most of their endeavors.
The problem faced by Catholic leaders was this: Which of the
two alternatives comes first, the preservation of the faith or
the pursuit of intellectual culture and influence? Both are

needed; but available resources will not suffice to provide both simultaneously. Our record of high scholarship and our contribution to the intellectual life of our country leave much to be desired, but we can be proud of our achievement in laying a foundation on which future generations can build.

It is no doubt salutary to have our deficiencies pointed out and to have a spur given to our efforts, lest we sink into a state of self-complacency. The immediate problem, however, is to formulate sound educational policies in view of our limited resources — limited at least by the exigencies of putting a roof over the heads of our elementary and high school students, as a first step toward bringing the Catholic faith into their minds and hearts. One of the most important steps which we could take by way of improvement would be to recognize certain necessary limitations on our efforts in the field of Catholic education. Obviously we cannot compete with the great state universities and the heavily endowed colleges in a continuous expansion of the curriculum, especially in respect to professional and vocational courses. There is a limit to our resources. We, as Catholics, have to distribute our financial contributions over the entire field of education, including elementary and high school as well as college and university. In consequence we should devote our energies to those aspects of education which are an integral part of the Catholic heritage and which are cognate to religion. This does not mean that we, as Catholics, are uninterested in the field of science or in the professions. It does mean, however, that we, as Catholics, should do for our students precisely those things which no one else can do, leaving to the great secular universities the things which our resources do not permit us to do well. This means concentrating our attention on the humanities, history, philosophy, theology, and the social sciences, and allowing others to bear the burden of vocational training in other fields.

A second step which we might take would consist in making more intimate contact with the intellectual life of our great secular universities, serving on their faculties, holding membership in learned societies, and contributing to scholarly publications. This means, in a word, that we must not remain isolated from the main stream of intellectual life, but rather seek to make our distinctive contribution as Catholics to the good of the nation as well as to the honor of religion.

The third step is to insist on the highest academic standards in the selection and training of our faculties, as well as in terms of achievement by our students. Where we are as yet deficient in any respect, we must explore the opportunities offered in graduate studies by the great European universities and by those in our own country. This has been done on an ever-increasing scale and notable results are being achieved. Witness the development of our scholarly magazines, such as *Thought, Theological Studies, Review of Politics, Worship, Social Order,* and others of a similar nature.

There are undoubtedly other practical suggestions which can be advanced, but whatever form they may assume, one attitude should be emphasized. The only justification of Catholic education is that it should reflect Catholic doctrine in all its wide and profound implications. Anything else would be useless duplication and a waste of resources. We must be careful, however, never to place a narrow construction on what concerns the welfare of souls or the good of religion. We must be realistic, not exaggerating our achievements, nor, on the other hand, deprecating them. We must grow in a sound appreciation of what intellectual leadership means for the Church and for human society. The words of Bishop Spalding, written in 1884, on "Higher Education" are still true: "When our zeal for intellectual excellence shall have raised up men who will take place among the first writers and thinkers of their day, their very presence will become the most persuasive of arguments to teach the world that no best gift is at war with the spirit of Catholic faith."

Part V

MAN IN RELATION TO OTHER MEN

IN PERFECTING HIS SOCIAL NATURE

*"By this will all men know that you are My
disciples, if you have love for one another."*

XXIII

JUSTICE BALANCED BY CHARITY

THE intelligent reader of the encyclicals of Pius XI can have no misunderstanding with respect to the value, the importance, and the utter necessity of re-establishing justice in our social relationships. No one, however, can read these encyclicals without at the same time being convinced that justice alone is not sufficient to re-establish unity and brotherhood among men. Something more is needed, and that essential something is the charity of Christ. "In effecting this reform [of the social order]" says the Holy Father, "charity, which is the bond of perfection, must play a leading part. How completely deceived are those inconsiderate reformers who, zealous only for commutative justice, proudly disdain the help of charity. For justice alone, even though most faithfully observed, can remove the cause of social strife but can never bring about a union of hearts and minds. Yet this union, binding men together, is the main principle of stability in all institutions which aim at establishing social peace."

In the days of tribulation which came upon the children of God of old, it was the voice of Jeremias, Isaias, and the other prophets which rang out clearly in Israel, admonishing them that it was their apostasy from the truth and the law of God which had brought them into captivity in pagan lands. In like manner, we shall do well to heed the voice of the Popes of this generation who have stood as the sentinels on the towers of Christendom and have warned the world of a similar apostasy from divine truth as it affects man's supernatural destiny.

There is a striking passage in *Quadragesimo Anno,* written in 1931, which reveals with something like prophetic foresight the sequence of disasters that engulfed the world in the following decade: "Unbridled ambition for domination has succeeded the desire for gain; the whole economic life has become hard, cruel, and relentless in a ghastly measure. It is patent that, in our days, not alone is wealth accumulated, but immense power and despotic economic domination are concentrated in the hands of the few. This accumulation of power, the characteristic note of the modern economic order, is a natural result of limitless free competition which permits the survival of those only who are the strongest, which often means those who fight most relentlessly, who pay least heed to the dictates of conscience.

"This concentration of power has led to a threefold struggle for domination. First, there is the struggle for dictatorship in the economic sphere itself; then, the fierce battle to acquire control of the state, so that its resources and authority may be abused in the economic struggles; finally, the clash between states themselves.

"This latter arises from two causes: first, because the nations apply their power and political influence, regardless of circumstances, to promote the economic advantages of their citizens; and because, vice versa, economic forces and economic domination are used to decide political controversies between peoples."

It was our Lord Jesus Christ who taught us both by word and example that the love of God and the love of our neighbor contains "the whole Law and the prophets." He made this lesson the central theme of His Sermon on the Mount, and

He illustrated it most effectively from the pulpit of the cross when, stretching wide His arms, He spoke in His agony the tender words: "Father, forgive them, for they do not know what they are doing." Christ began to preach from the very beginning of His divine mission that charity is the very badge of His fellowship. "By this will all men know that you are My disciples, if you have love for one another." Christianity, for the first time, in the words of Walter Lecky of Harvard, "made charity a rudimentary virtue." Prior to the advent of our Blessed Saviour there existed here and there noble sentiments of altruism and philanthropy, but there was nothing equivalent to what we understand by charity.

The act of the intellect by which we seek to comprehend the truth is indeed distinctive of our highest human nature, but the act of the will by which we love God and one another as children of God is the supreme act of the human personality, and constitutes, according to theologians, the very essence of Christian perfection.

In the modern world, however, charity has unconsciously become a caricature of the virtue Christ propounded under that name. Today it is regarded by some as nothing more than a sentimental attitude, a sort of praiseworthy emotion — nevertheless, a symptom not of strength but of weakness, endowed with a sort of feminine characteristic. Certain advocates of extreme nationalism sought in the recent past to eliminate charity from the spirit of their people and spoke blatantly and ignorantly of substituting force and vigor and even brutal harshness for this supreme virtue of love. There are others, and you will find them especially in the ranks of social workers, who have made charity synonymous with almsgiving, and that rather of an unintelligent kind. There are so-called reformers, who with pitiful misunderstanding declare loudly that what we want today is not charity but justice — as if justice could ever be a substitute for charity! None of these attitudes or positions manifest that comprehensive understanding of this virtue which Christ preached above all others. Charity is the very organizing principle of unity in human society and, as Pius XI declared, the very foundation stone of social stability.

St. Paul, in the famous thirteenth chapter of his first letter to the Corinthians, gives us the true interpretation of the majestic sweep of the nature of divine love: "Charity is patient, is kind; charity does not envy, is not pretentious, is not puffed up, is not ambitious, is not self-seeking, is not provoked; thinks no evil, does not rejoice over wickedness, but rejoices with the truth; bears with all things, believes all things, hopes all things, endures all things. Charity never fails, whereas prophecies will disappear, and tongues will cease, and knowledge will be destroyed. . . . We see now through a mirror in an obscure manner, but then face to face. Now I know in part, but then I shall know even as I have been known. So there abide faith, hope, and charity, these three; but the greatest of these is charity."

Charity, then, is rooted in the truths and mysteries of divine revelation, and that is why it withers and even disappears when it vainly tries to flourish in the uncongenial soil of secularism. Secularism dominates the spirit of our age. The great hierarchy of spiritual truths and supernatural virtues has been discredited, denied, and rejected in the high councils of the mighty ones of earth. Only a feeble humanitarianism remains, and necessarily it has failed to withstand the onslaughts of selfish individualism, ambitious nationalism, and world revolution.

St. John opens up to us a vision of true brotherhood, a brotherhood predicated upon the sublime fact that we are the sons of God. It was to make us participators in divinity, he tells us, that Christ, the Son of God, descended from on high and clothed Himself with human flesh. Through His Redemption we are incorporated by grace into His own Mystical Body and are made one with Him, and through Him one also with each other. "He was in the world, and the world was made through Him, and the world knew Him not. He came unto His own, and His own received Him not. But to as many as received Him He gave the power of becoming sons of God; to those who believe in His name: who were born not of blood, nor of the will of the flesh, nor of the will of man, but of God." This sublime statement of man's nature and destiny stands in glorious contrast to the spurious theory of Darwinian evolution or materialist biology. We are not brothers of simian anthropoids, but sons of God. We are indeed by nature children of the same first parents. Religion teaches the unity of the human family. But in the supernatural order, our kinship is something higher, nobler, and infinitely more sublime. By grace we are brethren of Christ. It is not the blood that flows in our veins that counts, but the grace of our Lord Jesus Christ which pulsates spiritually in mind and heart and soul. It is a spiritual bond of consanguinity that unites us to one another, and the blood of this relationship is the blood of Christ shed for a universal redemption.

The first and highest law of the Christian life is to love the Lord our God with our whole minds, our whole souls, and with all our strength, and then, for His sake, to love our neighbor as ourselves. Since the proper act of man's intellect is to seek truth and the proper act of his will is to love the good, it may strike us as a kind of paradox to hear that we should love with our *minds* as well as with our wills; yet there is profound truth in the terse statement of God's commandment. We must indeed love God with our whole minds so that no falsehood or perversion may become the object of our desires. The world has departed from this ideal and has fashioned for itself false gods, and in this apostasy you will find the secret of the present human tragedy. We dare not substitute false gods for the one true living God. We dare not set ourselves up in the place of God. We dare not substitute the nation or the totality of society as a supreme object of worship. We dare not impose an absolute value on earthly things or earthly life in place of eternal things and divine life. There can be no compromise with God and the imperious demands of divine love. We must love the Lord God above all things with our whole minds, our whole souls, and with all our strength.

We do not wish to imply that there have not been other periods of human history when wickedness arrogated to itself the place of virtue and seized the reins of power, but since the great religious revolution of the sixteenth century there has been a steady deterioration in the behavior of mankind. First the authority of God's Church was denied and private judgment substituted in its place. Then the revelation of God Himself was rejected in the period of the so called Enlightenment of the eighteenth century. But mere natural man, having rejected the supernatural, was not long content even to live according to the light of reason. His science became a perversion, and the goal of all his endeavors a mere quest of material and earthly happiness. Finally, God Himself was dethroned and rejected by materialist economics and biology. This is not an *ex parte* statement but the judgment of contemporary criticism, pronounced by an endless list of scholars, statesmen, and philosophers of history.

If we are to succeed in eliminating or lessening many of the ills that affect mankind today as a result of the accumulated evils of the ages and the godlessness of individuals, we must give due recognition to the basic importance of charity among men — the charity of Christ. We must pray, we must work so that Christ may dwell by faith in the hearts of men; so that, being rooted and founded in the love of God and neighbor, we may in time be able to find lasting solutions to many of our social problems, and one day be able to comprehend with the saints the breadth and length and height and depth of true charity, the charity of Christ "which surpasses knowledge."

XXIV

A BETTER SOCIAL-ECONOMIC ORDER

ALL sincere, thoughtful Christians are concerned with the problem of creating a better and more Christian social-economic order. A more thorough study and a deeper knowledge of the great social encyclicals *Rerum Novarum* and *Quadragesimo Anno* would lead to a more widespread and wholehearted acceptance of the principles therein set forth, and this, in turn, would show the way to a more just social order.

The aim of the encyclicals is the moral renovation of economic society through a new growth of social justice and social charity. The chief method proposed to achieve this aim is the re-establishment of a functional or vocational order, called in American terminology (for want of a better phrase) the "Industry Council system." There is need to clarify our position in respect to specific issues, and not merely to restate general and abstract propositions with which everyone is already familiar.

To focus attention on the immediate problems we face, let us consider them under two headings: first, the function of the Industry Council system; and secondly, its structure. The papal social encyclicals clearly presume that the existing social order is not in harmony with the requirements of natural law nor with the social virtues of justice and charity. Nor are the changes required to restore the social order to a sound moral basis merely changes of individual or personal attitudes on the part of capital and labor, helpful as this might be. The changes which the papal encyclicals call for go much deeper; they are changes in the very structure of our economic system. The Church's program consists, first in a rejection of the heretofore widely accepted socio-economic principles — namely, unrestrained competition, monopoly, dictatorship, and class conflict — secondly, in positive recommendations in favor of a new and higher form of co-operation based on the re-establishment of organized industries and professions, or, as they are sometimes called, guilds or vocational groups. The principle or bond of this unity and co-operation is the sharing on the part of both employers and employees, of a common economic function and the recognition by both of their common obligation to promote the general good.

The function of these Industry Councils in respect to economic problems is not specifically defined in the papal encyclicals. Serious differences of interpretation lead to grave differences of judgment regarding the extent and nature of the decisions which would fall under the jurisdiction of these Industry Councils. It is helpful in the understanding of our problem to differentiate three separate categories of decisions. First, there are decisions which affect the personnel of an industry, such as hiring, firing, upgrading, and seniority rights; second, there are decisions which affect the social policies of an industry, such as pensions, sick benefits, unemployment compensation, accidents, vacations, and in general, social security; third, there are decisions affecting economic policies, strictly understood — namely, what to make, where to make it, when to make it, how much of it to make; and such matters as investment policies, wages, prices, profits, and reserves for contingencies and expansion.

It seems generally agreed among Catholic social students that the function of the Industry Councils should definitely include the first two categories, namely, personnel policy and social policy. There is a difference of opinion, however, regarding the matter of economic decisions, strictly understood. Among these latter, one of the most significant would be the control of wages, prices, and profits. Some Catholic students advocate a system of control similar to that which we had under the Office of Price Stablization. The difference, however, would be that instead of the government exercising the control, this function would be taken over by the Industry Councils. In so far as it is possible to ascertain the facts, it appears that the larger number of Catholic authorities are opposed to this concept or interpretation of the social doctrine of the Church. The latter group contends that the control of wages, prices, and profits is definitely not a function of the Industry Councils; rather, its function is to control the broad economic conditions, so that monopoly, dictatorship, and ruthless competition can be eliminated. This control would be achieved both by government legislation and by regulations established by the Industry Councils themselves. Naturally, the latter would have to be invested with some form of juridical authority. In favor of this position, we can cite the names of such leaders as Father Gustav Gundlach, S. J., of the Gregorian University in Rome; Father Oswald von Nell-Breuning, S. J., one of the outstanding interpreters of the social encyclicals in Germany; Father John F. Cronin, S. S., of the Social Action Department, N. C. W. C.; and Father Leo C. Brown, S. J., of St. Louis University. All these seem to favor a free market, subject to social controls. In their judgment there should be no determination of wages, prices, and profits. Father Gundlach makes the following statement: "Here [speaking of conditions

in Europe] it is necessary to save the free market system. . . .
One can save the free market economy only by binding it again
to structures of order which are rooted in the territorial and
vocational groupings of production and which thus secure for
the economy the character of a social process. It is, therefore,
not its task to fix prices and directly interfere with the market.
No, its task is to influence, by a spatially and vocationally differentiated system of order, those factors which determine the
formation of the markets."

Later on, he adds the following statement: "The vocational
order — as a framework for a free market economy — assumes
forms which, at least in principle, are anchored in the right of
private property and with which society interferes only in a
co-ordinating way."

Obviously Father Gundlach, Father Nell-Breuning, and
others of the same school of thought definitely reject the concept of a planned economy or specific controls under a program
of nationalized industry. "Catholic social teaching constantly
demands," to quote Father Gundlach again, "that small and
medium-sized enterprises be founded in all sections of the
economy. Therefore the rejection of a centrally planned economy; for, by its very idea and in practice, it is naturally affiliated with large-scale enterprises and presupposes that human
labor be severed from property, isolated from the family, and
easily manageable." The following statement of Pius XII re-
inforces this same conclusion: "Meanwhile feverish attempts
are under way to work out other juridical types of organization
for the social economy; and at the moment, preference favors
state enterprise and the nationalization of industry. There can
be no question that the Church also admits — within certain
just limits — state ownership and management, charging that
certain forms of property may legitimately be reserved to the

public authority: those which represent a dominating power so great that it cannot without danger to the general welfare be entrusted to private individuals; but to make of this state enterprise the normal rule for public economic organization would mean reversing the order of things. Actually it is the mission of public law to serve private rights, not to absorb them."

Another question which needs to be determined is whether the Industry Council system functions on the local plant- or company-level — or whether it functions only on an industry-wide basis, such as in steel as a whole, in coal, rubber, etc. Most of the Catholic authorities reject the idea of an organized Industry Council system on the local plant-level; but there are some who seriously question the unlimited extent of this conclusion. This fact becomes evident when we consider the rather vehement division of opinion with regard to the development of so-called "co-determination," adopted in the coal and steel industries in Germany.

We might offer as evidence of the difference of opinion the opposing attitudes of Father Gundlach and Father Albert LeRoy, S. J., formerly of the International Labor Office. These two do not see eye to eye on this question. Father LeRoy seems to think that something can be said in favor of co-determination. He does not hold it to be an absolute right of labor to share in the responsibility of management, but he does hold that such a right, restricted to the formulation of decisions concerning personnel and social action, can be created by positive legislation on the part of the state. This would be particularly true in regard to mass industry, with its widespread stock distribution and its greatly limited responsibility of ownership under existing conditions.

It is true that the words of Pius XII, in his address on June 3, 1950, to the Catholic International Congress of Social

Studies and the International Christian Social Union, make it difficult to put a favorable interpretation on the German program of co-determination or co-management. He says: "For several decades now, in the majority of these countries [the old industrial countries] and often under the decisive influence of the Catholic Social Movement, social policy has been taking the form of a progressive evolution in labor legislation, with a corresponding subjection of the private owner of the means of production to juridical obligations in favor of the workingman. The desire to see social policy further developed in this direction encounters a limit, and that limit is reached where the danger arises that the working class may follow in its turn the wayward course of capital — which means, chiefly for big business, the withdrawal of personal responsibility from the private owner (individual or partnership) and handing it over to the responsibility of anonymous corporate groups. Such a development would suit a socialist mentality to perfection. It could not but prove disturbing to anyone who is aware of the fundamental importance of the right to private property in stimulating initiative and fixing responsibilities in economic matters. A similar danger is likewise present when it is claimed that wage earners in a given industry have the right to economic joint-management, notably when the exercise of this right rests in reality, directly or indirectly, with organizations managed from outside the establishment."

Something must be done to eliminate class conflict on the local plant-level. Collective bargaining does not seem to be the final answer, even though it be necessary under present conditions.

In *Quadragesimo Anno* Pius XI clearly states: "The contest between these divisions (hiring and offering for hire in the so-called labor market) turns the labor market itself almost into a battlefield, where, face to face, the opposing lines struggle bitterly. . . . Complete cure will not come until this opposition has been abolished and well-ordered members of the social body — industries and professions — are constituted, in which men have their place, not according to the position each has in the labor market but according to the respective social functions each performs."

Pius XI definitely refers in this paragraph to the conflict in the labor market between hiring and offering for hire; but it is precisely the individual company which hires men, and not industry as a whole. The same is true of offering labor for hire. The Holy Father, moreover, states that a complete cure will not come until well-ordered members of the social body have their place, not according to their position in the labor market but according to their respective social functions. Clearly the two concepts are related. We do not see how we can blink at the fact that class conflict at present exists not only between individual firms and companies within the same industry, but is particularly acute on the firm-level itself, especially in mass industries. It is precisely here that the conflict between owner-ship and labor becomes most vehement. To say that collective bargaining is the most satisfactory solution does not seem to hold true. In *Quadragesimo Anno* Pius XI warns us that the wage system (and therefore the capitalist system) is not in it-self unjust; but he does tell us that it would be highly desirable for the system to be modified "by a partnership in ownership or management or profits." We may indeed say that this latter is a secondary consideration in respect to the organization of the Industry Council system, but it is difficult to understand the words of Pius as excluding the organization of a functional order in regard to the individual firm or on the company-level.

We recognize that Pius XII, in his address to the Ninth Congress of the International Union of Catholic Employers on May 7, 1949, rejects the concept of any right to make economic decisions except by the owner himself: "The owner of the means of production, whoever he be — individual owner, workers' association, or corporation — must always, within the limits of public economic law, retain control of his economic decisions."

Father Gundlach holds that Pius XII, in this address of May, 1949, as well as in his subsequent address of June, 1950, definitely rejects the idea of co-determination as set up in Germany. Father LeRoy, reading the same allocution, emphasizes the phrase of the Holy Father, "within the limits of public economic law," and thereby reaches a different conclusion. Our purpose is merely to point out that as yet there does not exist a uniform judgment in the matter, and that further clarification is in order.

The second question to which we give our attention relates to the structure of the Industry Council system. It is an axiom that structure follows function; hence, before a specific method of organization can be created, we must have clear and definite ideas of the function to be performed. It is true that we do not need to start off with a complete blueprint, but it is equally true that we cannot start at all without some definite ideas as to the units of membership in the organization. Keeping in mind that it is agreed that the Industry Council system functions at least on an industry-wide basis, and finding agreement, furthermore, that the function of the Industry Council system is concerned certainly with personnel policies and social policies, then we are prepared to ask ourselves the following questions: What are the units of membership in the Industry Council system and, granting that the state (representing the public), the owner-management group, and the workers are all vitally interested, what is to be the relationship between them?

Leo XIII declares that the state is not merely "the guardian of law and good order, but rather must put forth every effort so that from the entire scheme of laws and institutions, both public and individual well-being may develop spontaneously out of the very structure and administration of the state." Pius XI, in *Quadragesimo Anno,* makes the following declaration: "When we speak of the reform of institutions, the state comes chiefly to mind . . ."; and he adds later: "The social policy of the state therefore must devote itself to the re-establishment of the industries and professions (*ordines et collegia ordinum*)."

It is also important to recall the words of Pius XII in his address *The Feast of Pentecost,* delivered June 1, 1941, commemorating the fiftieth anniversary of *Rerum Novarum:* To safeguard the inviolable sphere of the rights of the human person and to facilitate the fulfillment of his duties should be the essential office of every public authority. Does not this follow from that genuine concept of the common good which the state is called upon to promote? . . . If they [the employers and the workers] do not fulfill their functions, or cannot, because of special extraordinary emergencies, fulfill them, then it falls back on the state to intervene in the field of labor and in the division and distribution of work according to the form and measure that the common good properly understood demands."

According to Father Gundlach, "It is in the state that man finds the only institution which can permanently guarantee the use of all his personal rights and co-ordinate them with those of others."

In view of these various declarations, it seems obvious that the state has a highly responsible place in the organizational structure of the Industry Council system. Clearly, if the new social order demanded by the papal encyclicals is to come into being, there must be some public legislation which will authorize its existence, determine its purposes, and invest the Industry Council system with a juridical status so as to make its decisions effective. Secondly, since the state, in the words of *Quadragesimo Anno,* has the function of "directing, watching, urging, restraining, as occasion requires and necessity demands," it follows logically that the state must exercise some measure of supervisory power. Such power, however, could not be exercised unless the state retained at least a veto power over the decisions of the Industry Council system.

There is considerable difference of opinion as to whether the state should be represented officially with an active voice in the Industry Council system as one of the three partners — owner-management, labor, and the public. It is clear that the state should not dominate or control; hence, one of the most important considerations relates to the principle called "subsidiarity of function." The latter requires that lesser bodies be permitted to perform lesser functions, and so on, in graduated order, until the highest level is reached — namely, that of the supreme authority of the state itself. Although the social encyclicals do not specifically state that the public authority should be represented officially in the Industry Councils, nevertheless there must be some provision for representation of the public in order to safeguard the common good.

We should like to suggest that, in building an organization of Industry Councils, the possibilities of following the pattern set by the Federal Bank system be fully explored. There are certain aspects of the plan which might be adapted to the present case and which might win the favor of the public as something already tried and proved successful. It should be noted that every bank must be a member in order to qualify for Federal Deposit Insurance and other benefits. Every bank must take stock in the Federal Reserve in proportion to its capital. The regional and national reserve systems have a definite public or juridical authority to regulate the monetary needs of their areas. The controlling boards and officers, made up of both businessmen and bankers, are chosen by their respective member banks under government supervision and in part appointed by government. There is, therefore, a combination of private enterprise and public operation. In the Industry Council system it would be necessary, of course, to have labor or employee interests represented both in the right to vote and in the right to be board members and officers. This should not be too difficult to plan, even if it were less easy to sell the idea to the public immediately. Just as the Federal Reserve system regulates bank credit and monetary policies, so the Industry Councils might regulate economic policies, with rights and duties of members defined, in their respective areas of the economy.

In almost all discussions of the Industry Council system, it is presumed that the workers will be represented by their present international unions, either through their officers or through delegates chosen by them. This procedure raises the interesting question whether such an arrangement satisfies the papal concept of a functional order. If the bond of union is mutual interest based on common function, there must be provision for a selection of labor representatives from the individual plants or companies which constitute the industry, such as textile, coal, rubber, oil, and steel. We must be clear in our minds whether we are to reconcile class-interest groups by collective bargaining or by a new principle — mutual function and mutual interest. The latter requires active participation in the industry itself, just as the former makes desirable an independent status outside industry control. In attempting to answer this question, doubt and confusion arise concerning the nature and purpose of labor unions, as they now exist. Can they be classified as functional and vocational groups, as conceived in the mind of the Popes; or are they primarily class-conflict groups and class-interest groups? Let me hasten to state that there is no question here concerning the necessity for labor unions under present conditions, but only a question as to whether they are the proper units in the proposed new economic structure. Even if some other form of representation or unit of organization should be created for workingmen or employees in the Industry Council system, there still would be need of labor unions, in order that they might reach a decision separately concerning their own particular interests as workers. Father Leo Brown, S. J., commenting on the explanations proposed by a special committee on Industry Council systems, makes these rather pertinent remarks: "I find it hard to see where these principles [the principle of subsidiarity of function and the principles of social justice and social charity] compel us to throw the weight of Catholic thought behind a socio-economic structure basically composed of organized labor and organized capital, fused together in some way at a second or higher stage of the economic hierarchy. I do not think that such a fusion corresponds to the integration built around the community of action and interest which the encyclicals have in mind. Merely joining a large labor union to a large trade association does not, by the fact of juxtaposition, knit them together. It is entirely conceivable that such a structure would point up class warfare in a much more violent fashion."

Again we wish to point out that we have here another problem which needs further consideration and on which some agreement among our Catholic authorities is necessary. Otherwise we are unable to explain to the public with clarity the structure and operation of the Industry Council system.

We realize that our treatment of the subject of the Industry Councils, both with regard to their function and their structure, is somewhat negative. We think, however, that the questions posed must be answered before we can proceed to advocate, in an effective fashion, the organization of the Industry Council system. There is no doubt in our mind concerning the advantages and the urgent need of bringing about a better socio-economic order; nor is there any doubt in our mind that the Industry Councils could bring about this improvement. We are convinced, however, that there are definite dangers to be avoided. We must be on guard against the charge of Fascism and cartelization on the one hand, or of fostering a tendency toward socialism on the other. Until we have clarified our own definition of function, and provided more specific determination of membership in the structure of the Industry Councils, we shall be greatly retarded in making further progress.

XXV

A SPECIFIC CODE OF SOCIAL JUSTICE

THE charge is sometimes made that the Church talks a great deal about social justice, but that it does not give a clear and concrete program which the members of the Church can follow in their political, social, and economic lives. It must be clearly borne in mind that the Church is primarily the guardian of man's spiritual welfare and that it has been entrusted by Christ with a commission to teach religious truth and morality, both private and public. It is not the function of the Church to enter directly into the specialized fields of politics, sociology, and economics. The Church does not possess the competence or the technical skill and equipment to enter these specialized fields, but the Church does claim the right to teach authoritatively the principles of morality in so far as they affect the conduct of men in relation to these fields of activity.

To answer further the charge against the Church that it is content with talking merely in abstract terms or in proposing mere generalities, let us cite certain concrete propositions from the encyclical letters of Pius XI that throw some definite light on the matter under question. Here are some of the propositions which Catholic moralists, under the authority of Pius XI, lay down:

We recognize the right of private property but we declare simultaneously that it has a twofold purpose, both individual and social; it exists for the good of the individual owner and likewise for the good of society as a whole.

We assert that at the present time there is not too much private property but too little; there is too much in the hands of the few and too little in the hands of the many.

We assert that it is morally harmful to mankind when the social and economic organizations of society deny to a vast group of its citizens the effective opportunity to possess productive property.

We denounce these conditions which create, therefore, a proletariat — that is, a mass of propertyless citizens.

We recognize the right of private profit in business and industry. Without profit, business cannot exist.

We reject the claim of unreasonable profit for owners, gained at the expense of a family living wage for labor.

We declare, in accordance with social justice, that there should be a wider distribution of income among the masses.

We declare that our first concern should be to raise the income of the poorest paid laborers, and then advance the income of the better paid in due order, so that all ultimately receive a living family wage.

We recognize that a higher standard of living can be achieved only by increasing production of wealth. The chief reason why more wealth is not produced is bad economic organization causing unemployment.

We declare that unemployment is the worst enemy of man's material well-being and that it is the duty of the state directly to intervene for its elimination when private industry has failed to solve the problem.

We recognize the right of labor to organize freely into unions of their own choice.

We assert the right of collective bargaining with others through their own freely chosen representatives.

We acknowledge the right of labor to strike in extreme cases, but only when peaceful means have failed to obtain rights that are certain and definite, and where there is genuine hope of success.

We deny the right of mass picketing or the use of violence against persons or property.

We assert the right of the living family wage as the first charge against industry or business, having as it does a priority over rights of profit.

We recognize that competition in business is good when it leads to lower costs of production, better quality and more efficient service.

We denounce competition that leads merely to lower wages or longer hours of work, or work of inferior quality.

We recognize that in certain major industries competition is practically dead and that monopoly has taken its place.

We denounce monopoly that leads merely to higher prices through collusion, restraint of trade, or willful restriction of output.

We assert the right of government to supervise monopolies or to supplant them by public ownership.

We declare that our economic life can be best fostered by the organization of vocational groups in which both employers and employees participate.

We advocate, therefore, co-operation between industry and labor, such as vocational groups or guilds, as a substitute for ruthless competition.

We recognize that government is not merely a police force to keep public order but that it is vested with the duty of promoting the welfare of the citizens by positive social legislation.

We deny the right of government to exercise absolute sovereignty over the conscience and freedom of man or to undertake economic and social functions which can be well exercised by individuals or private associations.

We declare our conviction that the welfare of society can be best safeguarded by a Constitution which guarantees the rights of individuals and minorities and which permits the people to choose freely their representatives in government.

The Church, we see, is not content with speaking of social justice merely in general or abstract terms but, on the contrary, has set forth a clear and concrete code of social justice which its members can readily follow in their political, social, and economic lives.

XXVI

CAN SOCIAL SERVICE REPLACE CHARITY?

DURING the past thirty or forty years, many changes have been introduced which have clearly affected social problems and policies, both where private initiative is concerned and in the field of public or governmental action. Some think that these changes have modified not only the problems and the methods of solving them, but also the very spirit and attitude of society itself toward such problems.

There is a series of questions, in this regard, that needs to be answered analytically. Is the picture of the past changing? Shall charity occupy an honored place in the modern world such as it did in the historic past, or is there a new doctrine of social service which is to take its place? Are we in this modern age experiencing a conflict between social work and charity? Are these two in opposition to each other, or can there be co-operation? Is social service antagonistic to charity; and if so, can there be a reconciliation? Shall our appeal in the future be to the intelligence or to the heart; or can we appeal to both simultaneously?

There are some who hold that charity is no longer the authentic spokesman in the cause of human welfare; that it is no longer the exponent of the true brotherhood of man. The claim is put forth that charity has been superseded by organized social welfare; that a ministry of mercy was sufficiently well adapted to a primitive or simple society but that it is wholly inadequate in our complex and highly organized civilization.

253

We are told repeatedly that what is needed now is not charity but scientific social work; not an attitude of benevolence but an attitude of scientific inquiry.

There are others who think that social work has usurped the place of charity and is opposed to the spiritual values consecrated by religion. They look upon social work as upon something mechanical, uninspired, purely secular, occupied merely with a vision of man's temporal prosperity instead of a vision of man's spiritual nature and destiny. The problem does present a difficulty, but the difficulty can be overcome because it is founded essentially upon misunderstanding.

The misunderstanding is on both sides. The advocates of private charity at times misunderstand the nature and meaning of social work; frequently the partisans of organized social welfare or social service misunderstand the meaning of charity. Once the nature and function of charity and of social work are clearly grasped, not only are the two found to be reconcilable but what was mistakenly thought to be in opposition in them is seen to be altogether complementary.

To understand the nature of social work we must go back to the days of Auguste Comte (1798-1857), the French philosopher who first gave a name to and outlined a program for social science. Thrilled and inspired by the progress which had been made in the natural sciences, especially in physics, chemistry, and biology, Comte thought it possible to apply the scientific method to the behavior of man. Like Montesquieu, his predecessor, he wished to revamp the science of law and political economy. He wanted to know, not how human beings *should* act but how they *do* act. In consequence he studied human society under all conditions and circumstances. He studied poverty in all its forms: from the homeless hungry child to the decrepit and helpless old man. He studied sickness, mental disease, and death. He studied delinquency and crime. He studied the natural and social sciences. He gathered countless data and he wrote voluminously. At first he called his work social physics, but finally he hit upon the term "sociology."

The method which Comte introduced and which has been followed for more than a hundred years by his successors is described as the "scientific" method. Briefly this method can be summed up under four headings: the observation of the phenomena under consideration, the classification of the phenomena into their proper categories, the setting up of a hypothesis or theory to explain the phenomena, and finally the verification of the theory or hypothesis as valid in all circumstances by means of further experiment. The purpose and ambition of Comte and his successors down to our own day have been to reduce human conduct to scientific formulae.

At no time, however, during the past hundred years have we been able to develop a formula of human conduct like H_2O in chemistry, like "weight times velocity equals momentum" in physics, or like the Mendelian Law in genetics.

The reason, of course, is that man is totally different from inanimate nature. He is not composed of mere brute material. There is an element in him that defies calculation. He is, in spite of all attempts to prove the contrary, a spiritual being, a free agent endowed with liberty, whose conduct is unpredictable and whose behavior can never be compressed into a formula. In sociology, therefore, there will always be lacking that constant element which is essential to the creation of a natural or exact science.

We do not wish to imply that sociology has made no progress, but we do maintain that this progress is far short of the hopes and expectations of those who pioneered in this new field. Neither the conduct of individual man nor the conduct of men grouped as communities or nations can be definitely and certainly predicted. Sociology, however, is not the same as social service. While our progress in the former has been quite limited, we have, in the field of social service, learned a great deal in the past century about poverty and its causes and treatment, about sickness in all its phases, and about delinquency and crime in their individual and social aspects. Scientific method applied to social service and its administrative problems has been much more of a success than the scientific method applied to sociology in its study of the nature of man and his collective behavior.

In the historical development of social service, we can distinguish four separate stages of progress: the relief stage, the preventive stage, the scientific stage, and the political-economic stage.

Viewed in the light of history, social work began as a service to the underprivileged classes of society. Motivated by sympathy for the sufferings and inequalities of others, the social workers sought to provide the essentials of livelihood for various needy groups. Social service tried to remedy the condition of the poor, the sick, the delinquent, and the defective. It was concerned with supplying food, clothing, and shelter for various socially handicapped groups. Its chief problems were adequate relief, constructive treatment, and elimination of unwise philanthropy. This first stage in the development of social service is known as the relief stage.

As time went on, a new insight into the problems of poverty, disease, and delinquency was gained by social workers. They were no longer satisfied to deal with symptoms, but began to search out the causes of distress. They tried to get at the roots of their problems in much the same manner as the physician who diagnoses his patient's ills before he begins treatment. During this period in the development of social service, emphasis was transferred from the question of relief to that of prevention.

As a result of the discovery of the close relationship between the social sciences and the physical sciences, and the application to social development of new knowledge gained from medicine, biology, and experimental psychology, the field of social work itself became broader. In this third stage of development, which might be termed the scientific stage, the findings of the physical sciences were freely applied to the solution of social problems. The emphasis in social work now shifted to the fields of physical hygiene, social hygiene, and mental hygiene.

When social workers began investigating the basic causes of specific problems in the field of social pathology, they readily recognized the fact that many inequalities of social conditions had to be interpreted in terms affecting not merely an individual here and there, but as a plight of society affecting large groups of people everywhere. Some of the causes of poverty were to be found in the individual himself, physically and mentally handicapped from birth; but the more basic causes of poverty were to be found in the environment which was unfavorable to normal development, and which in consequence needed adjustment. If a remedy for such ills was to be found, and prevention made really effective, this environment must first be changed through new social legislation and new economic theory.

In social work today, emphasis is being placed on moral and spiritual values. The importance of an objective standard of morals, personal and social, political and economic, seems to have been rediscovered. Spiritual and religious motivation in the development of personality is accorded a more reverent attention than was the fashion a few years ago. Our under- standing of the development of personality has given us a new explanation of the forces which not only play upon the indi- vidual from without, but which also guide and direct him from within. It is apropos here to recall again the words of Friedrich Wilhelm Foerster, whose name meant so much in the past generation in the field of education, psychology, and sociology: "I know very well how far purely human inspiration will lead the world of youth. . . . I understand what a severe blow it must be to those who would replace religion by ethics when my convictions force me to oppose them with all my energy, when I assert that just my own thoroughgoing efforts in purely ethical instruction have convinced me that such instruction is insufficient — yea, that the ethical appeal, in order to become deeper, is forced by its own inner psychology to become reli- gious; that the natural disposition to good must be impregnated, clarified, fortified by superhuman ideals before it can cope successfully with the inborn tendencies to evil."

In order to complete our consideration of the contrast and the essential correlation between social service and charity, let us now turn our attention to the meaning of charity.

Charity is a virtue; social work is a method. Charity is an act of religion; social work is a science or profession. Charity, as a virtue, implies an attitude of benevolence, first toward God, and then toward our neighbor with a view to his spiritual and temporal good; social work implies an attitude of inquiry and research for the purpose of eliminating or alleviating human adversity. Social work is a thing of the mind; charity a thing of the spirit. This distinction, however, does not put social work in opposition to the virtue of charity.

No one would think of declaring, for example, that the profession of medicine is in conflict with the virtue of charity. Yet medicine deals with sickness in a scientific spirit rather than in a spirit of charity; charity, for instance, may prompt the nursing Sister to devote her life to the care of the sick. The doctor is not devoid of the spirit of charity, nor the nursing Sister devoid of the spirit of scientific inquiry and its application. These two things are complementary, not antagonistic. What is true in the field of medicine is equally true in the field of law. A lawyer worthy of the name must always be prompted by the virtue of justice; but the methods he uses are the methods of the legal science. Religion represents the most sacred bond which can exist between the creature and the Creator. As such it is a virtue. But it may also become a science. What else is theology in its various phases — dogmatic theology, moral theology, ascetic theology — what is it but the science of religion? In similar fashion the methods and rules of science may be applied to the practice of Christian charity without in any way derogating from its dignity and sanctity as a virtue.

Frequently social workers, as we have mentioned elsewhere, put a wrong interpretation upon the virtue of charity. They think it is synonymous with almsgiving of a rather unintelligent sort. Almsgiving is not to be confused with the great virtue of charity which is its root and source. It is merely one of the many manifestations of neighborly love. Unless almsgiving is actually rooted in the love of God and of our neighbor, it is worthless. "If I distribute all my goods to feed the poor, and if I deliver my body to be burned, yet do not have charity, it profits me nothing." It is important to keep in mind the distinction between charity and almsgiving, and between charity and social work; for this distinction eliminates confusion and provides a sound basis for reasonable and wholehearted co-operation.

There are three fundamental concepts and attitudes underlying all the various theories of social organization. At one extreme is the idea of individualism; at the other, the idea and program of Socialism or Communism. Both of these systems are purely temporal and secular in their outlook on life; both deny certain fundamental rights and duties inherent in human nature. The individualist believes in competition and in the strength of his own resources of mind and body and earthly possessions. The socialist theory substitutes social planning for competition in all social undertakings, but it does so at the expense of human liberty. It is forced to regiment human nature in its social planning and deny to man his essential freedom of choice.

Between these two extremes stands the comprehensive concept and philosophy of divine charity. It reconciles the hopes and the ambitions of individual effort with social responsibility. It teaches that no man lives for himself alone, but that he must love his neighbor as himself. It teaches that man is only a steward of his possessions, material, intellectual, and spiritual. It teaches him that Wealth must relieve Poverty; that Health must minister to Sickness; that Knowledge must instruct Ignorance; and that Strength must lift the load that Weakness cannot carry.

Charity has just as much place in the relations of mankind and in the structure of society today as in any of the ages past. Charity and justice are as much the cement in the structure of society, as much the warp and woof in the garment of Christian civilization, as they were when Christ spoke the words, "By this will all men know that you are My disciples, if you have love for one another."

It is religion which consecrates this ideal of unselfish service in the interests of Christ's weakest brethren. A spirit of charity must stimulate, motivate, and fortify those who would engage in any form of true social work. Unless social work is inspired with this spirit, it will remain sterile. In our efforts to alleviate the sufferings of mankind and to solve the manifold problems of modern society, we need social workers of the highest order; we need social vision, social planning, social action. To touch the souls of men, to lift the burden from their spirits as well as from their backs, we need the charity of Christ — the bond of all perfection.

XXVII

A HOUSE OF LOVE AND LEARNING

THE pages of the New Testament contain many illustrations of Christ's sympathetic concern for the sick. Again and again our divine Saviour manifested His tender regard for those who were afflicted in body or soul. In fact, Christ makes this concern for the afflicted one of the marks of His divine mission. When the disciples of John the Baptist put the question to Christ whether or not He was the promised Messias, He answered by quoting the words of Isaias the prophet: "Go and report to John what you have heard and seen: the blind see, the lame walk, the lepers are cleansed, the deaf hear, the dead rise, the poor have the Gospel preached to them." Thus Christ makes a direct appeal to His healing of the sick in order to establish His claim as the promised Redeemer.

The Church does the same today. As proof of the fact that to her was committed the mission of Christ, she points to her unmatched record in respect to the spiritual and corporal works of mercy. There is no suffering which she has not alleviated; no group of the sick whom she has not visited. With our divine Lord, she can say in realistic, even though figurative, words: "The blind see, the lame walk, . . . the deaf hear, . . . the poor have the Gospel preached to them." In her ministry of the sick, the Church has faithfully followed the example of our divine Master. Not only did Christ sympathize with bodily suffering but He was able to diagnose, with clear insight, the sickness of the soul also. Indeed, to Him the disease of the soul called for treatment more urgently than diseases of the body. When the friends and neighbors brought to Him the man sick of the palsy, Christ's first thought as He looked at the stricken body was to bring relief to this sin-sick soul. "Take courage, son," He said; "thy sins are forgiven thee." When the crowds murmured at this assumption of divine authority, Christ responded: "Why do you harbor evil thoughts in your hearts? For which is easier, to say, 'Thy sins are forgiven thee,' or to say, 'Arise and walk'?" In this dramatic fashion Christ linked together inseparably the spiritual and the corporal works of mercy.

In her long history, the Catholic Church has initiated a remarkable variety of charitable institutions. Unique among them, however, is the Catholic hospital. For the Catholic hospital is not only a manifestation of the spirit of Christian charity; it is also a manifestation of that harmony which should always exist between religion and science, and between state authority and voluntary effort.

In the pre-Christian era there was altruism but not charity. Altruism, as it was exercised among a limited number of cultivated pagans, was devoid of any dogmatic basis. It rested instead on personal sentiment; it lacked universality in its application to human needs, and it failed to sustain its efforts over any long period of time. It was nationalistic in concept and sentimental in motivation. Christ broadened its base when He proclaimed with divine originality that we should love not only our friends but our enemies also; that we should do good not only to those who help us but also to those who hate us. In the parable of the Good Samaritan the divine Master denounced by implication any such narrow interpretation of our neighbor as rested on a mere nationalistic basis or on selfish class interest. In the teaching of Christ, charity is founded on the common origin and destiny of man, and must be as far-reaching as human need and as impartial in its diffusion as the air we breathe.

From the beginning the Church played the part of the Good Samaritan in human society, pouring oil and wine into the wounds of its afflicted members. There is nothing extraordinary in the fact that as soon as Christianity emerged from the catacombs, the Church, in her organized religious life, should have institutionalized this doctrine of charity. Witness the example of the noble Roman lady Fabiola, who dedicated her own home as the first Christian hospital. True, this was only a primitive beginning. But with the march of time all Europe was so endowed with a far-flung network of Christian hospitals that a great medical historian, Professor Rudolf Virchow of Berlin University, could state with assurance that not a single town of five thousand inhabitants was without its benevolent institution to care for the sick. In spite of the brilliant progress of scientific medicine, it is doubtful whether any other period of human history has witnessed such excellent care in terms of human comfort as that which characterized the ages of faith. Faith plays a vital role in the founding and conducting of our hospitals.

In the busy routine of hospital life it is easy to become overwhelmed with such a multiplicity of duties that we lose sight of ultimate objectives. We must, at times, clear away whatever obscures our vision of spiritual purpose and eternal values. Catholic hospitals are not merely scientific or social institutions for the exemplification of medical practice. They are religious institutions. They set up no schizophrenia between soul and body; they do not isolate the germ of sickness from the germ of sin, but they see men as our Saviour saw them, whole and entire.

It is quite the fashion these days to glorify the achievements of scientific medicine and the benefits of social science. We do not wish to detract from their glories. Indeed, we reject any effort to disparage the benefits which have accrued to mankind from the advance of science. We nevertheless maintain that our Catholic hospitals are greater benefactors of mankind because of their religious motivation and inspiration than are merely scientific institutions. Catholic hospitals minister indeed to the sick with methods of science, but they do so in the spirit of divine charity and under the compulsion of religion. They lift the burden, not only off the backs of men but also off their souls.

There is no such thing as spontaneous generation in the development of virtue, any more than there is in the development of organic life. Benevolence, therefore, which eventuates in unselfish human service, must have an adequate cause. This cause, this root, this dynamic inspiration we find in religion alone. It is because our Catholic sisters and brothers wish to be followers of Christ, because they wish to sanctify themselves in the image of God, because they recognize that what they do for their least brethren is done for Christ Himself — it is for this that they consecrate their lives to the care of the sick. There is no time in life when people are so susceptible to the influence of religion as when they are prostrate in sickness. The Church exercises a great missionary function when, through the service of the sick, she makes religion resplendent not only in words but in action also. In her hospitals she invests divine truth with a most cogent appeal to the heart as well as to the mind.

Let it not be assumed that there is a conflict of purpose or any antagonism between science and religion. Religion itself requires that the service rendered the sick be of the highest order. Any failure to make use of the best scientific knowledge available, and any specious attempt to justify neglect of professional skill and technique would be unworthy of religion. Such conduct would be a denial of the virtues of justice, charity, and prudence which are inspired by religion. In the Catholic hospital there must always be genuine respect for knowledge and wisdom as being gifts of the Holy Spirit. Mere kindness of heart, no matter how valuable it may be in itself, can never be a substitute for professional competency. Diligent search for truth, both in diagnosis and in therapy, is a basic requirement of religion as it is of science.

In point of fact, the Catholic hospital is a unique institution, not so much because it is an effective expression of divine charity but rather because it is so intimately correlated with the development of science. In the Catholic hospital the old calumny that science and religion are in conflict with each other meets an effective refutation. Day by day, science and religion walk hand in hand through the corridors and wards of our hospitals. The wisdom of God derived from revelation is found to be in full harmony with the knowledge derived by man in the empirical process of science. As the Vatican Council emphatically pointed out, the only cause of discord or conflict between science and religion lies in the fact that either careless exponents of science proclaim as truths certain conclusions that are unwarranted by the premises, or else representatives of religion rashly claim as divine truths what the Church has never defined as such.

If, in the name of science, euthanasia, sterilization, artificial contraception, or other forms of attack upon human life are speciously advocated, we are forced to assert that such pretensions invade unjustly the field of morality. These are ethical questions; and they are to be answered not by the findings of the laboratory, nor by the attitudes of so-called social students but by moral principles made known through right reason and divine revelation. Life is not the property of man nor does man have dominion over it. Life is the gift of God and we are merely its stewards or trustees. The Catholic hospital, by means of its own code of ethics, defends without hesitation the inviolability of the right to life. It is not an arbitrary exercise of authority but an assertion of the immutability of moral principles.

To invoke the authority of the state in ethical questions leads to a lamentable confusion with respect to the proper functions of Church and state. The state has duties toward the common welfare. It must protect the right to life, liberty, and the pursuit of happiness against unjust attack; but it is not the business of the state to invade the field of morality and impose its dictates on conscience. Nor should it attempt to put the stamp of its approval on a partisan solution of difficult moral problems. Here in this country we have recognized the wisdom of separating the function of the state from the function of the Church. We hold that it is the business of the Church, not of the state, to render the verdict in questions of morality. The mandate of Christ is clear: "Render, therefore, to Caesar the things that are Caesar's, and to God the things that are God's." The Catholic hospital can no more tolerate a departure from the ethical code which protects human life than it can acquiesce in a breach of the divine commandment which says "Thou shalt not steal." In taking this position, the Church reveals herself as the champion of human rights against unlawful aggression.

The Catholic hospital is interested in the broad and comprehensive problem of public health. It is concerned with all the problems arising out of the correlation of hospital care with religion, with science, and with government. Because of this broad interest, the Catholic hospital is vitally concerned with the various health programs initiated by other voluntary organizations, and especially with the policies and programs initiated by our national and state governments. We are concerned with the future of the voluntary hospital and its legitimate place in the total program of health care. We recognize that government has a legitimate function in respect to health. We recognize that, in certain areas of health care, the government must take the initiative and bear the chief responsibility for financial organization and even administration. This is especially true in regard to chronic sickness and custodial care. We reject, however, the concept and the policy which would give to government a monopoly of social service or which would weaken and restrict the activities of the voluntary hospital. The principle which was enunciated by Pius XI in *Quadragesimo Anno* regarding social security has particular application and validity here. This is the celebrated principle of subsidiarity. It teaches that the state should not arrogate to itself functions and responsibilities which can be fulfilled by lesser associations of a voluntary character. Otherwise, in the words of the Holy Father, "social life loses its organic form" and the state becomes "submerged and overwhelmed by an infinity of affairs and duties. Of its very nature the true aim of social activity should be to help individual members of the social body, but never to destroy or absorb them." These words of the great Pontiff should be kept in mind when we are considering the needs of a national health program. They have special force in the question of compulsory national health insurance.

A Catholic hospital is something more than a social agency. Obviously its service is of inestimable social benefit in any community. But, as we have shown in the preceding chapter, social service is not the same as charity. Charity is a virtue; social service is a technique or a method. Charity is intimately associated with religion; social work is an adaptation of scientific knowledge. Charity implies an attitude of benevolence toward God and neighbor; social work implies an attitude of research and administrative efficiency. Charity is a thing of the spirit; social work, a thing of the mind. A Catholic hospital must be not only an institution of social service, but also an institution of charity.

To say that a Catholic hospital is an institution of charity is not to say that it is an almshouse. It cannot ordinarily render its services free or without cost, but it can and must render its services to all patients in a spirit of love and dedication. It is the spirit and the motive which count; and unless these reflect the mind and heart of Christ, no Catholic hospital would be worthy of its name. Christ identified Himself with the poor, the sick, the afflicted in body and soul, so that what we do for our neighbor is done unto Him. It is this spirit which must pervade a Catholic hospital and which gives to it its distinctive character.

The Catholic hospital must ever remain conscious of the fact that it is primarily a religious institution. It is a living expression of the spirit, the teaching, the example of Christ. The Catholic hospital is intimately associated with the broad and universal mission of the Church, and consequently it can never be divorced from its responsibility of extending the kingdom of God here on earth. The technical, professional, and administrative aspects of the hospital must never be permitted to take precedence over the spiritual and religious. Moreover, as an integral part of the divinely established Church, the Catholic hospital must in its development be subordinate in any diocese to the total organization set up for the welfare of souls. To be unhesitatingly responsive to the mind and the will of the Church is the surest way of bringing God's blessing on the efforts of any Religious community in its ministry to the sick. In these days there are so many standardizing and accrediting agencies, so many committees projecting surveys for community health, that it is well for us to remember that the Church is the final authority in formulating judgments and reaching decisions. She cannot abdicate her responsibility in determining her own program in the field of charity, nor surrender this right to a civic committee or professional agency.

We must not forget the corollary which flows from the fact that our hospitals are religious institutions. Never will the hospital be better than the individual Religious who staff it. Now the first duty of Religious men and women is to sanctify themselves. The active ministry, whether in charity or education, whether in the foreign or home missions, is only a means to an end. The sanctification of the individual, and through the individual the sanctification of human society, is the ultimate goal.

Catholic nurses also have a distinct code of ethics to safeguard, and a particular morale or *esprit de corps* to cultivate and maintain. The ethics which all Catholic nurses are obliged to observe is not a matter of mere etiquette in the sickroom or in contacts with doctors, patients, and hospitals; it is not a mere refinement of conduct but a stern demand of morality resting on divine and natural law.

Professionally, Catholic nurses are endowed not only with the scientific knowledge and professional skill to bring aid and comfort to the sick, but with the power to help the soul as well as the body. They are privileged to be messengers of God and angels of His mercy in disposing their patients to receive the benefits of the great Sacraments of Penance and Holy Eucharist. Because of the intimacy between them and their patients, and because of the confidence which is born of that intimacy, Catholic nurses can, as they go about their specific work of restoring health and strength to their patients' bodies, do much also to help their patients remove the burden of sin from their souls.

Idealism based on religion must always be a part of nursing and hospital work in general. There are those who, in our selfish age, would rob nursing of the lofty motivation and real purpose which religion has given to it. The vocation of nursing can never be merely a work compensated by the pay check. Nursing, of course, like all other fields of human activity, has its "bread-and-butter" side; but the function of the nurse can never rest on a purely materialistic basis. To insist primarily on placing shorter limits on the hours of duty, on increasing recreation time, and on making salaries the chief objective, can mean bartering the happiness and health of others for personal gains. What glorifies and sublimates the profession of nursing and the entire field of hospital work is the dedication to a human service, consecrated by Christ in the words, "I was sick and you visited Me." The record of our Catholic hospitals, year after year, in meeting and effectively dealing with the increasing problems of hospital administration and care is undeniable proof that the Church practices as well as preaches the corporal and the spiritual works of mercy. Our hospitals are truly houses of love and learning — of the supernaturally motivated love of God and neighbor and the studiously acquired knowledge and wisdom of medical science.

XXVIII

RESPONSIBLE TO WHOM?

AT A Catholic hospital convention some years ago we were
asked to deliver a paper on "Responsibility as the Basic
Safeguard in Hospital Service." We believe the reader will
agree with us that the subject at first sight neither captivates
the imagination nor stirs the emotions profoundly. If a speaker
were inclined to make a rousing appeal or to rise to great
heights of eloquence, he could choose few topics less suitable.
At first we were prompted to decline the invitation, but before
doing so we made further inquiry into the subject and found
that a problem deserving of consideration really did exist.

Considerable confusion has been created in the minds of
many people because of the loose manner in which the term
"responsibility" is being used in conventions, conferences, and
study groups. It is hard to determine from the remarks made
by speakers on public programs what is meant by the term
"responsibility"; to whom we are responsible and why; and
what constitutes the area of our responsibility. It may therefore be desirable and helpful to clarify the meaning of this
term and give greater precision to its content.

At the present time there exists a variety of agencies which
set up standards for hospital service. Some of these are endowed with public authority and some of them are the result
of voluntary action. We have, for instance, the American
Hospital Association, our own Catholic Hospital Association,
the American College of Surgeons, the American Medical As-

sociation — all these, together with the statute laws for various states and the regulations of state departments, are concerned in some way with medical practice, nursing service, hospital facilities, procedures, and policies. The question arises whether the term "responsibility" is to be interpreted primarily as a responsibility to these agencies or whether there is some other meaning which is even more significant and cogent for our Catholic hospitals and those who serve them.

The term "responsibility" if looked at etymologically, is derived from the Latin language and is equivalent to the English word "answerable." It involves the notion of obligation to a higher authority to whom we must account for our conduct and our actions. If looked at from the standpoint of ethics and theology, responsibility involves the question of a right conscience. A right conscience is the practical judgment of the mind as to whether a thing is right or wrong from the standpoint of morals. Responsibility postulates the existence of a right order established by God, the existence of an obligation or duty to observe that right order, and the existence of sanctions — that is, a reward for obedience and a punishment for disobedience. Responsibility in our Catholic hospitals, therefore, is a moral obligation binding in conscience.

All law which imposes an obligation in conscience implies the existence of a legislator who has rightful authority to make laws; the expression or manifestation of the mind of the lawgiver in some public manner called promulgation of the law; and the existence of reward and punishment. If we ask ourselves to whom we are responsible in this matter of hospital service, the answer must be, first to God, second to the Church, and, third, to the state. God is the supreme Lawgiver and He makes known His mind to us in the natural law written into our very nature and in the positive law through His revelation.

The Church, moreover, is a divinely established institution which is the representative of Christ on earth in all things concerning our spiritual welfare. The Church has been endowed by Christ with legislative powers and has the right to command our obedience in the field of her jurisdiction. The state also has legitimate authority. It has the right to bind us in conscience as long as it stays within its own field of jurisdiction.

It is Almighty God Himself who lays upon us the obligation of exercising the virtue of charity. Our divine Master has said, "By this will all men know that you are My disciples, if you have love for one another." Christ Himself exercised the virtue of charity particularly in behalf of the sick and infirm, and He left us the command to follow His own divine example. It is in order to fulfill this mission that Catholic hospitals exist. Their chief responsibility, therefore, is to follow the Master's example of charity to the sick. Certain Religious Orders have come into existence for this express purpose — to minister to Christ Himself in the person of the sick. It is for this reason that individual men and women consecrate themselves in the service of religion in order that they may devote themselves to the corporal and spiritual works of mercy, and in doing so sanctify themselves as well as benefit human society.

A Catholic hospital recognizes, therefore, a responsibility which is distinctive and peculiar to itself. It is a responsibility of an ethical character, operating through the individual conscience and looking far beyond any sanction of mere social approval, public accreditation, or standardization by some agency. We do not wish to imply that other hospitals which do not function under the auspices of the Church reject these standards, but rather that they do not place the same degree of emphasis on them nor do they specify them as their ultimate objective or as the motivating force in their service as do the hospitals conducted by Religious under the auspices of the Church.

The area of our responsibility is as broad and comprehensive as the service which a hospital is to render. The welfare of the patient must always be considered first and foremost; and, in order to serve the patient adequately, in what concerns both his bodily health and his spiritual well-being, it is necessary to establish right relations with the public and right relations with the staff; to provide proper scientific facilities, proper professional nursing service, and proper administrative policies and procedure. We have, therefore, the responsibility of observing not only the scriptural commandments of charity, not only the canonical provisions of Church law as they affect Religious and works of charity, not only civil statutes as they relate to non-profit corporations and medical and nursing practices, but also those standards of service as set by our voluntary organizations. We recognize responsibility in this entire field, but our responsibility is predicated upon a different and more fundamental principle than that of legal observance and social approval.

The very fact that our hospitals are so intimately correlated with the practice of religion and the manifestation of divine charity makes it incumbent upon us to see to it that our service is of the very highest order. Anything less than the best would be unworthy of religion. This holds good for types of equipment, professional skill and training, and all administrative procedures and policies.

Nursing, while it is subsidiary to the profession of medicine, is, at the same time, a true profession. As such it has its own scientific content, its own adaptation of knowledge to practice, its own professional literature, and that feature to be found in any true profession, the fact that its service is ultimately incommensurate with a purely monetary compensation. Since professional services can never, in the strict sense of the term, be bought, neither can nursing ever be honestly or completely commercialized.

In a Catholic hospital, nursing must be regarded as a vocation as well as a profession. A profession places primary stress upon intellectual qualities. In a vocation, however, moral qualities or virtues receive the major emphasis. Nursing, therefore, must lay particular stress not only upon the corporal but upon the spiritual works of mercy. It must regard the totality of the patient; it must restore health to body, mind, and spirit. To do this adequately, the virtues of social justice and social charity are of supreme importance.

When we speak of safeguards, we recognize indeed that there is a variety of means by which the standards of hospital service are protected; but when we speak of the basic safeguard, we imply that there is one which outranks all others in importance. It stands above any state requirements, any accreditation program, any form of approval by medical or hospital associations. The basic safeguard is the responsibility in conscience to maintain the highest service, which will benefit the patient both physically and spiritually. It is only when hospitals realize this responsibility that the standards of their service will be surrounded with basic safeguards for the patient and for society.

XXIX

THE JUDGE AND THE JUVENILE

FEW groups of men within the confines of a state exercise such a powerful influence on the lives of individual citizens as do our juvenile court judges. The destinies of thousands of future citizens are, in a large measure, affected by their decisions. Upon the wisdom, courage, and foresight which they display depend, in no small degree, the order and well-being of their respective communities. Of primary interest to us is their work as guardians of the welfare of neglected, dependent, and delinquent children.

In 1911 the Constitutional Convention gave us the Juvenile Court Code in Ohio. Since that time, the juvenile court, as an instrument of social control and an agency for the administration of social justice, has indeed indicated its right to exist. If we are to attain any success in our attack on the problem of crime, it is absolutely necessary that we begin our work of prevention among the ranks of the juveniles. Adult prisoners are largely recruited from the ranks of juvenile delinquents. In view of the importance of this corrective work with the juveniles, we might do well to consider the effectiveness of the judicial machinery that has been set up for the treatment of the juvenile offender.

During the past seventy-five years, beginning with Cesare Lombroso, we have been surfeited with a multiplicity of theories both in regard to the causes and the treatment of crime. These theories have followed one another in such kaleidoscopic fashion and have presented such contradictory attitudes and explanations, that it has been impossible to formulate any consistent and enduring policy for the legislatures, the courts, or public opinion. We have been very much in the position of the physician who tries to treat disease without any adequate or certain diagnosis and without any sure or positive knowledge of the efficacy of his remedial prescriptions.

We have traveled far since Lombroso announced his doctrine of the "born criminal." In Lombroso's theory, crime had a purely physical basis. According to his doctrine, the criminal could not help being what he was any more than a man can help being six feet or five feet tall, having blue or brown eyes. He was the victim of the uncontrollable laws of nature, a victim of heredity, a straggler in the onward march of civilization — the criminal or delinquent simply inherited a nature which had failed to keep step with the progress of human culture. He was a throwback to his savage ancestors, an atavist who could be recognized by physical stigmata such as protruding jaw, left-handedness, flattened nose, scanty beard, and misshapen head. This was a comfortable doctrine to the delinquent, who could plead the inevitability of his offense, but it held out small comfort to society at large in its age-old effort to control crime and provide self-protection.

Fortunately this theory was not permitted to pass unchallenged for long. Lombroso claimed to back up his theory by facts gathered with prodigious energy from a study of the prison population of his time. The fatal error in his study, however, was that he studied only criminals and failed to compare his findings with similar researches among the normal, law-abiding citizens. Gening, the famous English prison physician, did this very thing, however. He studied three thousand consecutive entrants into the prisons of England and then compared them with a like number of the non-criminal population. His conclusions flatly contradicted Lombroso. "Our results," he states, "nowhere confirm the evidence of a physical criminal type. They challenge the evidence at almost any point." The inevitable conclusion must be that there is no such thing as the born criminal. In fact, Gening reported that he found about the same differences in cranial measurements between the graduates of Cambridge and Oxford as between the criminals and law-abiding people.

We mention this theory of Lombroso, knowing well that it has been discredited and exists merely as an exhibit in the museum of criminal science, but we do so because it illustrates what has been happening in criminology for the past seventy-five years. One theory after another has lit up the firmament of science like a meteor; each, in its turn, acclaimed for a time as the final explanation of delinquent conduct, and then, upon further research, found wanting and scrapped.

Lombroso declared that the explanation of crime could be found in atavism — in physical stigmata or anomalies. Others have pioneered in different directions. Not so long ago we were told that the great majority of delinquents were mental derelicts, that they were as irresponsible as little children because they had not developed the faculties of their minds sufficiently to be able to distinguish right from wrong. Feeble-mindedness was the explanation. A more intense research into the situation, however, showed that the majority of individuals coming into conflict with the law were not at all mentally inferior to the average population. In fact they were reported in various surveys made in St. Louis, New York, and Philadelphia to be superior in ability to the average or median of the soldiers of the army draft. Furthermore, it is one thing to say that some delinquents are feeble-minded and quite a differ-

ent thing to say that all the feeble-minded are *ipso facto* potential delinquents. This latter statement is not at all true.

When feeble-mindedness or mental retardation was shown
to be unsatisfactory as an explanation of wrongdoing, the cause
was sought in a slightly different direction. We were told that
it was the emotionally unstable, the ill-balanced, the volition-
ally weak who formed the recruiting ground for the delinquents. A new term was invented to comprehend this group.
They were called psychopaths. Psychopathy was supposed to
indicate a discarded entity in the physical instrument or psychi-
cal structure of the mind. But here again we find the experts
in disagreement and many early enthusiasts retracing their
steps.

We began seventy-five years ago with atavism, then turned
to feeble-mindedness, next drifted to psychopathy, and now we
are in the midst of a new explanation of crime based upon the
glands in the human body. The functioning of the whole en-
docrine system is assumed to be closely related to all human
conduct as cause and effect. Some of us may be pardoned if,
as a result of past experience, we do not wax too enthusiastic
over this interpretation of human behavior.

To make the confusion worse, we are still struggling to
evaluate the merits of the old controversy between heredity and
environment. According to some, heredity is the all-important
factor in personality and character. These still read *The Fruit
of the Family Tree* by Albert Wiggan as if it were gospel, little
realizing that the whole question of heredity is filled with be-
wildering uncertainties. You would think the problem of inheritance was an open book when you read the story of Martin
Kallikek and his progeny, the Nan family, the Zero family,
and the tribe Ishmael, until you take up the considered statements of such an expert as H. S. Jennings of Johns Hopkins

University, who states categorically, "It is not true that what an organism shall become is determined, foreordained, when he gets his supply of chemicals or genes or germ cells, as the popular writers on eugenics would have us believe. Every individual has many sets of 'innate' or hereditary characters; the conditions under which he develops determine which set he shall bring forth."

On the other hand, there are those who maintain that environment is the all-important factor in personality and character. Environmental factors such as home and neighborhood, church and school, companionships and use of leisure time bulk large in the explanation of conduct and the diagnosis of the causes of crime, but can they be said to be all-important? Theories with even a goodly measure of truth in them are thus often of little help to the judge or social agency in their efforts to understand the personality of the particular and individual delinquent.

It is hard enough for the court to form any adequate concept of the causes of crime in the face of such complexity and disagreement in the theories offered. But that is not all. When it comes to treatment we are face to face with more theories. Some penologists hold that punishment as a method of treatment is out-of-date and should give way to newer methods of scientific social readjustment. What these latter are is not made clear, but the public is asked to give up not only its old attitude toward punishment of the criminal but to give up the very purpose and objective of punishment. Punishment is worthless, we are told, because it does not make the criminal any better. It does not restore him as a useful citizen. It is valueless for reformation. Yes, answer the opponents, but what of the public at large? How is it to be protected? Does not punishment act as a deterrent of crime? Does not the safety and protection of the whole community take precedence over the possible good to be done the criminal? Not only have we conflicting theories on the object and purpose of punishment, but we have the same uncertainty and confusion in respect to the qualities and means of punishment. The severity of the punishment is not so important as some of its other qualities. In order to be effective as a deterrent, punishment must be prompt, it must be certain, it must be impersonal, and it must be proportionate. This is true of any kind of punishment, private or public, whether in the home, in school, or in court.

All the theories about crime, its cause and treatment, have had some value even in their obsolescence, for they have been of help in enabling us to understand better the whole question of character and personality. The greatest difficulty with the theories, however, is that they are too general even when they contain a large element of truth. They constitute a classification of delinquents rather than an explanation of the personality and character of the individual delinquent who may happen to be before the court for disposition or treatment. In order to solve the problem of John Jones, the truant, and Mary Smith, the boy-struck girl, we have to face facts and not theories. The efficiency of any court or agency in its treatment of delinquency will depend upon facts, not general facts but precise, concrete facts about the particular boy or girl. And what is true in this respect of the problem of delinquency is equally true of the problem of dependency.

The organization and procedure in the juvenile court are quite different from that in the criminal courts because the purpose of the juvenile court is different. Its purpose is not to prosecute but to protect, not directly to punish but to reform and correct. In consequence, it follows the procedure of the courts of equity or chancery. It does not serve merely as a tribunal for the hearing of evidence and for applying the law to the facts presented. Instead, the chief business of the juvenile court is to procure the evidence, to institute inquiry, to collect information. Furthermore, the evidence it desires is not merely in support or denial of the specific charge made but rather in respect to the whole personality or character of the individual brought before the court. This distinction is vital in the whole concept and organization of the court. In criminal procedure, the contending lawyers submit the evidence or facts to the court either in prosecution or defense. In the criminal court the judge acts as umpire regarding the rules of evidence, the jury decides the facts, upon which the judge renders decision in accordance with the statutes. One of the difficulties which confront judges when first undertaking their duties in juvenile court, especially if they have been transferred from police court or common-pleas court, is to become accustomed to the new procedure or organization of the juvenile court. We remember hearing one judge state that the function of his court was not that of a court at all but rather the function of a social agency. In a sense this is true, and may represent an attitude highly commendable, but it is a serious mistake to forget that the court is different from any social agency in this: that it has genuine authority, that it speaks officially in the name of the community, that it can enforce its decrees. The function of the juvenile court, just as that of other courts, is to make decisions. It is a place where things are decided. It cannot leave questions up in the air, it cannot work in a hazy atmosphere, it cannot permit its decisions to remain unenforced except at the risk of incurring justly and fairly the suspicion of the layman, the contempt of the lawyer, and a realization of weakness and ineptitude on the part of the judge.

The judge of the court must still function in his original capacity as the one who renders decisions. He must, of course, know the law; but it is even more important that he know human nature, that he understand well the elements that go to make up personality, that he comprehend clearly the processes at work in the formation of character. It is not, as we conceive it, the function of a judge merely to deliver pious exhortations from the bench. It is a vain hope to expect to solve any problem of dependency or delinquency in such fashion.

Above all things, the judge must know the facts as they pertain to each case as it is presented in his court. Only in so far as he knows the total facts concerning each child can he render decisions adequately and constructively. It is the business of the probation officers or court workers to furnish the judge with the facts. These facts are physical, mental, social. They deal with the home, the neighborhood, the school; they deal with the social status of the members of the family, and their personalities; they deal with the whole question of character and conduct of the individual before the court — his complete background. These facts should be in the form of a written record and should constitute, like the lawyer's brief of a case, the basis of the judge's decision.

In order to get these facts it is necessary for the court to have a sufficient number of case workers or probation officers. Secondly, these workers must be qualified for the task. They must be people of intelligence, people of education, people with training; otherwise they will be totally unfit to recognize the facts that are really pertinent to the case or unable to discriminate between what is useful and necessary for the court and what is not. We recognize the different needs of the small rural counties and the great metropolitan centers, but even in the smaller counties there must be a proportion between personnel and the number of cases that must be heard. We realize, moreover, that it is difficult to obtain from the county commissioners and from an overburdened treasury sufficient funds to employ an adequate number of workers and to pay salaries that will interest properly qualified workers; but we submit that the need is urgent and that until it is met, our courts will not measure up to their full possibilities or even the expectations of the public. Furthermore, the sheriff's office and other county offices are far more liberally supplied than the juvenile court, and it is only a matter of time, effort, and persistence until the proper requirements of the juvenile court will be met. The judge must, however, lead the way.

We venture to make the suggestion that the judge return more and more to the old ideal of a court as a place where decisions are made. We do not advocate a return to the old formality of the criminal and civil courts, but we do suggest that there are advantages to be gained in having a court surrounded with proper dignity; that there be something in its conduct calculated to impress the layman; and that such informality as is practiced shall be for the purpose of facilitating the collection of facts and not result in creating contempt among lawyers or the feeling of weakness and ineptitude on the part of the judge or the citizens.

Part VI

MAN IN RELATION TO SPECIAL GROUPS

WITHIN THE CHURCH

"What could be more fitting than that the Holy Fathers should turn to the Catholic laity in order that the evil of laicism might, with divine paradox, be eradicated by the very action—the Catholic Action—of the laity themselves?"

XXX

THE AGE OF THE LAY APOSTOLATE

WHEN serious-minded men gather for discussion today, we often hear such phrases as "the crises of Western civilization," "the end of our times," "the decline of the West." It has become almost commonplace for our intellectual leaders to point out that our culture and civilization have entered upon a period of disintegration, that not only our political statesmanship, our economic organization, and our educational objectives are falling rapidly into a state of chaos and confusion, but that we, as a people, have become bankrupt in our intellectual, moral, and emotional life. This has happened largely because our whole social life has been loosened from its religious foundation, and severed from its roots of Christian grace. In consequence, there is urgent need of restoration. Pius X saw the problem when he chose as the motto of his pontificate: "To restore all things in Christ." Pius XI repeated the idea in more definite terms, choosing as his motto: "The peace of Christ in the reign of Christ." The problem is appreciated also by a host of Christian writers, such as Jacques Maritain, Peter Wust, Christopher Dawson, Belloc and Chesterton, Wyndham Lewis, and our own countrymen such as Harvey Wickham and Ross Hoffman, all of whom are lay children of the faith.

For a full century and a half there has been a steady movement away from the Christian source and origin of our culture. One after another the various fields of thought and action have been divorced from the guidance of Christian principles. First, it was economics, then politics, then education, then social service, until at present we may say that every province of human action has been impregnated with the spirit of secularism. Religion has been sent into exile. In the minds and hearts of the world's leaders of thought and action, there is no need of any priesthood; no need of the loyal priesthood of the laity co-operating with the priesthood of Christ; no need of divine redemption through a Saviour — man is sufficient unto himself and can rely absolutely on his own powers. It is assumed that man will attain ultimately to perfection. "Laicism" is the word coined in Europe to denote this progressive movement away from the foundations, the source, and the origin of Christian culture and civilization. The very word itself connotes rejection of the priestly office in human society. What could be more fitting than that the Holy Fathers should turn to the Catholic laity in order that the evil of laicism might, with divine paradox, be eradicated by the very action — the Catholic Action — of the laity themselves?

The most precise definition of Catholic Action is that given by Pope Pius XI: "Catholic Action is the participation of the laity in the apostolate of the hierarchy." The Holy Father makes clear the exact meaning of this definition in his encyclical *Ubi Arcano*, and in his letters addressed to various Cardinals. Catholic Action consists in "an extension and consolidation of the kingdom of Christ in individual personalities as well as in families and in the whole of society." Again the Holy Father speaks of it as "the whole group of movements, organizations, and works which pass under the name of Catholic Action." If we follow the Scholastic tradition and distinguish between matter and form in the definition, we might say that the two passages just quoted constitute the matter. The formal element is described in these words of Pius XI: "From the nature and scope of Catholic Action appears the necessity of its perfect adhesion and docility to the Catholic hierarchy, from which alone it can receive its mandate and its directive rules."

The word "action" has been chosen specifically in order to draw out the contrast between the faith which reveals itself in good works and action, and a faith which remains merely passive or dormant. Catholic Action, moreover, implies something official. It is much more than a mere approval. It is a reaching out to the laity for the necessary assistance in extending Christ's kingdom or consolidating it, by investing the laity with an official or formal character as co-operators in what is essentially a divinely authorized undertaking. Although many organizations and movements may, by their nature, be suitable for designation as Catholic Action, only those movements, organizations, and works that are undertaken at the direct command of the Bishops, that follow a program specifically outlined by the Bishops, and hold themselves completely responsible to them are entitled to the term "Catholic Action" in the fullest and strictest sense.

The word "apostolate," in its original significance, implies not only the commission received directly from Christ but also a definite function. The first apostles received not only their authority from Christ for their mission in the world but also their program of action. The apostles were sent to the missions to teach, to sanctify through the sacraments, and to rule, direct, and guide the faithful. They were to be the shepherds of the flock. Consequently, the participation of the laity in the apostolate of the hierarchy involves something of each of these three functions. The Holy Father is careful to say that Catholic Action is a participation of the laity only in a certain sense. There is no intention of minimizing the unique and exclusive character of the priesthood, but rather of indicating that this priesthood does not stand alone and unassisted. There are to be in the Church other co-laborers with the apostles, or as St. Paul describes them, those who "have devoted themselves to the service of the saints" or who are in the "ministry of the Church"; "fellow workers in the kingdom of God," as the same apostle writes to the Colossians.

The definition of the Holy Father, moreover, might be regarded as a mild reproach or a challenge issued to the laity. The Holy Father insists that Catholic Action is nothing new, but he implies that in recent generations the laity have left altogether too large a responsibility to the formal priesthood of the Church in their efforts to extend and consolidate Christ's kingdom. The Holy Father is likewise quick to dissipate any misunderstanding that might arise from the fact that Catholic Action among the laity originates solely in the mandates of the Bishops and proceeds only with perfect adhesion and docility to the Catholic hierarchy. He rejects vigorously the thought that this imposes undue restriction upon the laity or that it robs them in any way of their initiative or responsibility. The two are quite compatible in his mind, and in fact are necessary in order to present a united front in defense of Christian truth or in the launching of a new crusade to re-Christianize society.

Catholic Action begins with the individual, but it does not stop there. It begins by setting the individual right with God and his fellow man and then it proceeds through the individual to translate the principles of Christ's teaching into the life of society. The individual Catholic, if he is to advance the kingdom of Christ, must put his faith into practice, first of all, in his own private life and then publicly and corporately in society at large. This does not mean that the individual who wishes to participate in Catholic Action must ally himself with all the social-welfare movements which promise to eradicate injustice, hatred, and greed from our social organization. We must be consistently on guard against the blandishments of those who try to win our favor and our support in behalf of a mere mechanical reorganization of our society. We are not going to bring about a "restoration of all things in Christ" or "the peace of Christ in the reign of Christ" by merely subscribing to a new social-security law or a new banking act or an additional treaty. Something much more radical and fundamental must be attempted and achieved. We must go all the way back to Christian truth and principles. We must reckon once more with God, His law, His grace, and His direction, whether it be in politics or economics, in education or in art, in social service or domestic ethics.

As we have shown in an earlier chapter, the character and quality of any civilization can be readily determined by certain fundamental social attitudes and values. When you know the attitude of a people toward human life, whether it is recognized as belonging to God or to man, then you will know whether life is safe and sacred or whether it is held cheap and insecure. When you know the attitude of a people toward the institution of private property, then you will know the attitude of that people toward wealth and poverty; whether human rights are subordinate to property rights or not. When you know the attitude of a people toward marriage and the family, then you will know whether its unity can be broken by wanton divorce and its purpose frustrated by the suicidal practice of artificial birth control. When you know the attitude of a people toward work and leisure, then you will know whether there is a bitter class struggle between a proletariat and a *bourgeoisie*. When you know the attitude of a people toward authority, whether it be from God or from man, then you will know their attitude toward government; you will know whether the state will be a responsible sovereignty or whether it will be a totalitarian state with absolute and tyrannical power. When you know these and other similar basic attitudes of any people, then you will know the character and quality of its civilization and culture.

Catholic Action implies a knowledge of these social phenomena; it implies a knowledge of the inherent nature of man, his origin and destiny; and also a knowledge of the kind of world in which man lives. It implies knowledge of man as an individual and as a social being. Catholic Action implies, furthermore, that there is a solution to be found in the Christian Gospel both for the problems of the individual man and for social man — that is, human society. It proclaims a redemption to be realized in part here on earth and fully in heaven. This goal can be achieved provided we arouse a sufficient number, not only to believe in Christ and His teaching but also to believe wholeheartedly, intensely, vividly; to put their faith into practice in their own private lives, and then to translate this faith into their public and social lives. Only in this way shall we effect a restoration of society and achieve "the peace of Christ in the reign of Christ."

In order to understand the reason or the motive for stressing so forcibly the need of Catholic Action, we must understand the full implication of the modern heresy which denies *in toto* the supernatural element in life. The solution offered by Catholic Action to this problem of secularism depends for its fuller understanding on a deeper apprehension of the doctrine of the Mystical Body of Christ and the place which the Sacrament of the Holy Eucharist occupies in the new dispensation of grace.

There can be no social reform until there has been individual reform. There can, however, be no individual reform until each individual has been set in right relationship to God according to a divinely conceived and divinely revealed plan. Society as such has no value in the sight of God except in so far as it is made up of individual human beings, each one of whom has been created by God, redeemed by God, and destined to an eternal participation in the life of God. It is the individual that counts. Now it is only through Baptism that the individual is regenerated. There is no other way. And this regeneration is above all things necessary, for only thus is man made perfectible or capable of sound growth or progress. The waters of Baptism must first flow on the foreheads of the individuals who compose human society before we can have any fundamental social reform. It is through Baptism that we are made one with Christ, partakers of His divine life, and members of His Mystical Body. As Pius XI explained it: "Among the members of this Body there must be solidarity of interests and reciprocal communication of life. As every Christian receives [in Baptism] the supernatural life which circulates in the veins of the Mystical Body of Christ, so he must transfuse it into others who do not possess it or possess it too little."

While we begin in the Sacrament of Baptism this supernatural life which is the earliest source and origin of Catholic Action, we must not forget that it is in the Sacrament of the Holy Eucharist that we nourish and perfect this life of grace. Our membership in the Mystical Body of Christ is thereby continued and completed. There can be no forceful expression of Catholic Action without intense devotion to the Holy Eucharist; for "I am the vine," says Christ; "you are the branches. He who abides in Me, and I in him, he bears much fruit; for without Me you can do nothing." While the other sacraments give an increase of grace, this sacrament contains the very Author of grace, Christ Himself.

The Holy Father's call has gone out to all Catholics to enlist themselves in the cause of Catholic Action. No one may exempt himself. The chief responsibility rests, of course, with those who by natural endowments and by educational opportunity are constituted leaders among the people. Pre-eminently, therefore, our Catholic college men and women who have these advantages must be regarded as the chosen apostles of Catholic Action.

Considering the thousands of young men and women who during the past decades have been graduated from our Catholic colleges, we have reason to complain of the tardiness with which the ranks of militant Catholic Action are being recruited. It is not merely that these graduates lack as yet maturity or seasoning but rather that they lack a flaming zeal and burning conviction. They have not become as yet conscious of the spiritual crisis which is a present threat nor of the full import of the program of Catholic Action which is its solution.

Keeping in mind that Catholic Action has its genesis in personal sanctification and that this individual aim is primary and the social aim only secondary and consequent upon the first, we should like to recommend certain practices.

The first is frequent attendance at daily Mass. Sunday Mass is a matter of obligation, but daily Mass is voluntary and as such indicates the measure of our understanding of the great mystery of the cross and the depth of our personal loyalty and devotion to Christ our King. Our age has lost its consciousness of sin and its sense of the supernatural; it needs very badly a spirit of reverence to replace flippancy and cynicism. There is no better way to provide a corrective than to increase attendance at daily Mass, which is a community function, a high social act, a public worship testifying to our intimate relationship with God. As Pope Pius XI said in 1929 to a pilgrim group: "What our age needs is social or communal prayer," and again in 1931, "The first element of Catholic Action is prayer."

The second recommendation is a full and complete participation in the Holy Sacrifice. It is not merely frequent Communion but frequent Communion in the frequent Mass. Partaking of the sacrifice has always been regarded as an essential element in establishing a community of worship between priest and people as well as a union with the Divine Majesty through the intimate joining of the Victim of sacrifice with those who offer it. Without Holy Communion the Mass lacks completeness and without the Mass, Holy Communion suffers from the same defect. The two belong together and form thus an integral act of worship which is both public and private in character and social and individual in its implications of grace and spiritual benefit.

For almost half a century there has been a movement in the Church in favor of a better understanding of the liturgy. This does not mean merely more careful adherence to prescribed forms and ceremonies; better church architecture and ornamentation; linen surplices instead of lace; one hundred per cent beeswax candles in place of oleo or stearic acid; Gregorian chant instead of modern syncopation. The liturgical movement means much more than that. It means, as Pius X intended it to mean, an essential part of the great plan of the restoration of Christian society. It means that our religion consists of three essential parts, not merely two. It consists not only of a creed and a code but also of a cult. It has faith and the commandments, but also — and very emphatically — worship.

Everyone knows the force of example given by the leaders of society. The pattern of human conduct is set by those who have intellectual and social pre-eminence. Hence, if they will set the example in their own lives; if they will be the leaders in their respective parishes in frequenting daily Mass and in participating fully in the sacrifice by receiving Holy Communion; if they will show an understanding of the liturgical movement and foster public worship or communal prayer, they will be doing what is best adapted to promote Catholic Action.

If they do this, they will likewise be ready to enlist in the great adventure of rescuing human society from a ruin which secularism seems to threaten. The Christian man or woman who keeps close to Christ in Holy Mass and Holy Communion will "walk out from public worship," as Gerald Ellard, S. J., remarks, "into the thousand situations of everyday life carrying a Christ-germ within him, capable of expansion at every breath he draws until he attains to the full knowledge of the Son of God, to the perfect man, to the full measure of the stature of Christ."

XXXI

KNOW THE MIND OF THE CHURCH

UNITY is one of the distinguishing marks of the Church.
This unity extends beyond the confines of doctrine,
morals, and discipline. It is inherent in the membership of
the Church. There is no body of men and women in all the
world more intimately united than the members of the Catholic
Church. Together they constitute the Mystical Body of Christ.
Catholic men and women are one, because they acknowledge
"one Lord, one faith, one Baptism; one God and Father of all."
They are one because they constitute a vast cohesive organism,
united mystically with Christ, their Head; they are one because
they share the same supernatural life of grace. They are one because they participate in the same sacraments, and are nourished
in Holy Communion by the same Body and Blood of Christ.
They are one because they have a common discipline under the
authority of their Bishops united with the Vicar of Christ,
the Supreme Head of the Church. Now, in spite of this genuine unity, there is no body of men and women having a common life and purpose which, at least in one sense, is so poorly
organized. There are some who will object and say that we
are already well organized; there are some who might even
think that we are overorganized. That contention can be both
true and false. It is true if we speak only of our spiritual life;
it is true if we speak only of our parishes organized for divine
worship and the administration of the sacraments; it is true
if we speak only of our religious societies with their spiritual

conferences, retreats, novenas, and missions. But it is far from the truth if we speak of their influence and effective action as Christians in all those things which concern our social and public life. Our Catholic men and women too often have no forum in which they can discuss their mutual problems, and no effective program of action to implement their ideals.

We have only words of commendation for our existing Catholic societies. They are invaluable units in the larger organization which the Church desires to see established under the name of Catholic Action. Circumstances and conditions change from age to age, and the Church must therefore establish new institutions or organizations to make the principles of the Gospel effective in meeting new conditions. The Church, especially in the encyclicals of Pius XI and Pius XII, has emphasized the need for our Catholic laity to assume greater initiative and a large measure of responsibility for the welfare of religion and the preservation of our Christian civilization.

The layman is to be the effective, although unofficial, representative of Christ; the liaison between the Church and the public. To perform this function well, he must be instructed in the doctrine, the laws, and the life of the Church. Knowledge, or what is called a Christian formation, is an essential prerequisite; but, standing alone, it is not enough. There must be a lively sense of realization on the part of the laity that they share in the mission of Christ, and that the work of the apostolate belongs not only to the clergy but to the laity as well. There are indeed two levels of responsibility. To the Bishops of the Church, Christ confided the work of the apostolate by divine commission and by means of sacred orders. To the laity, however, belong both the right and the duty of participating in the apostolate of the hierarchy.

The chief task of lay organizations today is to know the mind of the Church. When we say this, we are thinking not of any one particular doctrine, nor of certain moral obligations, nor of the liturgical worship of the Church, but rather of the sum total of these things. Together they constitute the life of the Mystical Body of Christ. A passive acceptance of the faith is not enough; there is required an active enthusiasm and zeal to make these truths of religion come alive and be effective as practical guides in the life of the individual and in the lives of all those with whom he comes in contact.

As we have often stated, the great problem which Christianity faces today, and which it has faced for several generations, is the divorce or separation between religion and ordinary day-to-day life, both private and public. Religion has come to be regarded as comprising only one phase of man's existence rather than its very substance. Where religion is alive and operative, it determines, shapes, and forms our entire culture. If genuine, it will control our personal conduct and also our social institutions, our laws, and our public policy. This cleavage between religion and what people think and do day by day, in business, political life, education, family life, and economic life is what we mean by secularism. It is the theoretical denial, or at least the practical denial, of the sacred order of things as God wants them to be, and the substitution in their place of purely human, temporal, or secular ideals and outlooks. If Toynbee, the great historical scholar, is wrong in many things, he is right at least in pronouncing emphatically that religion is the matrix of every culture or civilization. The thing that is wrong with the world in which we live today is that religion has ceased to exercise effectively this kind of influence. This is the obstacle, the difficulty, or the problem to which the Popes ever since Pius IX have addressed themselves with ever-increasing insistence. It is the reason they have issued the call to Catholic Action on the part of our lay organizations.

In order to make a program of Catholic Action effective, lay leadership is an absolute necessity. There seems to be no lack of willingness on the part of our Catholic lay people; but they are hesitant and often confused. And there does seem to be a need of greater emphasis on their responsibility to be active, and greater need of clarification concerning objectives and methods. There is need also of better or tighter organization. One of the first requirements, in view of the multiplicity of our Catholic lay societies, is a clear definition of the purpose or function of each. The purpose should be specific and definite, or there is bound to be confusion and duplication of effort. The second requirement is that each society adhere strictly to its own business and not wander into extraneous fields. A Parent-Teacher association, for instance, should not engage in the work of a hospital guild or a peace association. The Confraternity of Christian Doctrine should not campaign for an orphanage. Catholic Charities should not try to solve the problems of the educators. The St. Vincent de Paul Society should not try to reform the liturgy. The Family Life groups have a very broad field, but they should not allow themselves to become enmeshed in community action such as the Red Cross, the United Appeal, or other similar activities. The old axiom should hold true: "Keep your eye on the target."

So far, we have been speaking of the traditional Catholic societies, those that we have had for a long time in our parishes and dioceses. In recent times, however, something new has been inaugurated by the Popes — the movement that we described and analyzed in the preceding pages — Catholic Action. This envisions a new kind of function and structure for our Catholic lay organizations. It takes a broader view of the world's problems than is possible on the part of the societies with specialized functions. Catholic Action is concerned with the fundamental Christian principles which affect our social attitudes, our social institutions, and our social policies. It is concerned with the problems which affect our political, economic, and social life.

There is a close relationship between the social order and the spiritual order. The Church is vitally interested in both, for the one affects the other, and together they determine man's eternal as well as temporal destiny. The overriding issues which engage the attention of the world today are to be found in the political, social, and economic order; and because false principles have been followed in the solution of these problems, there has been a progressive dechristianization of our society. Communism, secularism, racialism, nationalism are some of the concrete manifestations of this departure from Christian principles.

The new type of Catholic lay organization has its own distinctive function and structure, comprising both an elite and a mass movement. As an elite movement it is designed to meet the present need for leadership — those qualified to be leaders must be awakened to their responsibility. As a mass movement, it is set up to meet the need for concerted action — action to be had by federating all Catholic societies into a single unified body.

A frequent complaint heard among pastors is that the Catholic men and women who have had the privilege of a college education do not show an interest in the parish societies, or exercise the leadership which in justice might be expected of them. Perhaps the fault lies as much with the parish and the kind of program encouraged or tolerated by the priests of the parish as it does with the Catholic college graduates themselves. Mere entertainment or recreational diversions on a parish level will not capture the interest of an intellectual or serious-minded group of Catholics. Many parishes, moreover, are made up of heterogeneous groups having their own distinct class interests. Some of the parishioners are lawyers, some doctors, clerks, truck drivers, businessmen, or labor leaders. It is hard to find a common denominator either in their interests and activities or in their intellectual equipment. They have, indeed, the faith in common, but not much else. Hence it is desirable to follow the vocational principle in our organizing efforts, a principle advocated by Pius XI — namely, the principle of "like to like."

A parish is, in a sense, the fundamental unit of Catholic life. It is a unit, however, for religious and sacramental life rather than a unit for Catholic Action. A parish as such does not meet for discussion or for action. It meets at church for divine worship, reception of the sacraments, and religious devotions. Parochial life as a community is conducted by and through various parish societies. Some of these are for purely spiritual ends — namely, for the sanctification of the individual members rather than for the sanctification of the environment in which they live. Both are needed, but the technique or method of procedure will differ in each. Many parishes are too restricted in numbers, too impoverished in the quality of their leadership, and frequently too divergent in their class interests to constitute a satisfactory unit for fruitful discussion and effective action.

It is here that the principle of vocational groupings and the principle of federation come into play. There may not be a sufficient number of natural leaders such as lawyers, or doctors, or businessmen, or labor leaders in any one parish to form an effective group; but such groups could be recruited from a wider area, such as the particular city or deanery of which they are a part, and which allows intimate contact and easy communication. Since these groups follow the same vocation they necessarily have much in common. It should be far easier by means of this procedure to arouse their interest and co-operative effort in applying Christian principles to the broad social problems which affect the life of the community. By following this principle of organization, it may be possible to create an elite or a type of leadership which represents the Church at its best. The intention is not to bypass the parish, but rather to stimulate, by means of vocational groupings, the interest of natural leaders in the problems which the Church faces, and as a result to have these leaders seek outlets for their zeal and devotion eventually in and through the parish societies. Moreover, these vocational groupings should be represented on Deanery and Diocesan Boards of the Councils of Catholic Men and Women.

There seems to be no other way of recruiting qualified leadership on the parish level, at least in the beginning, than for the pastor or priest-chaplain to select a small but competent committee from within the parish who can assist him in formulating a worth-while program. The program must provide subject matter of a challenging nature which lends itself easily to discussion by the group. It must have sufficient continuity so that the subject may be explored adequately. There must be a discussion leader who will keep the debate from becoming desultory and who will guide the meeting toward some fruitful resolutions or form of action. Once the laity have assumed responsibility, they must be free to develop their own initiative. There will be no consistent effort unless the leadership is allowed to remain in their hands. Unless the parish is well organized toward the Christian development of its members, there is little hope of Catholic Action in the Church's sense of the term.

No matter how much we may depend on leadership on the parish level, we still need the strength which comes from numbers. We need to pool our resources, to apply the principle of federation. By bringing all the interparochial societies and the parish organizations into one federated group, it should be possible to find a qualified leadership for the larger undertakings, and at the same time put the weight and strength of large numbers behind a project of broad scope or significance. (It was for this reason that the Bishops of the United States called into being the National Councils of Catholic Men and Women.) The separate or individual units may be parish societies, interparochial societies, organizations diocesan-wide or even national; but whatever be the size of the units, the function of the federation itself is national in scope and outlook. In consequence it can act as a national clearing house for other Catholic societies and serve also as a channel of communication between the hierarchy as a whole and the general public. The foregoing principles of good organization can be summarized under four headings — namely, specialization in function, vocational groupings, subsidiarity or hierarchical order, and federation for massive strength. At present the weakest link in the chain of command over our forces is that of vocational groupings and that of the formation of an elite who are qualified to observe, plan, and act in accordance with the exigencies of the times.

A second complaint often mentioned is that the lay organizations are not allowed sufficient initiative or autonomy. This may be true at times and, if so, it is a defect which should be corrected. Complaints also arise from the opposite angle — namely, that the parish priests do not take enough interest in

or give encouragement to the lay organizations. It is not easy
to find and steer a middle course between these two extremes.
The function of the priest-chaplain or moderator is not to conduct the meetings, or to dictate the program, but rather to act
as referee; to supervise, encourage and guide the action of the
lay organizations, so that they truly reflect the mind of the
Church. No worth-while results can be obtained if our Catholic
lay leaders are kept in hobbles or under too tight a rein by
priest chaplains or moderators. Nevertheless there is an element of risk involved here which, as long as we are aware of it,
can lead to no harm. It arises from the fact that the Church
does have an official position or policy in certain instances, and
so no commitment should be made by a Catholic lay society
without the sanction of official Church authority. Granting that
there is at times debatable ground wherein freedom of judgment is permissible, still it can happen that, on some important
matter of Church policy, two Catholic societies may take exactly
opposite positions. Unless they first clear the matter with an
authorized central agency, their procedure will obviously be
self-defeating and will lay us open to the charge that Catholics
do not know their own mind.

The encyclical letters of the Popes within the past seventy-
five years have treated many questions of public interest; treated
them by giving clear doctrinal instruction and moral directives.
The Popes have spoken on Christian democracy, the right relation between Church and state, the rights of the working
class, the reconstruction of the social order, international peace,
education, and family life. Such questions as these must be
taken up and answered in a Christian context, if our environment, social institutions, laws, and public policy are to be in
harmony with Christian religious conviction. Unless these public issues are judged in the light of Christian principles, they

will inevitably be resolved according to the arbitrary views derived from secularist principles. Our Catholic lay organizations must be familiar, therefore, with the teachings and directives of the Church, if their contribution to our spiritual and social well-being is to be effective and beneficial.

In formulating a course of action, Catholic lay organizations must be guided by prudence. Their purpose is to be constructive, not merely critical; positive rather than negative. We wish to create a wholesome social atmosphere and Christian environment for ourselves and for our neighbors. We are mindful that we are a minority and that in consequence we must achieve our purposes by persuasion and not coercion. Coercion would be undesirable under any circumstance. We do not seek to dominate, even if we could. Our strength rests in the cogency of our arguments, not in numbers. Co-operation with all others who recognize the sovereignty of God and the primacy of the moral law is our method of procedure. Such co-operation, however, must never lead to any confusion or compromise of religious truth; for the unique position of the Church as the official witness of Christ and His revelation must at all times be maintained.

Membership in the Church of Christ is both a privilege and a responsibility. The privilege is that of being incorporated into the kingdom of Christ; the responsibility is that of serving the kingdom with loyalty and devotion. It is not enough to have the faith. We must safeguard it against its enemies and we must preach it to every creature. The laity share this responsibility with their Bishops; not in the same measure, but by participating in the apostolic work of the hierarchy. They are called upon to discharge this responsibility by becoming apostles to their fellow men in those areas of public life which belong primarily to the laity. To achieve this goal they must be made more and more conscious of the fact that Christ has a claim upon their allegiance. He became the Head of the human race — the One who holds the primacy in all things, the One whose word is law, the One who is judge both of the living and of the dead. It is to this high vocation that your Bishop is calling you in order that you may join with him in restoring all things in Christ.

XXXII

MEN AND WOMEN WITH INFLUENCE

MANY changes have taken place in the world since the National Council of Catholic Men, and its counterpart, the National Council of Catholic Women, were organized about forty years ago. At that time we were still suffering from the aftermath of the first World War. Hunger, sickness, and poverty were the immediate and overwhelming problems in Europe. The United States had escaped most of the ravages of the war. The emphasis here at home was put on a return to normalcy and on the restoration of a policy of national isolation in world affairs. Neither effort was effective for long. In the face of the mounting threats of Communism, Fascism, and Nazism we were forced to retreat from our position. Because of a coalescence of these evils, the second World War with all its horror soon engulfed mankind. Nothing has been the same since. The cold war which ensued has divided the world into two opposing camps. The issues at stake are nothing less than the survival or death of our Christian civilization.

An aggressive nationalism has made its appearance in a large part of the world. Raw and inexperienced nations have tried to leap the gap of centuries and overnight to gain a new standard of living equal to that of the old industrial nations of the West. No matter how we may sympathize with their legitimate ambitions, we cannot ignore the immediate problems which have arisen from this attempt to achieve such goals. This world of ours has never before witnessed such widespread upheaval; certainly none which so profoundly challenges the fundamental values consecrated by Christianity. Our Holy Father Pope John XXIII, following the practice of Pius XII, and conscious of the transcendent importance of the issues involved, has asked us to mobilize all the moral forces of the Christian world, to tighten our ranks, to broaden the horizon of our interests, and to engage with all our energy and spiritual strength in this struggle for Christ and the Church.

About forty years ago the Catholic men and women of this country, under the leadership of their Bishops, were taking their first faltering steps in creating national federations which could speak out boldly in defense of Christian values. Their chief aim was to orientate the minds of their members toward dealing with those wider problems which could not be met effectively by local small-scale organizations. Their success in achieving a status of national significance during the intervening years is a matter of public record. The National Council of Catholic Men and the National Council of Catholic Women have grown in proportion to the expanding interests of the nation. Their influence has extended beyond our own boundaries and reached out, at least in some measure, to the entire world. There is scarcely a problem of importance which these two organizations have not effectively worked to solve. They have been active in the fields of human rights, family life, Christian marriage, child care, immigration, race relations, and in a variety of other areas both national and international.

As we take inventory of past achievements and survey the pressing problems of the immediate future, we are more and more conscious of the wisdom and urgency of the directives given by the late Holy Father in his allocution to the World Congress of the Laity in 1957. Pope Pius XII, on that memorable occasion, stressed the importance of a thorough preparation on the part of those who would guide society toward the reconstruction of a Christian social order. The indispensable requirements for effective action are, he stated: first, a sound spiritual formation, and, secondly, expert or technical knowledge. The first is necessary in order that Christian principles may supply both the motivation and the objectives. The second is necessary so that the right means may be chosen to accomplish the ends desired. Genuine leadership presupposes an intellectual preparation as well as a spiritual formation. Zeal, devotion, and good will are necessary, but of themselves they are insufficient. They must be supplemented by hard and painstaking efforts to know more fully the mind of the Church in its social doctrine and to grasp more clearly the causes and remedies of the problems to be solved.

These problems, moreover, have taken on a new dimension. They are no longer restricted to the local or national levels, but have become international in their impact on our Christian culture and civilization. In consequence, the interests and the efforts of our Catholic laity have had to keep pace with the expanding interests and activities of the Church. We have learned that responsibility is inevitably associated with power. This is true not only in the temporal order of things but also in the spiritual. The defense of human rights, of religious freedom, of Christian social principles must now be carried out in a world-wide forum by means of international co-operation. Our Catholic men and women must not fail to inform themselves thoroughly on the basic principles involved in questions of public dispute. They must be aware of the essential differences and the tensions which exist between religious groups. Then they must use this knowledge to promote charity and better understanding among all.

There has recently been an upsurge of religious sentiment which has expressed itself in a great increase in church affiliations. Competent students of the facts tell us that never before in the history of our country has church membership increased so fast and so extensively. At the same time, these observers tell us that the secularist spirit was never more in evidence. If we measure its pervasiveness by the attitudes, interests, hopes, and ambitions of the great body of the American people, we have reason to be concerned. It is obvious that their interests are not other-worldly, but are centered rather on this world. Religion is frequently nothing more than a social welfare program. It often lacks clear and definite doctrine, and, in consequence, fails in its understanding of the supernatural. It is a man-centered religion rather than a God-centered one. We do not wish to discount all values in this movement; we welcome the general trend but we cannot fail to note its shortcomings. In the judgment of acute observers, it has been described as religiosity — a combination of religious sentiment and secularism.

One of the striking features of this new development is that people no longer identify themselves in their respective communities by the traditions of the past, such as language, custom, and national origin, but primarily by their religious affiliation. In consequence, the lines of cleavage based on religious differences are beginning to show signs of hardening. A strong group-consciousness is becoming apparent, with overtones of divisive tendencies. The unfortunate result is a growth of religious tensions in our population. These tensions manifest themselves in various ways, but particularly in respect to religious tolerance, state and Church relationships, the public school system, and censorship.

If we seek an explanation of this social phenomenon we can find it, at least in part, in the changed position of Catholics in this country. We are no longer a negligible minority; neither do we lack today the prestige or influence which comes from education and social position, as was often the case in the early days of immigration. Our separated brethren feel instinctively that they have been challenged in their traditional dominance of public life and in their former easy assumption of a superior status. There is a certain latent resentment on their part at this loss of preferment. We can readily understand the nature of this reaction, but it does not become thereby less injurious to good relations. We do not wish to create invidious distinctions, but we should like to remind those of our fellow citizens who think the Church is an alien institution, that the early discoveries and explorations by Catholic pioneers are a witness to the fact that the Church is indeed indigenous to this country. The very names of our cities, our rivers, our valleys have stamped their Catholic origin indelibly on the geography and history of these United States.

There is a second explanation which accounts for much of the tension that exists between religious groups. It consists in the almost complete failure to understand the Catholic position on the meaning of "the Church." To most of those outside the fold, the Church is nothing more than a voluntary organization of those who believe in Christ. In their estimation it differs little from other forms of mutual co-operation, even though it is concerned with sacred things. To their way of thinking, the Church is by its nature pluralistic, admitting of many forms or denominations; flexible in its accommodation or interpretation of doctrine; and fluid in its membership. Church affiliation for them may be desirable, but it is not necessary.

What the Catholic has in mind when he speaks of the Church is something utterly different, as we showed at length in previous chapters. To us within the fold, the Church is a unique institution, unlike anything else known to man. It is divinely established. It needs no charter from any state or the permission of any government to exist and to fulfill its mission. It has rights and duties conferred upon it by Christ, and occupies, therefore, an independent status in society. It is a complete or perfect society in terms of membership, means, and end. It bears within itself the mark of perpetuity. It speaks with authority in matters of religion, as did Christ its Founder; it claims to be His sole authentic representative on earth; it admits of no rival claim with which it shares responsibility. In the language of St. Paul, the Church is Christ; it is His Mystical Body functioning now in human society as Christ did when He walked on earth.

Obviously, then, with such widely divergent points of view, there is bound to be confusion when we begin to discuss, for instance, the question of religious tolerance. The Church can never be indifferent toward religious error nor countenance any deviation in the deposit of faith. There is only one Lord, one faith, one Baptism. Toleration in doctrine, therefore, is inadmissible for Catholics. Unfortunately, however, some of our fellow citizens jump to a wrong conclusion. Since we hold such an inflexible position in doctrine, they think that we would be equally intransigent in respect to civic and political tolerance and would, if circumstances permitted, impose our religious belief on others. This is illogical and false. We repudiate any such conclusion and we reject absolutely the notion that physical force or legal compulsion can ever be rightly used to establish religious conformity. The sacred canons of the Church uphold "freedom of conscience," if rightly understood, and denounce coercion as a means of religious conversion. It is our firm belief and our unchanging doctrine that the state has no jurisdiction or competence in the field of religion. The First Amendment of our Constitution, therefore, which denies to Congress any right to make a law respecting the establishment of religion or to forbid the practice of religion is quite consistent with our own convictions. The Church, as we have emphasized often, requires nothing more than freedom to exist, freedom to teach the Gospel of Christ, freedom to choose her own pastors, freedom to use the normal means of communication, and freedom to possess the visible and tangible means of normal support in order that she may give continuity to the mission of Christ. If, in addition to these things, the state takes a benevolent attitude toward religion, so much the better.

In a pluralistic society such as ours, where a wide variety of religious denominations exists, there always will be grave differences in respect to the ethics of family life and education. As long, however, as we are free as Catholics to follow our own convictions in practice, and free to express our honest judgment publicly on the moral issues involved, we ask no more of the law of the land. Obviously we should be happier if others could be persuaded to see eye to eye with us in these matters.

There is one area, however — one which we have already treated — in which we entertain a certain sense of grievance. We hold that freedom of education does not now enjoy equal status with freedom of speech and freedom of assembly; and we regret that freedom of education is not recognized with the same liberality in our national policy as it is in many other democratic countries. We reasonably contend that where the burden of school taxation is universally imposed, there should be a universal application of the principle of distributive justice. We as Catholics are not opposed to public schools. We endorse the principles of universal and free education. We regret the absence of religious instruction, but are conscious of the difficulties involved. If there were no public schools, we would have to help create them; not that we would need them, but others would. We do ask one thing: namely, that freedom of religion in education be not penalized by our being forced to bear a double burden of taxation, and that social or auxiliary services be not denied our children simply because they do not attend tax-supported schools.

Another one of the areas in which tensions derive from a difference in views among religious groups has more recently made its appearance in respect to censorship. There are few questions which involve so many complexities. It is a touchy question. Censorship which involves nothing more than the public expression of a moral judgment cannot be legitimately attacked. Every book review or evaluation of a screen play, every radio broadcast and television program automatically falls into the same category. Normally this excites no adverse comment. It is only when legal coercion or economic boycott is involved that we find objections raised. Our opponents claim that we have no right to impose our particular views on others. But, by the same token, they have no right to impose their views on us. It seems obvious to us that the state has a responsibility to protect the moral health of the community even as it does the physical health. To forbid and punish lewd and obscene attacks on the moral standards of a community is not censorship but a legitimate and necessary exercise of police powers of the state. If a proper distinction were kept in mind between these two separate attitudes, the specious charge of undue censorship would cease to carry any weight.

Certain aspects of the problem of pornographic literature need to be emphasized. The first is related to the fact that we are faced with a serious moral problem which affects the well-being of the entire community. It is not an imaginary problem envisioned merely by emotional people with a puritan or prudish attitude of mind. It is a real problem, which is recognized by good, solid citizens as an insidious attack on the home, the family, and the community. It would take no more than a ten-minute exposure to an exhibit of this moral filth to convince any decent normal person of the vicious nature of the pornographic literature that is being widely circulated.

Attention should also be called to the nefarious way in which unsuspecting youth is enticed into the trap of these commercial exploiters of pornographic literature. Innocent-looking advertisements are used as a bait for the unwary. Peddlers often work the neighborhoods of our schools and places where youth forgathers for recreation. These evil practices are nation-wide, and constitute big business running into hundreds of millions of dollars. The harm that is done to our youth is as widespread in its pernicious effects as is the size of the business itself.

We are not concerned here with censorship in any ordinary acceptance of that term. We have no intention of invading the traditional freedoms which are guaranteed to us under the First Amendment. The Supreme Court has settled that question. It has decreed that pornographic literature which violates the accepted moral standards of a community does not enjoy the protection of the First Amendment. Just as the public health is safeguarded from charlatans operating in the field of medicine, so the public morals can and must be protected by public law and its enforcement agencies. To do this effectively, the police and the courts need the active and articulated support of the community.

There is a definite connection between the widespread distribution of pornographic literature and the overall problem of juvenile delinquency. To support this contention we can cite the testimony of eminent sociologists and social psychologists. The studies of the Judge Baker Foundation in Boston have demonstrated that where there is a breakdown in moral standards in one area, almost inevitably the contagion spreads to other areas, so that theft, lying, dishonesty, and violence are frequently associated with sexual indecency. Pornography poses a serious threat to the moral standards of our nation. We heartily commend the firm stand taken by our Postmaster General, by the Citizens for Decent Literature, and by the general public.

Tensions in the mutual relations of religious groups will continue to exist no doubt in some measure, but there is no reason why we should not strive to create a better climate of public opinion and remove misunderstanding of the Church and her teaching. It seems reasonable and even urgent that our Catholic laity should assume the major responsibility of meeting this situation and that its members should interpret the mind of the Church to their own associates. Explanations will come with better grace from the laity because of its status, and will carry more conviction than if proffered by the clergy, no matter how cogently the case be argued. In order to be effective, however, Catholic men and women must, above all, have accurate information on the facts involved and on the precise teaching of the Church. They must guard against the mere expression of personal opinion. They must rely on the authentic sources of doctrine, and not substitute what some individual holds or what is merely advisable or expedient for what is obligatory and binding in conscience. Nothing will be gained if they allow themselves to become engaged in angry denunciation of their opponents, for the task is one of persistently, patiently, and calmly explaining the position of the Church. They might well be mindful of the advice that it is easy to win an argument but easier to lose a friend; easy to criticize but not so easy to correct. Generosity of mind, therefore, in our approach to others can and should be our policy; it is at the same time a true exercise of charity.

We must convince our fellow citizens that we are not reaching out for power; that we have no desire to dominate public life in our own selfish interest, but that our sole purpose is to share the blessings of a Christian culture and civilization with our neighbors. To have our laws, social institutions, and public policy impregnated with Christian principles of peace, justice, and charity; to restore all things in Christ — this is surely a worthy objective, and it is toward such a goal that the National Council of Catholic Men and the Council of Catholic Women should bend their every effort.

XXXIII

LIFE ON THE LAND — A PARTNERSHIP

THERE is a well-known philosophic axiom which states that "things are not to be multiplied without necessity." A corollary of this truth is that new organizations or societies are not to be formed unless there is adequate justification for their existence. How does the existence, within the framework of the Church, of a special group dealing exclusively with rural life fit into this rule? What does the Church, whose purpose is spiritual and other-worldly, have to say about rural life as distinct from urban life? What is there about life on the land that warrants any specific attention on the part of the Church? In other words, why should there be a Catholic Rural Life Conference? To answer this question let us consider certain parallel situations.

That there should be a National Catholic Educational Association is fairly obvious. We believe, for instance, that moral and spiritual values are an integral part of any comprehensive system of education. We believe, moreover, that religion is an essential prerequisite in any program that seeks to inculcate these values in the minds and hearts of youth. Since, therefore, we have a distinctive philosophy of education, and since there are distinctive problems affecting our schools, a Catholic organization in the field of education is an obvious necessity. The same can be said of our Catholic Charities Conferences, our Catholic Hospital Association, and our Catholic Social Action Congresses. There are distinctive Catholic principles

derived from the Gospel of Christ which are decisive in formulating our policies, methods, and purposes in all these fields.
It is not, however, equally obvious that the problems affecting
rural life fall into the same category. Some explanation, therefore, seems to be in order.

Life on the land is a vocation which represents a more intimate partnership with God in the work of creation than any
other form of economic activity. To provide mankind with the
essential elements of food and clothing is a way of life which
is basic in the divine dispensation of maintaining the existence
of the human family. The Church wishes to give due recognition to this fact, so that life on the land will have a place of
honor within the wide variety of human avocations.

The land itself is such a primary source of God's bounty
in maintaining life that the soil and its products must be regarded as gifts of God. They belong, not to one generation or
to one nation only but to all mankind. "The earth is the Lord's,
and the fullness thereof." As a consequence, we must cultivate
an attitude of respect toward the land and treat it with provi-
dential care, so that it be not wasted and rendered sterile
through neglect or misuse.

As long as mankind continues to exist on earth there will
be men who till the soil. There are two ways of looking upon
this most necessary of all human avocations. One is to regard
it as pure drudgery, to which men give themselves reluctantly,
without inspiration or spiritual imagination. The other is to
see it as a partnership with God in the great work of creation,
lifting the souls of men in a spirit of awe and reverence to
the marvels of God's providence, and gratifying the human
spirit with a sense of dignity and worth-while achievement.
In order to help create such a wholesome regard both on the
part of those who farm the land, and on the part of urban

people who must live off the land, the Church gives its cordial approval to the work of the Catholic Rural Life Conference.

There are other considerations which prompt the Church to give moral support to a program of social welfare for people living in rural areas. Ever since the days of Leo XIII and Pius XI we have been made familiar with the problems of industrial society. We have been warned against the evils which create a proletariat in the cities, with the consequent danger of social revolution and religious apostasy. There is a similar danger, however, of fostering the formation of a rural proletariat, if we are not on guard against certain evils which can and do develop in rural areas.

Tenant farming, absentee ownership, depressed prices, soil erosion, and climatic disasters are some of the hazards of agrarian life. The virtues of social justice and social charity have a valid and appropriate application to life on the farm, just as they do to life in urban industry. The farmer is entitled to a decent living, with security against the hazards of his life and occupation, just as much as the industrial worker is. Pius XII has taken pains to point out some of these problems in his allocutions, wherein he prescribes certain remedies that will help correct the evils. The business of the Catholic Rural Life Conference is to study these recommendations in the light of our own national experience and to make suitable application to the particular problems of our own areas.

Much has been said and written about the deterioration of the family as a social unit in recent years. The criticism, however, does not apply so much to the rural family as it does to the family living under the conditions of city life. In the country, the family continues to be the economic unit, the recreational unit, and the cultural or educational unit. On the land father and mother and children work the farm together and share a mutual interest and activity in providing for the economic well-being of the whole family. The son learns his way of life from his father by working with him on the soil. The daughter learns her domestic duties from her mother under the family roof-tree. In the city, by contrast, the father leaves the home each day and engages in an occupation which has no vocational value for the other members of the family. The only active interest in his work is likely to be in the weekly pay envelope or monthly salary check. Sons do not often follow the father into the shop or factory, or learn from him the skills and understanding whereby they may make their own living in the future. The modern organization of industry tends to disrupt the family, not only by taking the father out of the home throughout his workday hours, but also by its instability, causing him, at times, to move about from job to job in such a way as to necessitate frequent moving on the part of the whole family. The result is the weakening of family ties. From these disturbing influences the rural family is for the most part free.

What is true of the rural family in respect to unity and mutual interests in the economic order is also true in large part in the cultural and recreational aspects of life. The open country affords opportunities for genuine neighborliness; families join one another not only in their work but in social diversions centered in the family rather than in the individual. When the family engages in close co-operation in its daily living and routine duties, it is easier to inculcate the practice of family prayer, the observance of feast days, the use of ritual blessings, and a sense of immediate dependence on the overruling providence of God. It is a noteworthy fact that in rural areas where Catholics constitute a majority of the population, a genuine Catholic culture is to be found. The faith impregnates the thoughts, words, and actions of the people and finds outward expression in social practices and traditions. In rural areas there is far less danger of religious indifference and less temptation than in the cities; there is greater opportunity for the parish, by exercising its influence not only in religious things but also in social matters, to create an environment which is conducive to wholesome living.

Conditions in rural life are, of course, not always ideal, not even in Catholic neighborhoods. The parish, however, that is truly mindful of the Church's wish to promote whatever is conducive to the good life here on the land, where conditions are most favorable, can readily become the true center and focus of all rural interests and activities. In the matter of soil conservation, of establishing credit unions, of co-operatives for purchasing or marketing, of 4-H Clubs, the parish should concern itself, seeing to it that what otherwise might be only a matter of economics becomes an area for the exercise of the great Christian virtues of social justice and social charity.

It is an interesting fact that in the course of our national history radical changes have taken place in the relative preponderance of rural and urban populations. The first national census of 1790 shows that ninety-five per cent of the population was then living in rural areas. In 1860, just before the Civil War, fifty-nine per cent of the total working population was engaged in agriculture. By 1950 this figure had been reduced to twelve and a half per cent. These figures are valid for the Catholic population shift as well.

If we examine the religious situation of our country, we will note that only a small proportion of our Catholic population lives on the land. We are, in fact, preponderantly an urban people. There are in this situation advantages which favor the growth of the Church. It is a fact that the influence

of the cities — as centers of education, the sites of our colleges
and universities; centers of communication, such as the press,
radio, and television; centers of dynamic public opinion, such
as is crystallized ultimately in laws, public policy, and social
institutions — dominates and fashions the spirit and character
of our national life. And so it follows that the influence of
the Catholic Church, since the Church is predominantly urban,
is the strongest in our great metropolitan areas, and thence
radiates into every part of the country. Not that this is the
ideal situation, however. The steady retreat from the farms
and the rapid migration of people to the cities have constituted
a significant social change which has had a disturbing influence
on family life. In so far as it involves Catholic families it is
a movement that should be discouraged. It is, in fact, one of
the purposes of the Catholic Rural Life Conference to do just
this, by using all its power to make life on the land more
interesting, more satisfying, and more wholesome, both for
the good of the individual and for the good of religion. Its
effort is toward keeping Catholics on the land, because the
rural family has more stability, a better-controlled environment,
and in the end a more secure spiritual future.

At the same time it is equally true that the area in which
the Church is least understood and most feared is precisely the
rural area. There are immense geographical sections of our
country where personal contacts with Catholics are few and
far between. Where there are no face-to-face relationships,
ignorance and fear and prejudice thrive unhindered. In the
states of the deep South the ratio of Catholics is less than five
per cent, and in some instances only one per cent. These rural
areas, moreover, are the reservoirs of our future population, for
it is their excess of population which, in a steady flow of
migrants, populates our industrial cities of the North and so

tends to undermine the strength and lessen the influence of the Church, even in the cities. To protect ourselves against harmful reactions, we must bring knowledge of the Church to these backward areas that constitute such a vast section of our country. That, however, is not the chief reason for our interest or concern. We have a higher motive and a more urgent obligation. As followers of Christ we have the duty of bringing the full message of the Gospel to all our brethren, making them sharers in the blessings that we ourselves possess. The command of our Lord was to "preach the Gospel to every creature."

The Catholic Rural Life Conference should be one of the great agencies of the Church in the work of conversions. One of its aims is to be just that. The Glenmary priests (the Home Missioners of America) and the Glenmary Sisters (the Home Mission Sisters of America) are in fact an outgrowth of the Catholic Rural Life Movement. Missionaries must be sent into the hundreds of priestless counties of the United States so that the Church may become known for what it is — the true instrument of salvation established by Christ. Toward this end we sorely need, first of all, an apostolic spirit among those who live on the land, so that they will be convert-minded; and, backing them up, a truly vitalized Catholic Rural Life movement to pursue the work systematically. Rural America must be given an opportunity to learn the full truth of the Catholic faith; and what group should be more interested in accomplishing this purpose than those Catholics who share the same way of life?

XXXIV

THE YOUTH OF THIS GENERATION

YOUTH is always more interested in the future than in the past; more concerned with the shape of things to come than with an analysis of past successes or failures. Obviously it is hazardous to venture into unknown territory and to forecast the conditions which will surround our future lives, but at least such an attempt has the merit of an intellectual adventure. And so we turn our mind's eye to the future and ask: What kind of world will our young people face?

Uppermost in the youthful, questing mind, affecting all its hopes and aspirations, is the uncertain prospect of whether there will be war or peace. There have been two world wars in our own times and various localized conflicts of major proportions; there has been, moreover, during the last decade so much tension in our international relations that we have spontaneously recognized the situation as "a cold war." What, then, we ask is the probability that the present generation will be called upon again to mobilize for another Armageddon? Will the youth of the land again be thrust into the fiery ordeal of war, with all the consequences which the new machinery of death makes so terrible? The answer to that question cannot be given with assurance even by our best-informed statesmen. There are, however, certain considerations which offer some encouragement that the second half of this century may be more peaceful than the first. At least we may hope that the conflicting national interests will not find their solution in a contest of arms. With the atom bomb, the hydrogen bomb, and intercontinental ballistic missiles, has come a completely altered concept of war. Nations have come to recognize that war is no longer an effective instrument in the pursuit of national interests; it is decidedly a total disaster for any nation, whether victor or vanquished. The period of *successful* wars is a thing of the past. Even aggressive nations, with no moral inhibitions and with a policy of world revolution and domination, such as Communist countries, hesitate to assume the terrible risks of wars.

War conducted in terms of the hydrogen bomb and intercontinental ballistic missiles creates such a frightful threat of retaliation to an aggressor as to cause even the Kremlin to think twice before it dares to challenge the United States and the NATO powers. Add to this the fact that the situation in the countries which now groan under the dictatorship of Soviet Communism — East Germany, Poland, and Hungary, for instance — is so threatening that Russia must know full well that it would face a civil war within its own boundaries if it should begin an aggressive march toward the West. It comes down to this: there are today only two possible world antagonists — Russia and the United States. Other nations are too weak to initiate World War III.

It can be stated categorically that the people of the United States abhor the prospect of war and most certainly will not provoke one. Our country has endured insults; it has tolerated the wanton rupture of treaties, and it has suffered the humiliating abuse and imprisonment of its own citizens — without resort to arms. It would be only in the case of clear necessity and in self-defense that our government would accept the challenge of another war. These facts constitute a certain measure of safety, and the prospect of peace in the future is therefore somewhat brighter than might otherwise be supposed. We offer this as something to encourage the youth of the present generation.

The second question concerns the future economic prospects of the youth of today. Will there be an opportunity for gainful employment for the six hundred thousand young men and women who each year enter the ranks of the labor force? Again the answer cannot be an absolute affirmative. But there is ample evidence that we are entering an era of an expanding economy. Those who talked lugubriously of a mature economy during the depression are today outmoded and in retreat. The discovery of atomic energy and its practical adaptation to industry and commerce are introducing a new factor into our economic life, which will be significant for social progress, as was the development of electricity during the last century. The new field of applied chemical science — as yet in its infancy — is another important factor in an expanding economy which will no doubt provide many additional opportunities for employment despite the trend toward automation in some of the older industries.

There is another situation which cannot be overlooked. The population growth during this past decade will exercise a decisive influence in the immediate future. There was a time during the late twenties and all through the thirties when our population seemed to have reached a static condition. Then, with the close of World War II, there was a sudden and startling boom in the population. During the war years, many marriages had of necessity been postponed; but, beginning with 1946, new families were established in ever-increasing numbers and the birth rate jumped from seventeen per thousand to twenty-five per thousand. This meant that new millions of human beings were being added to our population over and beyond the normal increase. Contrary to all expectations, this rate of increase is continuing and we shall soon be a nation of 185,000,000. The immediate effect on the economy was something utterly unforeseen. The huge increase of births gave an unexpected boost to all the industries which supply the multifarious needs of childhood. New jobs by the tens of thousands came into being. That was only a start. As we look ahead we see the inevitable consequences of this population growth in other areas of our economic life. It means a need for more food, more clothing, more furniture and equipment, more houses, more schools, more transportation — more of everything in order to supply this expanding capacity for consumption. As a result of this new and unprecedented condition there must of necessity be generated an intense and widespread economic activity. With it there will develop new opportunities everywhere for useful employment. It is good to be once more a nation of young people, with all the dynamism which that implies.

If we turn now from a consideration of purely temporal things and give our attention to the things that count most, the spiritual and religious, we find it less easy to interpret for our young people the signs of the future. Our uncertainty arises from the fact that there is no systematic program in our national life to provide for a continuation of the distinctly Christian culture and civilization which we have inherited from the past. Ordinarily it is the primary responsibility and function of an educational system to preserve the religious and spiritual traditions of a people. In this respect our great national system of public education has failed us. As we have shown in a previous chapter, it has become almost completely secular in its orientation, in its philosophy, and in its curriculum. One hundred years ago the most articulate and dynamic leaders in the field of education, with high motives but questionable results, determined to make schools and knowledge universal and free for all our citizens. In itself that purpose was good; but the method which was chosen leaves much to be desired. In divorcing the control and the direction of education from the care of the Church, and making it a state monopoly as far as public support is concerned, they opened the way to secularism. Religion and spiritual values could not in such a system be given an effective place in the curriculum. It was considered impossible to satisfy the conflicting interests of so great a diversity of religious denominations, and religion, therefore, was eliminated. Today there is a mounting concern among educators about the place of religion in the public schools; it is recognized more and more that religion has a definite and valid place in any comprehensive system. It is one thing, however, to recognize the need for religious instruction and quite another, under existing conditions, to devise a system which will be adequate and at the same time safeguard the rights of conscience and the demands of distributive justice. Four generations of children have grown up under the existing educational handicap, and today, in the fifth generation, we find unfortunately that a great number of our people are practically illiterate in the matter of religion. Under these conditions our Christian heritage is placed in jeopardy. This is a problem with which our young men and women, the future leaders of our society, must come to grips. Unless the problem is solved fairly and adequately, we face a steady deterioration in our Christian culture.

There are other serious problems which this generation must face and for which it must find a solution. In our international relations there is the question of what we shall do about the United Nations. How can we modify and improve both its structure and its function? Obviously it has not achieved any notable success in eliminating war and securing the peace. There have been, however, certain collateral benefits which should not be discounted. There are definite advantages in having a world forum for the expression of opinion, even though the results have been largely negative. At least we know where the leaders of the nations stand and can measure the strength of the opposition.

The Catholic Church, both by reason of her doctrine and by reason of her structure, is profoundly sympathetic to the idea of a world-society. We hold that all men are brothers, sharing a common destiny. In this world-society there must always be room for the expression and preservation of legitimate national interests and cultural values; but there are also common international problems, such as war and peace, problems of transportation, communication, health, scientific progress, education, and many others, wherein there exists a common interest and in regard to which we need an organized agency to initiate and direct our common efforts. Until we find something better, let us hold on to what we have and make a sustained effort to improve the functioning of the United Nations. In particular we should work to develop a structure of international law on sound juridical principles — not to supersede our own Constitution but to supplement it. Let us work, moreover, to strengthen the powers of the Assembly of the United Nations as against the war-inspired hegemony of the Security Council; and let us work to open the United Nations to all the nations without a veto power on the part of the Security Council concerning their admission. Here at home we have a problem in our national economic life which has been growing more acute over the past twenty years. It is the question of who shall exercise the dominating power in our industrial life. Shall it be business management? Shall it be organized labor?

Or shall it be government? Obviously, if the selfish interests of only one group or class is allowed to dominate the others, the common good inevitably suffers. To place the controlling power in the hands of either business, or labor, or government alone, will ultimately destroy our free economic system. We must be on guard, therefore, against the concentration of both political and economic power in the hands of any single group. There is no better solution to the problem than that which was advocated by Pope Pius XI in his celebrated encyclical on the social order. He advocates a combination of all three elements, business, labor, and government, all working together for the common good. The responsibility for this development of Industry Councils, both in regard to their structure and their function, rests with the young men of this generation.

There are other problems great and small, but these seem to be the most significant. Sometimes we hear it said that we should all be optimists, placing the brightest and most appealing interpretation on the prospects of the future. We disagree. That attitude smacks too much of Pollyanna and wishful thinking. We do not think that we should be optimists; nor by the same token do we think that we should be pessimists. Let us be realists, facing the facts with clear vision and proper courage, neither minimizing the difficulties nor exaggerating advantageous prospects.

The youth of this generation would do well to adopt as a guide of their actions an axiom which is ever ancient and ever new, the axiom of St. Augustine, who understood well the difference between uniformity and unity: "In sure things, unity; in doubtful things, liberty; in all things, charity."

XXXV

STUDENTS WHO ARE CRUSADERS

THERE exists between one American Catholic student and another a powerful bond of unity; a bond that transcends their common language and national traditions. For not only do they speak the same language and share the same national traditions, but they are the beneficiaries of a Catholic education and respond to the same ideals of the Catholic apostolate of youth. Over and above all other things that make them one is their common faith, their common purpose, and their common motivation. They are members of the Mystical Body of Christ, bound together not by ties of blood but by the much stronger and more enduring ties of supernatural affinity. They are sons of God, not by a mere figure of speech but by the adoption of grace through Jesus Christ our Lord.

The common purpose which should animate the minds and hearts of Catholic students is to build the kingdom of God, the new Jerusalem, not only here at home but throughout the world; not only for themselves but for God's children everywhere — no matter what their color, their race, or their language. They should try to envision what this world ought to be in the far-reaching plan of God: one human family, "one Lord, one faith, one Baptism, one God and Father of all." They should still hear the echo of Christ's words when He spoke to the apostles: " ... Make disciples of all nations. ... Preach the Gospel to every creature."

335

Catholic students know the meaning of those words. They spell salvation; they also spell happiness, contentment, culture, civilization for all mankind. They hold out the only hope for a release from the dark prison of ignorance, hate, strife, and war. They alone contain the promise of a real and lasting United Nations.

To accomplish this purpose, Catholic students have enlisted in a great crusade, the Catholic Students' Mission Crusade. They want to win back not only the Holy Land, made sacred by our Lord's footsteps, but the whole world for Christ. They want to see consecrated men and women in ever-increasing numbers carry the Gospel into the lands which are still alien to Christ's teaching. They want to stir a lively interest among all Catholic youth in achieving this project by earnest prayer and generous alms and even by personal dedication. For these things we salute them as crusaders in the cause of Christ.

We recognize that language, color, and race can be divisive influences in human relationships. We know well that there are differences in culture, traditions, and customs, all of which make for differences in outlook, preference, and judgment. But we also know that all men were created equal by God — equal in the sense that they were all made to the image and likeness of God, endowed with intelligence and free will, destined to a supernatural life by grace, and to the same everlasting union with God in the beatific vision. We know that Christ suffered and died for all men; that He wants all men to be saved. For this purpose He established a Church — one and the same for all men; one flock and one Shepherd. We know that He prayed for unity in His last discourse with the apostles on the night before He died. "Yet not for these only do I pray, but for those also who through their word are to believe in Me, that all may be one, even as Thou, Father, in Me and I in Thee; that they also may be one in Us, that the world may believe that Thou hast sent Me."

International unity, so much to be desired, can never be made effective by mere mechanical organization or by establishing a universal parliament, if it lacks decisive authority. There must be first a basic unity of principles, a sincerity of purpose, and mutual agreement concerning fundamental morality. Unless these postulates are recognized as imperative, there can be no genuine basis for unity. As long as the nations fail to accept at least as a minimum the sovereignty of God and the primacy of the moral law, there can be no unity of minds or purposes, and hence no united action in implementing a program of peace or in promoting the common good.

Our criticism is not directed against the concept of unity, nor is it one of disparagement of any and every human effort to achieve this unity; but rather it is a criticism of the ineptitude of a procedure which tries to reconcile what is by nature irreconcilable. It is more hopeful to sacrifice the concept of universality in the representation of the nations and choose instead the principle of consistency of purpose. Let those nations alone unite for common action which accept and abide by common principles. Anything else must end in frustration or serve the cause of specious propaganda.

True religion alone can supply the deficiencies in the current attempts to create unity in the human family, for it alone supplies a common denominator amid all the diversities of human nature. Until the whole world is converted to God's plan for unity, mere human efforts will remain for the most part sterile and abortive.

What is true in respect to international relations is even more true in respect to religion. In any attempt to achieve religious unity we must start with the concept that God Himself has willed that there be such unity among men. Unless God has decreed a definite plan for this purpose, it is futile for men to try to search for it, and even more absurd to try to invent one.

If there was no divinely established Church in the beginning, then there can be none now. But if, in fact, Christ did establish such a Church, then it never could have ceased to exist; for to assume that a divinely established Church had failed would be to charge God either with lack of wisdom to provide adequately for future needs, or — what is equally unthinkable — with lack of power to safeguard His Church from error or destruction. The point of the argument is that there is no possibility of unifying the Church by human compromise or by some form of mechanical organization. It was *always* one by divine decree, or it cannot be made one now. The only thing that can be done by sincere-minded men who are not yet members of the one flock is to go back to the beginning and find the Church as Christ established it.

We believe with the utmost conviction that there is such a divine plan. We believe that Christ established a Church, one, holy, universal, and apostolic; and we believe furthermore that Christ wants all men to be members of this Church which He founded. It is the sole instrument of salvation as it is of unity. He declared that this Church would be watched over by His Holy Spirit to keep it free from error; and that He Himself would remain with it even to the consummation of the world. This Church, therefore, must have existed from the beginning; it continues to exist now, for unless this be true, it could never come into existence by some human effort. The business of every honest mind is to find it and cling to it, and not try to invent some substitute for the divine plan.

Members of the Catholic Students' Mission Crusade understand these things, and therefore their program for world unity,
for world peace, for world progress, rests upon a solid and
indestructible foundation. They know that as the Gospel of
Christ is spread through the world by missionary effort, the
divine plan for unity of the human family, for world peace and
order, is being constantly advanced. They are helping to build
the kingdom of God here on earth and are thus promoting the
common good of the whole human race.

Pius XII, the incomparable leader of the Mission Crusade,
summarized the situation which we face today in a brief but
trenchant sentence. He declared in his encyclical *Heralds of
the Gospel* (*Evangelii Praecones*): "The human race is involved
today in a supreme crisis which will issue in its salvation by
Christ or in its dire destruction."

Certain periods of history are revolutionary in character.
Spiritual attitudes and ideas, as well as political, social, and
economic conditions, then undergo transformation. Our own
particular period of history reflects such a condition. The times
are out of joint. Much suffering and many evils are associated
with these periods of violent transition. Nevertheless there can
be fresh opportunity to preach the Gospel to minds and hearts
set free from previous bonds of prejudice. New methods may
have to be adopted. A new approach may have to be used to
create a favorable hearing. We can call it missiology or anything else; but nothing can ever be substituted for the primary
objective, which is spiritual and supernatural. "Seek ye first,"
says our Lord, "the kingdom of God and His justice; and all
these things shall be added unto you."

Counting only the years since 1940, this generation has witnessed a mighty social upheaval. Germany and Japan were
devastated in war and their empires destroyed. Russia, by con-

trast, has advanced its frontiers by force and conspiracy, and has become a gigantic threat to peace and security. China, the largest nation in the world, has lost its independence and has become a satellite of Moscow imperialism. India, the second largest nation in the world, has gained its independence but has suffered a serious split of personality. Pakistan and Congress India are rent asunder. The Dutch colonial empire has broken up. Great Britain and France have ceased to exercise the hegemony in Continental Europe and have suffered serious loss of face in other parts of the world. The Middle East is in turmoil. And brooding over all these changes is the menace of atheistic Communism.

The most frightening event in this period, perhaps, has been the conquest of China by the Communist revolutionaries. No one can estimate the fearful consequences which may ensue. If, during the past one hundred years, more attention had been given to the conversion of China, there might have been a sufficient basis of Christian truth on which to rear a bulwark of defense. There would have been, no doubt, Catholic leaders in education, industry, and public life who would have corrected the evils of excessive poverty on the one hand and special privilege on the other. The fact that China offered little resistance to the advance of Communistic theory and practice was due to the spiritual vacuum which existed, and in large measure to the past spiritual inertia of the Christian peoples of the West. It was due in part also to a popular misconception of what constitutes a true missionary program.

The missionary objective of the Church is not a glorified program of social welfare. It is not merely a movement to redress the grievances of underprivileged nations. Its chief purpose is not to feed the hungry, clothe the naked, nurse the sick. Our purpose is not the advancement of democracy, nor the emancipation of backward peoples. These are the inevitable and invaluable by-products of Christian truth and practice. They are not its essence. It is the spiritual salvation of the world at which the Mission movement aims. The first and most imperious demand on our efforts and attention is to make known the revelation which Christ brought to earth.

When our Blessed Saviour gathered the apostles around Him for the last time, He stretched His hands over them in blessing and said: "Go, ... and make disciples of all nations, ... teaching them to observe all that I have commanded you." This is the mission of the Church. No other task can take precedence over it. We must "preach Christ and Him crucified." There is no salvation under heaven in any other name. So St. Peter declared in the beginning of the apostolate, and so it is today.

We understand very well and we cherish the achievements of missionary effort as expressed in terms of civilization, culture, and social betterment.

All too often even Christian men and women put too narrow a construction on the words of Christ: "Go into the whole world and preach the Gospel to every creature." They interpret the command of Christ as an exclusive direction to the clergy. Pius XI, however, emphasizes the universality of the application. The laity have a work to do. It is not merely to furnish alms to support the efforts of the missionaries, not merely to pray for vocations, but to aid the work of the missions by active participation.

The mission countries need teachers, doctors, nurses, social workers, and experts in agronomy, economics, and other allied fields. Point IV in the program of the United Nations needs a spiritual interpretation and motivation. It needs to be implemented by supernatural means. This above all is the work of the laity. Let us commend this phase of the work to the Catholic Students' Mission Crusade.

Pioneer work has already been done. Witness the program of the Grail Movement. There has gone out from Grailville, in the Archdiocese of Cincinnati, a missionary team of professional nurses — laywomen who are dedicating themselves for a period of three years to the cause of the missions. Let us quote for you the words of our late Holy Father Pius XII, taken from his encyclical *Heralds of the Gospel* (*Evangelii Praecones*): "Likewise all know that the Gospel followed the great Roman roads and was spread not only by Bishops and priests but also by public officials, soldiers, and private citizens. Thousands of Christian neophytes, whose names are today unknown, were fired with zeal for promoting the new religion they had embraced, and endeavored to prepare the way for the coming of the Gospel. That explains why after about a hundred years Christianity had penetrated into all the chief cities of the Roman empire."

The whole world is our missionary field. We cannot be partisan in our choice of territory, preferring one country to another, nor selective in respect to the particular Religious communities which are entrusted with the work. But when this has been said, we cannot overlook the fact that an individual community, an individual agency or movement, cannot spread its interest effectively over the whole world; it can, therefore, very properly take a major interest in some specialized area. We recommend to you, then, a special interest in the mission countries of the Western world. Let that be the subject of intensive study.

The Catholic Students' Mission Crusade, organized by Catholic youth some two-score years ago, is dedicated to the threefold objective of prayer for the missions, study of the mission problems of the Church, and personal sacrifice for the missions both at home and abroad. The Crusade never has placed and never will place in contrary or contradictory positions the missionary Church at home or abroad, for to do so would be contrary to our teaching of unity in the Mystical Body of Christ.

In 1925, the constitution and organization of the Catholic Students' Mission Crusade was approved by Pope Pius XI. The Crusade is, therefore, a pontifically approved society with specialization in the field of mission education. As a national organization, the Crusade does not itself collect money for the missions (other than a nominal amount — by way of dues — to maintain the national office). Not one penny of the students' sacrifices for the missions reaches Crusade Castle, the national headquarters. By the Constitution, each unit is autonomous, and the Crusade urges the units to make their contributions of sacrifice to the Pontifical Society for the Propagation of the Faith; and, in the case of elementary school children, to the Pontifical Association of the Holy Childhood.

The purpose of the missions, according to the mind of the Church, is to plant the faith, to nourish the young Church in her infancy to the point of maturity, which is reached when native sons and daughters replace the missionary, so that he can go to new lands to renew the process of the conversion of the world. The Church is a living, vital organism, dynamic and purposeful in her objective. The Church is Christ in the twentieth century, gathering the children of men and making them sons of God. In carrying out her divine purpose, she meets her enemies, who breathe forth hatred for her. Millions of Catholics in other parts of the world are proving their loyalty to Jesus Christ and His teachings in the face of persecution and death. The Catholic Church has remained erect amid the ruins of every form of civilization, struggling for the preservation of human and divine values. Even when cruelly attacked with every type of weapon from false propaganda to violent persecution, she struggles on for the preservation of human freedom and divine truths. Snares are set for young people and even for small children. Prisons close their doors on her laity, her sisters and priests, her Bishops. But she remains strong in the conviction that her eternal values cannot perish. She is confident in the promises of her divine Founder, always convinced that though her martyrs may be struck down by the lightning bolts of persecution, the storm will pass, and the sun of justice and truth will return in splendor. She hears the words of her divine Founder: "I am with you all days, even unto the consummation of the world."

Part VII

MAN IN HIS RELIGIOUS

AND DEVOTIONAL LIFE

"The Christian religion is not merely a code of conduct which we must follow, a mode of worship which we must practice, a creed which we must believe; it is far more than that. It is a series of profound mysteries illuminating the relationship between God and man."

XXXVI

THE PERSON OF CHRIST

I

In His Birth and Life

TO SINGLE out any one event in the life of Christ, any one aspect of His existence, any one statement which He made, and to attempt to hang thereon a discussion of His divinity is to rob the argument of its full force and cogency. We must take Christ's life in its entirety from Bethlehem to Calvary; from the resurrection to His glorious ascension. Never was there a story such as this; it is utterly unlike anything else which has appeared in history. This is not legend or hearsay. It is a record of events witnessed by Christ's contemporaries and vouched for in authentic documents. With the shedding of their blood, His followers bore testimony to the fact of His life and the truth of His teachings.

If we compare all the prophecies of ancient times with the facts of Christ's life; if we consider the miracles wrought by Him, the sublime beauty of His doctrine, the sinless purity of His life, and the testimony which He gave of Himself, there is no other conclusion possible but that He was indeed the Son of God, the Messias, the Christ anointed with divinity. No other explanation makes sense or harmonizes the facts into a coherent whole.

Christ was indeed God, but He was also man. Because He had two natures He could, in His own Person, bridge the

347

gap between heaven and earth. Because Christ was human, a brother of ours in the flesh, He could make atonement for our sin; because He was divine, the merit of His sacrifice was more than equal to the penalty incurred by the sin of His human brethren. When we contemplate this mystery, we cry out in breathless admiration as did St. Paul: "Oh, the depth of the riches of the wisdom and of the knowledge of God! How incomprehensible are His judgments and how unsearchable His ways!"

The mission of Christ on earth was one of peace and reconciliation. He came to restore what had been lost; He came to renew the offer of that supernatural life which had been forfeited. "I came that they may have life, and have it more abundantly." It is of this life that St. John speaks when he says: "He came unto His own, and His own received Him not. But to as many as received Him He gave the power of becoming sons of God; to those who believe in His name: who were born not of blood, nor of the will of the flesh, nor of the will of man, but of God." It is not the life of the body nor the life of the mind, but the supernatural life of sanctifying grace of which the evangelist speaks. Unless we understand this exalted truth, we do not understand the Incarnation.

We who have the faith understand well the original plan of God for the salvation of mankind. We know that man in the morning of creation was destined, not for suffering and death, but for happiness and immortality. We know that the fulfillment of this original plan of God was conditioned on man's free acceptance of the divine will; we know also that the plan of God was frustrated by the overreaching ambition and prideful disobedience of our first parents. St. Paul tells us that through the disobedience of "one man sin entered into the world and through sin death, and thus death passed unto all men because all have sinned." The present world with its mystery of pain, defeat, and death is an insoluble riddle to the unbeliever and the agnostic. We who know the message of divine revelation have an adequate explanation of the miseries and contradictions of the present life. Others may sink into blind despair or be forced into indifference; we of the faith have grounds for an uplifting hope.

Recall the prophecies of ancient times. It was foretold that there would come a Redeemer who would set things right. He would break down the wall of separation between heaven and earth; He would put an end to the unnatural estrangement between God and man; He would blot out the indictment of guilt which stood against us; He would restore our inheritance as children of the heavenly Father.

When our first parents fell into sin, God in His mercy promised a Redeemer. This promise was kept alive through all succeeding generations. The prophets foretold not only the time but the place; not only the tribe but the family in which the Messias was to be born. Isaias, seven centuries before the event, proclaimed the startling fact that a virgin would conceive and bring forth a son whose name would be Emmanuel, which means "God with us." He was to be of the race of Abraham, of the tribe of Juda, and the family of David. His birth was to take place in Bethlehem, as all Jerusalem knew. This was the word given subsequently to the Magi, indicating the official interpretation held by the rulers of the temple: "And thou, Bethlehem, of the land of Juda, art by no means least among the princes of Juda; for from thee shall come forth a Leader who shall rule My people Israel."

When, therefore, the fullness of time had come, God sent His angel to the Blessed Virgin Mary to announce that the Holy Spirit would overshadow her and that He who was to be born of her would be the Holy One of God, the Son of the Most High: "And the Lord God," said the angel, "will give Him the throne of David His Father, and He shall be king over the house of Jacob forever; and of His kingdom there shall be no end."

We of the faith believe that the Infant born of Mary, wrapped in swaddling clothes, and laid in the manger is truly the Messias — the Christ, the Son of the living God, foretold by the prophets through the ages. We know very well how stupendous a thing this is that we declare. We know that the Incarnation, the union of God and man in one person, surpasses the most exaggerated flights of fancy of pagan antiquity. We know that it meets with incredulity from some today just as much as in the past. We ourselves are not credulous; we do not oversimplify the problem; we are not unacquainted with the difficulties which this mystery imposes. For four centuries the Christian world itself wrestled with this problem.

If God Himself had not vouched for it, what mortal man would dare to conceive such a manifestation of divine love as is revealed in the mystery of the Incarnation? We can easily understand the attitude of the skeptic or the unbeliever. We admit that it does indeed require a tremendous act of faith on our part to believe that the infinite God — God who put the stars in the firmament, who calls forth the myriad forms of life, from the simple cell of the amoeba to the complex organism of man; God who rules the world with unending wisdom and power and is sufficient to Himself in all things — that He would stoop to our lowliness and clothe Himself with human flesh. When confronted with such a seeming contradiction between the finite and the infinite, the human mind rightly demands some incontestable proof.

And where are we to find this evidence, and what is its nature? To be sure, it is not some form of empirical demonstration or proof, such as might be discovered in a science laboratory. Rather, it is proof of that kind which is required to establish a historical fact. It is evidence in the juridical or moral order, such as might be found valid in any court of law. It is the testimony of the prophets, who, as we have stated, foretold the event with a precision which named the time, the place, the tribe, the family, and the circumstances and did so hundreds of years before the angel made his announcement to the Blessed Virgin Mary.

When Christ did come into the world, He left no doubt that the prophecies were verified in His own Person. He made good His word by the miraculous works He wrought, the superhuman example He set, and the sublimity of the doctrine He preached. There was no doubt in the minds of His apostles as to Christ's identity. St. Peter, St. John, St. Matthew, St. Paul — all knew Him for what He was: the Son of the living God. The four Gospels, the Acts of the Apostles, and the letters of St. Paul are unanimous in their direct and indirect testimony to the fact that He was the Messias, the Saviour, the divine King of kings and Lord of lords.

There was no doubt in the mind of the early Christian Church concerning His nature and personality. Again and again, whenever the mystery of the Incarnation came up for discussion, the overwhelming voice of the Church was heard proclaiming that Christ was the only-begotten Son of the Father. From Nicaea, where the first Council of the Church was held, down to this very day, the words re-echo in the Credo of the Mass: "Deum de Deo, lumen de lumine, Deum verum de Deo vero — God of God, Light of light, true God of true God." When skeptics in the early centuries questioned Christ's real humanity, the answer was the solemn proclamation: "Et incarnatus est" — Christ is truly man just as He is truly God — one person, two natures, a divine mind and a human mind, a divine will and a human will. Gnostics, Arians, Nestorians, Monophysites, and Monothelites are the ancient heretics who tampered with this truth and left only their names on the pages of history. The Incarnation in an ineffable mystery and no human mind will ever fathom its depth. But the fact itself is clear and unmistakable.

Each year at Christmas we recall with wonderment and awe the historical events of Bethlehem. We do more than that. We relive the sacred mystery and we share once more in the fruits of the divine mission of Christ. The Mass we celebrate is the sequel of the Incarnation. Christ who is present on our altars is the same Christ who lay on the straw in the stable of Bethlehem.

The spirit of Christmas is revealed in a multitude of popular traditions and sacred memories long since crystallized into song and story; but the most authentic expression of the Christmas spirit will be found in the liturgy of the Church. On this day each priest is permitted, by way of exception, to celebrate Holy Mass three times: once in memory of the first coming of Christ as the Infant Saviour in the crib of Bethlehem; once in thanksgiving for the rebirth of supernatural life in our souls through divine grace; and once in premonition of the glorious second coming of Christ in the day of judgment.

In earlier times, it was the practice at Rome for the entire papal court to observe the great festive days of the Church by marching solemnly in procession from the Lateran Palace to some particular church where Pontifical Mass would be celebrated. These special churches were called the Roman Stations. Their names are incorporated in the titles of the

Masses on great feasts and are still found in our present-day missals.

On Christmas, the church designated for the Pope's midnight Mass was that of St. Mary Major, the most celebrated church of Our Lady in Rome. It was chosen for this purpose not only because it was fitting so to honor the mother of the Infant Saviour on the anniversary of His birth, but more particularly because the reputed crib in which Christ was born was preserved there since the days of the seventh century.

In the liturgy of the midnight Mass, the Church directs that we read the Gospel of St. Luke, in which we find the simple and unadorned story of the events which took place at Bethlehem. Because the event is one of such tremendous historical significance, St. Luke establishes for the record the exact time, place, and circumstances of our Lord's birth. The great mystery of the Incarnation is revealed to us by the evangelist in an almost prosaic narrative, with no more excitement than would accompany the recording of an ordinary birth. It is, however, this very simplicity of statement which makes the recital of the events so extraordinary and which creates immediately a persuasion in favor of their authenticity.

The second Pontifical Mass in Rome on Christmas day was celebrated, according to ancient tradition, in the church which bore the name of St. Anastasia. This church belonged to the Greek-speaking people in Rome, and was frequented by the Byzantine officials who were members of the imperial court. The Popes wished to honor this particular group because of the important contribution made by the Greek-speaking people to the early history of the Church. At the same time, this gesture of good will signalized the universality of the Church, whose membership includes both Jew and Gentile, Greek and Scythian, learned and unlearned. We in this day are apt to forget that the Church had first taken root in the Hellenic areas of the Mediterranean world. The New Testament was originally written, for the most part, in Greek; and the first eight General Councils of the Church were held in Eastern cities where the Greek culture predominated. There is an ancient tradition, moreover, that this particular Roman church — that of St. Anastasia — was sacred to the memory of the resurrection; hence the purpose in choosing it may well have been the desire to contrast the simplicity and poverty of Bethlehem with the final triumph and glory of Easter morning.

This second Mass at the Church of St. Anastasia was celebrated ordinarily at dawn and was known as the Shepherds' Mass. In the Gospel which the Church appoints to be read, the story of Bethlehem is continued, but with the same calm and matter-of-fact treatment. There is no straining after effect, even when St. Luke describes the apparition of the angels before the bewildered eyes of the shepherds. There is as yet no interpretation of the meaning of this stupendous mystery and no attempt to impress his readers with this extraordinary revelation of God's goodness and mercy.

The third Mass of Christmas day was celebrated for a time in the great Basilica of St. Peter, but because the distance between it and the Lateran Palace was too great for convenient access, a change was made and the Pope returned for the climax of the Christmas feast to the Church of St. Mary Major. In this third Mass, the keynote of the celebration is found in the opening chapter of St. John's Gospel. In view of the fact that the Gospel of St. Luke had established, in the first two Masses, the historical record of events, now the Church in her liturgy leaves behind the incidental details of Christ's birth and soars aloft to the empyrean. The words of St. John constitute no doubt the most sublime statement of the mystery of the Incarnation to be found in the whole of Sacred Scripture. "In the beginning was the Word, and the Word was with God; and the Word was God. . . . In Him was life, and the life was the light of men. And the light shines in the darkness; and the darkness grasped it not. . . . He came unto His own, and His own received Him not. But to as many as received Him He gave the power of becoming sons of God; to those who believe in His name: . . . And we saw His glory — glory as of the only-begotten of the Father — full of grace and of truth."

The vivid contrast between the elaborate ritual enacted by the Church in her Christmas liturgy and the primitive simplicity which surrounded the manger bed of the Christ Child has evoked much comment. In our churches at Christmas, our hearts are stirred by the sound of trumpets and the majestic roll of the organ. In far-off Bethlehem there was only the quiet rustling of the wind in the stable loft and the stamping of the cattle in the straw. We have a pageantry of glowing color, of solemn music, and stately movement; on the distant hillside of Judea there were only the dim shadows, silence, and passive contemplation.

The contrast is indeed obvious, so obvious that some uninspired persons are ready to call it a contradiction or anomaly. They think that we invest our celebration with too much splendor in contrast to the simplicity of the first Christmas. They forget that the full story of Bethlehem has not been told when they leave Mary and Joseph bending over the crib of the Infant Saviour in the company of dumb beasts. They forget the mighty chant of the angels' choir thrilling in the skies; they forget the awe-stricken shepherds, rushing headlong to behold the mystery in the crib; they forget the wondrous star, divinely appointed, to guide the Wise Men from the East; they forget the gifts of gold, frankincense, and myrrh. They forget that this Child, wrapped in swaddling clothes, is God as well as man.

We are first of all mindful of the dignity and majesty of the divine Guest whom we entertain. We desire to emulate the angelic host who gave their royal salute to the newborn King with rapturous song. "Glory to God in the highest" was the burden of their chant. There is nothing too good, too lavish, or too splendid to express the joy, the gratitude, and the loving adoration which we feel in the depths of our hearts. We are mindful too of the fact that this newborn Child is man as well as God. He is human, as we are human. He came to share our lowliness, our helplessness, and our sorrow. He clothed Himself, therefore, with all the weakness of human nature — save sin — in order to set us an example of encouragement and resignation. What, then, could be more fitting than that He, being God, should trample underfoot our perishable grandeur? As St. Paul says, He "emptied Himself, taking the nature of a slave and being made like unto men." He had no need of earthly glory because He possessed glory in its essence as the second Person of the Trinity; He had no need of ceremonies or pageantry — but we do. We need to use these earthly things as means of proclaiming effectively the birthday of the King of kings and Lord of lords.

If we want to understand the real meaning of Christmas, we must look behind the tinseled façade which has been erected by commercial enterprise and see beyond the mere humanitarian sentiment which is popularly associated with this great festival. We must not forget that the warm and human sentiment which pours itself out in an all-embracing kindliness at this season of the year is nothing more than a corollary or by-product of the profound mystery of the Incarnation.

What meaning does the mystery of Bethlehem hold for us today? The answer can still be found in the message which the angels brought from heaven. That message contains a directive as well as a promise. The directive or divine mandate is addressed to all mankind, reminding us that our first duty as creatures is to recognize our Creator by giving Him glory, honor, love, and obedience.

The message of the angels contains not only an injunction but also a promise; it is a conditional promise, however. The promise is one of peace, but peace only to men of good will. The peace of which the angels sang is not merely the cessation of war and conflict between the nations here on earth, but rather that tranquillity of mind and soul which comes from a right order between heaven and earth. As long as sin intervened in our relationship with God, there could be no real peace. For this reason the meaning of the Incarnation consists, above everything else, in the re-establishment of a right order or a bond of union between the creature and the Creator.

The Incarnation means even more than that; it means that the human race was to have a new start, a new lease on life. We must sublimate our vision of man and his destiny before we can fully understand the import of Christ's advent into human history. It is a glorious vision which is held out to us. It is nothing less than the creation of a new humanity. It is the establishment of a new order of being, wherein the vital principle is spiritual and supernatural. Christ often speaks of this new society as the kingdom of God here on earth. He Himself is the Head of this kingdom, sharing our humanity but infusing into it a share of His own divinity. St. Paul says: "But God, who is rich in mercy, by reason of His very great love wherewith He has loved us even when we were dead by reason of our sins, brought us to life together with Christ (by grace you have been saved), and raised us up together, and seated us together in heaven in Christ Jesus, that He might show in the ages to come the overflowing riches of His grace in kindness toward us in Christ Jesus." This is a sublime concept as St. Paul expounds it in his eloquent letter to the Ephesians.

If, however, this concept is too exalted for the uninitiated to grasp, there are other meanings which even the average man can understand. He can understand the importance of that spirit of humility which is exemplified in the stable of Bethlehem and which offers such a sharp contrast to the overweening pride of man. Pride is the sin by which the angels fell. Pride is the besetting sin of the world in all its tragic history. Pride is the sin most repugnant to God. It may be pride of intellect, which rejects the simple truths of faith; it may be pride of achievement and self-sufficiency, which usurps the honor due to God; it may be the pride of wealth and power, which treats with contempt the weak and poor, or refuses to exercise a proper stewardship of God's gifts to men. "Blessed are the poor in spirit" is the first beatitude mentioned in the Sermon on the Mount. It is also the first lesson we learn at the crib of the Christ Child.

Good will among men is the inescapable condition of peace. It may not be in our power now to organize peace among the nations, for peace is the fruit of justice, and the will to achieve justice is not yet apparent among our adversaries. But this much we know — that only the spirit of Christ, the Prince of Peace, will furnish a sure foundation for that tranquillity of order which spells genuine peace. For this we can pray; for this we can work; for this we can meet in international conference, ready to make concessions so long as the principles of justice, the rights of God, and the responsibility to honor our pledged word are safeguarded. In these momentous times we can give our cordial support to every reasonable international effort to reduce tensions and prepare the way for peace. We can incorporate the spirit of Christ into our own lives, schooling ourselves, as the Scriptures say, "to forgo irreverent thoughts and worldly appetites, and to live in the present world a life of order, of justice, and of holiness."

II

IN HIS DEATH AND RESURRECTION

In the springtime of each year we witness a recurring mystery. From the grave of winter, nature stages an annual resurrection. The bountiful harvests of fruit and grain which fill our granaries each autumn are mysteriously pregnant in the tiny seeds which lie dormant in the bosom of winter. The stalk of wheat growing in the fields becomes bread upon our tables. The bread which we eat becomes flesh and blood in a mysterious process which we can name, but which no man fully comprehends. Light and air, time and space, motion and inertia are phenomena which we can describe but never fully understand. All these things are mysteries but they cause no wonderment because they are of regular and frequent occurrence. The phenomena which excite our interest and arouse our curiosity are not those which are marvelous in themselves, but rather those that are of rare occurrence or which interrupt the ordinary course of nature.

Religion has always been correlated with mystery. Without mystery, religion would never rise above that which is merely human. Since religion is both a revelation of God and an interpretation of life, it must of necessity contain mystery.

Mystery is not an escape from reality. It is a recognition of the fact that God in His essence must forever remain incomprehensible to any finite intelligence. If this were not true, God's wisdom and power would be no higher and no greater than those of man. Such an assumption would empty the divine revelation of its meaning and would reduce religion to mere humanism. It would clip the wings of the spirit and stop short the flight of the soul toward a vision of heavenly things.

The Christian religion is not merely a code of conduct which we must follow, a mode of worship which we must practice, a creed which we must believe; it is far more than that. It is a series of profound mysteries illuminating the relationship between God and man. The resurrection of Christ, in the mind of the Church, is the highest mystery of our holy religion. It is the climax of Christ's life, the sublime summation of the Gospel.

If Christ had not risen from the dead, His mission on earth would have been declared a failure. If the stark reality of His death had not been followed by the startling fact of His resurrection, there would have been no authentic proof of His divine mission and no future for the Christian Church. His enemies would have pointed to His shameful death on the cross as proof of the fact that He could not make good His promise. Men of succeeding generations might have given Him credit for good intentions; they might have paid Him a tribute of admiration for His sublime doctrine, but they would have said that ultimately it lacked the seal and sanction of divine approval. The resurrection is the vindication of Christ's promise and the irrefutable evidence of His claim to divinity. It is the testimony of heaven itself. St. Paul refers to this sign of approval when he says: "Christ ... emptied Himself, taking the nature of a slave and being made like unto men. And appearing in the form of man, He humbled Himself, becoming obedient to death, even to death on a cross. Therefore God also has exalted Him and has bestowed upon Him the name that is above every name, so that at the name of Jesus every knee should bend of those in heaven, on earth and under the earth."

The resurrection of Christ is indeed primarily a historical fact. If it were not an indubitable fact, it would have no significance. Christ made sure that the fact itself would stand out with compelling conviction. He appeared under such diverse circumstances, in so many different places, to so many varied individuals and groups, that there can be no uncertainty concerning the fact that He was risen from the grave. The proofs recorded in the Scriptures — spread out over forty days during which He appeared repeatedly to the apostles, to Mary Magdalene, to Thomas, to the five hundred — are overwhelming evidence that He was alive and glorified after His death on Calvary. But the resurrection is more than a historical fact. The resurrection is both the fulfillment of prophecy and a manifestation of divine power. As such it marks the triumph of Christ. To speak of the resurrection as both a fact and as a mystery may seem to involve a confusion of mind or at least a confusion in the use of words. Such is not the case. The resurrection is the great climax of that drama which began at Bethlehem and ended, not on Calvary but at the ascension of the glorified Christ.

To understand the significance of the resurrection, we must read not only the Gospel record, but must also familiarize ourselves with the ancient prophecies and the historical prefigurations which foretold the future and find fulfillment in the events of Holy Week. Easter is the Christian "Passover." As the Israelites were saved by the blood of the lamb and delivered from the bondage of Egypt, so Christians are delivered from the bondage of sin and saved by the blood of the Lamb of the New Testament, shed on the altar of the cross. As the Israelites were fed by the heavenly manna in the desert, so the followers of Christ are fed by the Manna of the New Testament. "I am the living bread that has come down from heaven," says our Lord; "If anyone eat of this bread he shall live forever. . . . He who eats My flesh and drinks My blood has life everlasting and I will raise him up on the last day." We recall how the night before He died Christ took bread into His sacred and venerable hands and said: "Take and eat; this is My Body." This action was intimately associated with the events which were to follow the next day on Calvary. For our Lord continued: "This is My Body, which is being given for you, . . . and My Blood of the New Covenant, which is being shed for many unto the forgiveness of sins." This was a new sacrament, instituted to commemorate forever His death upon the cross, and also His triumph in the resurrection.

No wonder that Christ, from the very first day of His resurrection, repeated this significant action of the Last Supper; for the Scriptures tell us that the two disciples on the way to Emmaus recognized Him in the "breaking of the bread." We too, as members of this same household of the faith, still recognize Christ in the "breaking of the bread."

In recent years, there have been some who think they have discovered an explanation of the Christian celebration of Easter in the survival of some pagan spring festival marking the resurgence of nature into new life. Such an interpretation would empty the feast of its sublime significance. The elemental truth is that Christ, who was certainly dead on the cross, has, by His own power, surely risen from the grave. This is the supreme truth which constitutes the very substance of the feast of Easter. The day of Christ's resurrection is historical in fact or it is nothing. It has indeed an overwhelming spiritual meaning; but it treats of fact, not fancy.

One of the worst errors that has ever afflicted mankind is the theory that man is self-sufficient in the attainment of happiness or in the achievement of his own perfection. The assumption that man, by the exercise merely of his own intelligence and will power, can achieve uninterrupted progress toward the good life is as deceptive in theory as it is false in fact. Witness the misery of the present world with its wars and savage brutality in spite of unparalleled scientific advancement; witness the futility, in large part, of the elaborate political and social organization for world peace and order. The fact is that man suffered a disastrous defeat in his search for happiness at the very beginning of human history. The bitter consequences of this defeat have plagued mankind ever since. The whole concept of the Redemption rests on this primordial fact. Man suffered an original fall from grace through his own self-seeking. Man had to be restored to his original status of immortality and friendship with God through the direct intervention of God Himself. The mysteries of the Incarnation, the Redemption, and the Resurrection constitute an essential part in our understanding of human history. These truths are the premises on which we form a correct understanding of the world in which we live. They are truths grounded in religious faith.

The spiritual climate of the past one hundred years has not been favorable to a belief in the supernatural. The extraordinary advance of the physical sciences has created in the minds of many people the rash supposition that man no longer stands in need of religion. Immature theories of evolution, pseudo-scientific criticism of the Bible, and a crassly materialistic approach to the subject of anthropology have succeeded in creating an atmosphere of skepticism and secularism. All the phenomena of the world, so it was thought, admit of a purely natural explanation, independent of God and His revelation.

The intellectual leadership of the world, in consequence, passed from the care and protection of the Church to the control and direction of secular-minded scholars, scientists, and statesmen. Faith itself, as a rational expression of man's relationship to God, became progressively weakened and religion almost disappeared as a vital force in our civilization. Conditions, however, have changed recently, and there is now a new respect for and appreciation of the value of religion. The disastrous experience of mankind since the beginning of this present century has convinced it once more that science alone is insufficient; that we need superhuman ideals, fortified and impregnated with divine truth and grace, before we can cope with man's innate tendencies to evil.

From the earliest apostolic times, the resurrection was regarded as the cornerstone of the Christian faith. Whether it was St. Peter addressing his first congregation on Pentecost day or whether it was St. Paul preaching to the sophisticated Athenians on the Areopagus, it was the fact of Christ's resurrection which formed the central theme of their discourses. "If Christ has not risen," writes St. Paul to the Church of Corinth, "vain then is our preaching, vain too is your faith." There is no rational and coherent explanation of the empty tomb on Easter except the realistic one that God manifested His power in the resurrection of His divine Son. Self-deception, collusion, hysteria — all abortive attempts to explain away the mystery — are utterly lacking in consistency and openly contradict the manifest record of eyewitnesses.

"Without faith," say the Scriptures, "it is impossible to please God." St. Paul, writing to the Romans, emphasizes the fact that "he who is just lives by faith." The very first requisite for a right relationship with God is the belief that He exists and that He sent His divine Son into this world to save us from sin and to restore us to supernatural life.

Faith is not merely an act of the mind, but an act of the will also. Because it is a virtue and not a scientific demonstration, it requires docility of mind and a ready submission of the will. Ordinarily when we speak of faith, we have in mind the divine virtue of faith. There is also a human faith that rests on authoritative testimony. It is a source of knowledge just as legitimate as scientific demonstration. All that is required for credibility is that the witness be trustworthy and endowed with integrity of character as well as sureness of knowledge. If he has these qualifications, we believe his testimony. It is testimony of this type that is recognized in every court of justice. Now, while divine faith differs from scientific knowledge, it is by no means to be confused with mere sentiment. It is not a leap in the dark. It has its own rules of evidence — namely, miracles and prophecy, sublimity of doctrine and purity of life; all taken together to produce a cumulative argument. Science rests upon empirical evidence; faith rests upon the credibility of witnesses who know what they are talking about and whose veracity is a guarantee of their statements. Just as it is rational to believe the evidence of our senses, so also it is reasonable to believe the testimony of witnesses. Without human faith there could be no knowledge of human history; and without divine faith there can be no adequate knowledge of the things of God.

Faith without works is dead. Unless faith is impregnated with the spirit of divine charity it will profit us nothing. "The devils also believe and tremble"; they do not believe and love, and so their faith is futile. Faith genuine and sincere will inevitably lead men to the performance of good works. Faith must be associated, by its very nature, not only with the love of God, but with love of our neighbor. The two are inseparable, as St. James and St. John tell us. For a man to say that he loves God, whom he cannot see, and, at the same time, hate his neighbor, constitutes a glaring contradiction. It was religious faith which down the centuries created not only the visible monuments of our civilization, but its inner spirit and driving force. It is the chief factor in producing the intellectual, political, and social progress of the Christian world.

Easter, like all other feasts of the Church, has its characteristic note. It is a day of triumph and victory for the Christian, because it marks the end of the long estrangement which existed between God and man. St. Paul states that Christ, by His sacrifice, broke down the wall of partition which stood between heaven and earth, and blotted out the handwriting of the decree of guilt which stood against us, making peace in His own Blood on the cross. The desire for peace is uppermost in the minds and hearts of men everywhere and at all times; at least as the ultimate objective. War and strife are suffered only as a means to peace. Peace is the tranquillity of order; and order is the result of a right relationship between the elements of any society. There must be right order, however, between God and men before there can be right order here on earth. Today we are searching desperately for order and peace in the world, but we shall find it only if we follow God's will rather than our own. Peace will come when men keep the commandments, not only as individuals but as nations. The same law which binds the conscience of the individual must bind the conscience of the nation, if there is to be order.

Peace will come only when we substitute love for hatred, truth for deceit and hypocrisy, and justice for expediency and self-seeking.

XXXVII

THROUGH MARY WE COME TO CHRIST

THE Christian attitude toward womanhood is a subject of particular interest. Prior to the advent of Christianity, both the legal and the social status of woman was one of inferiority and definite subordination to man. This was true not only in respect to the place which a woman occupied in the family circle, but also as regards property rights, the rights of her children, and her rights within the marriage bond.

From the very beginning, Christianity gave woman an equal place at the side of man. While recognizing the father and husband as head of the family, the Church, following her divine Master, taught that woman was equal to man in creation, in redemption, in her final destiny, and in other rights and prerogatives. In the words of St. Paul, husbands were to love their wives even as Christ loved the Church and delivered Himself up for it. Men were taught to reverence, respect, and cherish their wives even as their own bodies. No longer could woman be treated as a chattel as in pagan antiquity or dismissed at the will of her husband. The marriage bond was as sacred and compelling to the one as to the other.

When we call up before our mind a picture of the ideal woman presented in the pages of Sacred Scripture and in Christian teaching, we think of one endowed with gentleness, with modesty, with purity of soul and body; we think of one possessing loyalty and devotion, truth and righteousness; we think of one having a spirit of self-sacrifice and a heart overflowing with charity toward God and man. To find such a woman may be difficult, for we know and understand the limitations of weak human nature. In His providence, however, God raised up for us an exemplar of womanly virtue in the person of the Blessed Virgin Mary. To her whom He had chosen to be His Mother because of her exalted virtue, He sent His angel with the salutation: "Hail, full of grace, the Lord is with thee. Blessed art thou among women."

In ancient times the ideal of womanhood was one of physical charm; in Christian times, the true ideal of womanhood is one of spiritual beauty. In ancient times, artists worked with brush and chisel attempting to portray their ideal of woman in the classical statues of Venus and Athena, clothing them with beauty of form and grace of movement. In Christian times, artists work rather to express the soul of woman in the person of the Blessed Virgin Mary. From the Madonnas painted by Raphael and Michelangelo, Botticelli and Ghirlandajo, there shines forth an inner beauty of supernatural grace and spiritual attraction. This is the ideal which the Church holds up for all women to imitate.

In the person of Mary, the Mother of Jesus, we have a combination of all the charm, all the glory, all the virtues both of maidenhood and of motherhood. She is the Virgin Mother whose mission was foretold in the Old Testament by the prophet Isaias; the Virgin saluted in the New Testament by the Archangel Gabriel. She is the woman "above all women glorified, our tainted nature's solitary boast; purer than foam on central ocean tost," as the poet Wordsworth so beautifully expresses it. When we review the life of our Blessed Lady we are impressed with this one fact above all others — her fidelity to her vocation of maidenhood and of motherhood, her life as a virgin and a mother. In fulfilling that vocation, Mary summed up in her own person all that is most admirable in womanhood.

Virginity has not always been regarded with favor in this world of ours. In ancient times, virginity was a concept quite foreign to the pagan mind. Yet even in pre-Christian days there was one exception. The vestal virgins at Rome, who kept the sacred fire burning without interruption in the temple of their goddess, were obliged to lead virginal lives. There was something appealing in the thought of virginity in the midst of pagan superstition. Chastity invested these pagan priestesses with a touch of the divine.

Our Blessed Lady, however, by her example of virginity spread a new aura around the practice of this virtue, changed the whole course of tradition for all future generations, and set a new ideal of womanly beauty. In response to the angel's message that she had been chosen to be the mother of the Messias, Mary replied with a simple question: "How shall this happen, since I do not know man?" With these words a new ideal of spiritual and inner beauty was substituted for that mere external and vanishing beauty which was embodied in the art of ancient Greece and Rome. Ever since that day tens of thousands of young women have emulated the example of the Blessed Virgin Mary and have dedicated themselves to the service of God in a state of virginity.

There is need to emphasize once more the value of chastity and modesty in the ranks of the rising generation. In the face of the many temptations that beset youth in the areas of entertainment, dress, books and periodicals, and especially in the unrestrained freedom of social intercourse which secular attitudes and customs sanction, it becomes progressively more difficult to maintain a Christian standard of purity and decency. Mere human appeal is insufficient to cope with the innate forces of evil. Social standards of decency must be imbued with spiritual ideals; and our youth must be fortified with supernatural grace if they are to be rescued from the sharp descent into lustful self-indulgences. The example of our Blessed Lady and her powerful intercession are the most effective means to ensure the practice of the virtue of chastity, which sublimates and ennobles both body and soul. "How beautiful is the chaste generation with glory; . . . it is known both with God and with men."

Mary is known, loved, and honored under two distinct titles: we address her reverently both as the Blessed Virgin and also the Mother of God. It was at the Council of Ephesus in 431 that the Church, after intense debate with the Nestorian heretics, vindicated this latter title of Mary's as incontestable for all future times. She is indeed the Mother of God by reason of the divinity of Jesus, her Son. She is also our Mother by reason of the gift that Jesus made to us from the cross: "Behold thy Mother. . . . Woman, behold thy son."

Motherhood is the high vocation to which the majority of women are called. The degree in which they are faithful to the responsibilities of motherhood marks the high or low level of our Christian culture and civilization. From time immemorial, the heritage of faith has been in the keeping of the home. It is in the home that the lessons of faith and virtue are first learned. Authority rests with the father, and the duties he performs reflect the overruling providence of our Father in heaven; but the most persuasive and lasting influences in the home, especially during the children's formative years, are the gentle ministrations of motherly love. The lessons which a child learns from a mother's lips, and even more from her example, leave an indelible mark.

There are some who seem to take offense at the sight of thousands honoring Mary, as if the honor due to her divine Son were lessened by the honor paid to her. But this is not so. Wherever devotion to the Blessed Virgin has flourished, there also the divine prerogatives have been safeguarded. It is inherently impossible to separate the Mother from the Son. True religion, with its emphasis on the doctrines of the Blessed Trinity, the Incarnation, the Redemption, the Church, and the entire sacramental system, is inevitably promoted, strengthened, and made vital in proportion as Christians invoke the name of Mary and pay her homage.

It may rightly be said that love and devotion to Mary is a mark of the universality of the Church. Wherever the true religion flourishes, there inevitably the names of Jesus and Mary will be joined together. When we review the history of Marian devotion, we are reminded of the words of the Magnificat: "Behold, henceforth all generations shall call me blessed; because He who is mighty has done great things for me, and holy is His name."

There are many celebrated shrines of the Blessed Virgin Mary scattered throughout the Catholic countries of the world: Lourdes, Fatima, Loreto, Einsiedeln, Czestochowa, Walsingham, and others come readily to mind. Those who are not acquainted with Catholic devotions frequently misinterpret the purpose of a shrine or the meaning of a pilgrimage. There are some who think that a shrine is a place where miracles take place, or that people go thither on pilgrimage to be cured of physical illness or disease. It is true that many times, through the intercession of our Blessed Lady or the saints, God has been pleased to manifest His power and His mercy, but ordinarily the chief purpose of a shrine is to focus attention on a particular devotion, a particular saint, or on some particular mystery of religion. The benefits obtained at a shrine or a place of pilgrimage are primarily spiritual: special supernatural graces which beget an increase of Christian virtues and a closer union with God.

A hundred years ago the little peasant girl Bernadette Soubirous saw Our Lady poised in dazzling splendor on a shelf of rock in the hills outside Lourdes. Repeatedly the Virgin appeared to her chosen client and always the burden of her message was the same: Do penance and pray! The prayer which Mary recited with Bernadette was the Rosary, indicating a certain predilection for this great devotion. For more than a hundred years that hallowed spot in southern France has been the scene of marvelous benedictions; from every part of the world the children of Mary have gone in pilgrimage to that shrine to pay her homage.

Forty-three years ago our Blessed Lady again made another appearance here on earth. This time it was at Fatima in Portugal, and the recipients of her favor were three shepherd children from the nearby village of Iria. On the thirteenth day of six consecutive months, from May to October of the year 1917, the Mother of God appeared to these children and told them that great calamities threatened the world unless there was repentance for sin and conversion to God. Again the burden of the heavenly message was: Do penance, and pray. In spite of the overwhelming evidence which testified to the truth of the apparitions and the genuine character of the revelations, the world remained skeptical or inattentive. As a result, the evils which were foretold have been visited on us in these latter days. People did not take the practice of their religion seriously; they did not do penance; they did not pray. Russia in consequence has not been converted, but instead has flooded the world with her evil propaganda and has begun a ruthless aggression against both the spiritual and temporal welfare of mankind. At Fatima our Blessed Lady once more pleaded that we practice devotion to the Rosary as a powerful means of intercession with her divine Son.

The beautiful devotion of the Rosary has had a long and venerable tradition in the history of the Church. It goes back to St. Dominic and his heroic struggle against the Albigensian heresy in southern France. The power of the Rosary to bring help and to avert evil is based on the merits of the Redemption and the honored place which Mary occupies in the whole plan of our salvation. Saints and sinners have extolled her praises in the telling of the beads. Scholars of the Church have waxed eloquent over the mysteries of religion which the Rosary recalls so vividly to mind. Children of every age have lisped the Pater Noster and the Ave Maria with sincere faith and simple devotion. In times of crisis, when the forces of evil were on the march and the fabric of Christian civilization was threatened with destruction, the Popes have again and again summoned the faithful to take the rosary in hand and appeal to Our Lady for protection and succor.

The feast of the Holy Rosary, originally known as the feast of Our Lady of Victory, was inaugurated by the saintly pontiff Pius V after the great Christian victory at the battle of Lepanto. After the lapse of centuries it is difficult for us to recapture the thrill of joy which animated all European nations at the news of this signal defeat of the age-old enemy of Christian civilization. For eight centuries a life and death struggle had been waged between the forces of Islam and those of Christianity; between the crescent and the cross; between the narrow fanaticism of Mohammed and the universal charity of Christ. Islamism began its march of conquest in the eighth century after

Christ and in a brief span of years laid waste the garden of the Church. Asia Minor, North Africa, and Visigothic Spain, where Christianity had long flourished, came under the domination of the Moslem hordes. Fire and sword swept away the entire structure of the Church and its Christian institutions in this area. All Europe was aroused to combat the peril; one crusade after the other was organized to defend Christian truth and morality.

Anyone who looks upon the crusades as a mere adventure of romantic chivalry, or a mystical nostalgia for ground made sacred by the living footsteps of the Saviour, fails utterly to interpret the comprehensive mind and high Christian statesmanship of the Papacy. The very existence of the faith under the providence of God was at stake in this mighty struggle. The battle of Lepanto was the climax and victorious consummation of these centuries of Christian effort. When the Turkish fleet was destroyed by Don John of Austria in the Gulf of Corinth in 1571 at the battle of Lepanto, the Mediterranean was once again made safe for peaceful commerce; but, more important, the Christian faith was safe at last from Mohammedan perversion.

As happens so often in sacred history, the great issues of divine right and human freedom were finally settled not so much by force of arms as by humble prayer and simple trust in God's protecting providence. While the contending fleets clashed in battle and great deeds of heroism were recorded, Pope Pius V was exhorting the faithful to follow his leadership in prayer and penance. For days the Christian populace marched in procession to the churches, devoutly reciting our Lady's Rosary. As David, clad not in military armor but in God's protection, fought Goliath, so the Christians fought at Lepanto. No wonder God gave them victory!

Incarnation is utterly impossible without an understanding
of Mary's part both as Virgin Immaculate and as Mother of
God. That which was true in earliest Christian times is true
today. Through the Mother we approach the Son; through
Mary we come to Christ.

XXXVIII

SAINTS AND THE RELIGIOUS LIFE

IN SECULAR tradition it is customary to memorialize the
birthday of the great men of the world. In the tradition
of the Church it is not the birthday which counts, but rather
the day of death. The glorification of a human life, in the eyes
of the Church, belongs not to its beginning, but to its end. Only
if the end denotes a final victory over sin and confirms the
sure attainment of virtue, can we speak of triumph. Man
begins his earthly existence estranged from God through
original sin; but through the grace of Jesus Christ he can
finish his earthly sojourn as a son of God. When a man or
woman completes a life of heroic virtue, the Church celebrates
the fact by placing the name of the individual in the calendar
of the saints. We honor and revere the saints both because
of what they were and because of what they did. They are
God's noblemen and they lived as such.

No two saints are alike. Every one of those whom the
Church has raised to the dignity of the altar has something in
common with all other saints, but he has something also which
is distinctively his own. St. Peter and St. John were different
from each other in many ways, but they were alike in their
intense love of Christ. St. Benedict, St. Francis, St. Dominic,
and St. Ignatius, the founders of the great Religious Orders of
the West, were both alike and different. Their objectives were
the same, their methods were not. Their differences stem not

379

only from their distinct personalities, but also from the different problems they faced.

St. Benedict was the founder of religious monasticism in the West of Europe. He lived in an age when the old Roman empire had broken up; its unity had been destroyed by invading armies of barbarian tribes; its center of law and order completely dissolved. The problem he faced was one both of Christianizing and of civilizing the great mass of people who swarmed into the old Roman states from the outer world of pagan barbarism. To achieve his purpose he adopted the principle of establishing at regular intervals, throughout Europe, monastic centers from which religion and culture could radiate. We still have historical remnants of the old system, especially along the East coast of England from Canterbury to Durham. Here in our own country in California we have an illustration of the same system. Junípero Serra, who followed the Benedictine pattern, established his mission centers about forty miles apart, from San Diego to San Francisco.

Every Religious Order has its distinctive spirit. That of the oldest, the Benedictines, is set forth in their motto: "Orare et laborare." Their great objective was to establish model communities of Christian civilized life which could serve as shining examples for the disorganized life of the country about them. For centuries their monasteries constituted green and fertile oases in the desert of European barbarism which followed close upon the breakup of the Roman empire. A fixed center of activity was needed for their purpose, and hence the Benedictine monks took a vow of stability in their respective monasteries. From these centers radiated their Christian culture.

About seven hundred years after St. Benedict came St. Francis of Assisi. His was an age of rapid social change. People were moving from the open country into towns and cities. Prosperity was on the increase, and with it came a spirit of pride and luxury. The old settled communities, living on the land, had depended to a great extent upon the Benedictine monasteries as the religious, social, and cultural centers of their lives. The new towns and cities, however, were not within the reach of this monastic influence. St. Francis became more and more aware of this situation. In order to bring the Gospel and the ministrations of religion to these uprooted people, he established an order which would have great flexibility of movement. Instead of adhering to the policy of remaining in one place, emphasized by the Benedictines with their vow of stability, he bade his friars to disperse far and wide over the entire country and go to the people wherever they might be, rather than have them come to him and his followers. He insisted on humility and simplicity to counteract luxury and pride; on detachment from property and its responsibilities in order that his community could always travel light like scouts instead of as an army weighted down with heavy baggage. He wanted no fixed monasteries that would handicap the free and easy movement of his disciples in their roving campaign for Christ.

St. Francis of Assisi captured the imagination of his own and succeeding generations by his humility, simplicity, and overpowering love of his fellow men. He was the troubadour of Lady Poverty at a time when the world had grown fat with riches and self-indulgence. He was the knight errant of God, singing in lyrical phrases the beauty of God's creation and calling on all nature to offer homage to its Lord. Francis made the highways and the byways of the world his pulpit and his parish. He brought Christian truth and ideals out of the cloister into the full stream of human life. His concepts of

Christian living were perhaps too ideal to stand the wear and tear of a practical world, but they served their purpose of lifting up the minds and hearts of men from material things to those that are spiritual and supernatural.

St. Dominic was a contemporary of St. Francis, but his mission in the Church was totally different. The problem which he faced was one of heresy; and the heresy which he was charged to combat was one of a peculiarly malignant character — the heresy of the Albigenses in southern France. If this heresy were allowed to spread, it would dissolve not only true religion but all social order and morality. There was need of a body of preachers who could counteract the insidious doctrines of the Albigenses by vigorously proclaiming the ancient truths of the Christian faith. St. Dominic had to make his appeal to the mind as well as to the heart. His religious community, therefore, became known as the Order of Preachers. Ever since the days of Dominic the emphasis of the Dominican Order has been on doctrine; its strongest appeal to the intellect of man.

The Dominicans devoted themselves to intellectual pursuits and framed the great synthesis of knowledge, both human and divine, at a time when the long night of learning had ended and the sun of intellectual advance burst with full effulgence over the thirteenth century. St. Thomas Aquinas and St. Albertus Magnus were the great luminaries of the Order at the universities of Paris and Bonn.

It was more than three hundred years after the time of St. Francis and St. Dominic that St. Ignatius appeared on the scene of history. The conditions of the times are a key once more to an understanding of his character. His mission in the Church was to counteract the evils of the Religious Revolt of the sixteenth century. The place of his Society was in the

forefront of the campaign to defend the faith. There was a new
ferment among people, something akin to the spirit which
dominates our own times under Marxist Communism. Whereas
in previous periods of religious upheaval, some particular doctrine was called into question, in this case the very principle
of unity was assailed. The authority of the Church itself, under
Christ's Vicar, was repudiated; the priesthood was attacked
as a usurpation of power; the sacramental system was denied
for the most part; and the principle of private judgment was
proclaimed as a source of a new religious freedom. Mixed up
in a hopelessly tangled fashion was a multiplicity of political,
social, and economic factors, all of which intensified the religious confusion and spirit of revolt. The need of the times was
a return to a deep interior spiritual life and a recognition of the
principle of loyalty and obedience to divinely established authority. This St. Ignatius was quick to understand. Like every
true reformer, he began first with himself. He retired into deep
solitude in the cave of Manresa. Solitude is the home of greatness. He made his own soul right with God, and then, when he
had made himself ready, he proceeded to help others. From
his meditations came the *Spiritual Exercises* — one of the greatest means of sanctification for the human soul which the
Church has ever developed. From his organizing genius also
came the Society of Jesus, built upon the principle of unquestioning obedience and loyal devotion to the Pope. His was a
soldier's attitude transferred from the military to the spiritual
order. Under their military leader turned saint and scholar,
the Jesuits captured once more the citadel of learning, and
beat back the waves of Lutheran and Calvinist revolutionary
errors.

There have been other saints who founded great Religious
Orders. For example, we might mention the Order of Cister-

cians, exponents of an austerity of life and a fiery eloquence, which became, in the persons of Bernard of Clairvaux and Peter the Hermit, one of the instruments of the great crusades. The defense of Christendom against the onslaughts of Mohammed's fanatical followers was in great part the fruit of their efforts.

In considering specific Religious Orders and their saintly founders, however, we must never lose sight of the basic fact that it was Christ Himself who laid the ground plan of all Religious Orders when He recommended as a way of Christian perfection the voluntary pursuit of poverty, chastity, and obedience. The saintly founders of the great Religious communities merely chose different methods to activate these counsels of perfection. They also chose different objectives according to the exigencies of time and place.

The needs of the Church differ from age to age according to the fluctuating pattern of human existence. At one time the emphasis will be on works of charity, at another it will be on the work of education and Christian scholarship, at still another it will be on the work of the foreign missions; but always it will be first and foremost on the work of personal sanctification.

All exponents of the Religious life stress the importance of detachment from the world in order that there may be attachment to the things of God. The human heart has always found satisfaction and comfort in earthly possessions, in family life, in the assertion of self-will, autonomy, independence. It is because we are weighted down with the effects of original sin that these normal desires and natural inclinations impede our spiritual progress and rise up as obstacles in our path toward perfection and the attainment of our ultimate destiny as sons of God. Concupiscence is the enemy within; the Evil Spirit himself is the enemy without. Against these enemies

the great weapons are the religious vows: against the concupiscence of the eyes (avarice) there is the vow of poverty;
against the concupiscence of the flesh (lust) there is the vow
of chastity; and against the pride of life there is the vow of obedience. Total abstinence from lawful things is a heroic measure,
and although not mandatory in God's commandments, it is
nevertheless most effective in warding off the danger of excess,
and most helpful in concentrating on the one thing necessary.
That "one thing" is salvation, perfection, holiness. The vows
of poverty, chastity, and obedience remove effectively the great
hindrances to perfection and set the soul free to seek God. In
the Religious life there is indeed mortification of the senses
and self-denial; but these things are negative and avail little
in themselves unless they are the prelude to a greater growth
in grace and wisdom before God and men.

As we look back over the past, we can see in better perspective the problems which the Church in general has faced —
problems which entered also into the cloister. One of these
problems was that of maintaining unity and coherence in Religious life in spite of the differences of language, attitudes, and
traditions inherited from the past by the Catholic immigrants
who flooded the shores of this country. The danger of schism
was always present in the organization of Religious life in
general; it was not always easy, even in the monasteries and
convents to avoid the nationalist influences which would lead
to friction, discontent, and possible dissolution of community
life. We owe it to the wisdom, tact, and charity of our early
pioneers that we came through that period successfully.

Then there was the equally grave problem of making the
transition to the life of a new country. There was a new
language to learn, there were new conditions to meet, new resources to develop. It was an age of brick and mortar as well

as an age of adaptation and assimilation. New techniques had to be learned in the administration of schools, hospitals, and a variety of charitable institutions. All of this had to be done without losing sight of the ultimate objective, which is, and always will be, personal holiness. To undertake too much would have been rash; to progress too slowly would have been shortsighted. There was always a nice balance to be maintained between courage and prudence. Thank God that the Church and our Religious communities came through these difficulties with undiminished zeal and untarnished ideals!

Today we face the future with a considerable measure of anxiety. This anxiety is precipitated more by the spirit of secularism which pervades our national life than by the external enemy which is bent upon the conquest of our historic Christian civilization. We can defy the enemy outside our gates if we are strong within. Our strength, however, rests not so much in military power, necessary as that may be, but in our virtue. It is our Christian principles, and our consistent practice of them, which count most. In this ominous struggle the Church not only in her official capacity, but in the life of her Religious communities, must be alert to the danger, and active in preparing to meet it. This is a time of penance and of prayer. It is a time for translating our faith from a mere passive possession into an active and public manifestation of Christian truth; a time for impregnating our laws, our policies, our social institutions with the spirit of Christ. To help do this effectively, members of Religious Orders must create a stronger impact on the minds and hearts of their novices and students. They must help to create a deep sense of personal responsibility in the ranks of our youth, a responsibility that will flow over and exert an influence on the total social environment of which they are a part. There has been too much spiritual self-complacency and not enough dynamic conviction that Christ is the only source of salvation and that there is no other name under heaven by which we can be saved. This holds good for the kingdom of God here upon earth and for our temporal welfare, as well as for the fulfillment of our eternal destiny. We must replace secularism with the spirit of Christ and make religion once more a vital influence in public as well as in private life. This is the great vocation to which all of us, and especially the members of Religious Orders, must be wholly dedicated.

XXXIX

FAITH PUT INTO PRACTICE

NO ONE who gives serious thought to the matter can fail to recognize the great pastoral value of promoting a fuller understanding of the sacred liturgy and a more active participation in the public worship of the Church. Interest in the sacred liturgy is not a matter of personal choice. Man's first duty is to worship his Creator. The sacred liturgy is worship; it is the highest form of worship, for it is the united worship of Christ, our Head and High Priest, with His ordained minister and the faithful who, as members of Christ's Mystical Body, have the privilege of participating in His worship. Since the holy sacrifice of the Mass, the sacraments, and the divine office constitute the essential liturgy, the liturgy, as such, must be regarded as the indispensable source of that spirit by which the Christian is formed.

The liturgy, then, is and was intended to be a divinely ordained means of Christian perfection; and, therefore, when the full significance of this fact is overlooked by both priest and layman, as it has been to some extent in modern times, a restoration in accordance with the mind of the Church is clearly in order. It was just such a restoration that St. Pius X officially inaugurated more than half a century ago when he took certain initial steps toward the reform of Church music, the practice of frequent and early Communion, and the reorganization, in part, of the breviary according to its original structure. The saintly Pontiff indicated that this was only a beginning, but he expressed his mind clearly when he stated that the liturgy is a "primary and indispensable means of Christian perfection." What St. Pius began, his successors have continued; and step by step the faithful are coming to a better understanding of, and a more profitable participation in, the liturgy. Today the missal has become in large part a handbook of devotion at Mass for the faithful, in contrast to the almost complete oblivion with which it was surrounded fifty years ago. The *Missa recitata* has stimulated the active participation of the laity in the Eucharistic liturgy; and the congregational responses, together with congregational singing of the parts of the Mass, as yet only begun, mark another advance in the revitalization of the liturgy.

In his celebrated encyclical *Mediator Dei*, Pius XII elaborated a full treatise on the liturgy. He gave positive instructions to the Bishops of the Church, calling for the establishment of liturgical commissions in their respective dioceses. This instruction presupposes that there are specific functions which such commissions are to exercise. Evidently there exist certain deficiencies with respect to a right understanding of the liturgy and its full significance in the devotional life of the Christian community; otherwise there would be no need of such commissions. Private devotions, although good in themselves whenever approved by lawful Church authority, are nevertheless not to be given equal status with the official liturgy of the Church. What the Supreme Pontiffs wish to achieve is not only a better understanding of the public and official worship of the Church, but also a more active participation of the laity in the liturgy itself.

It is important at the outset to rid our minds of certain misconceptions. When we speak of the Church's liturgy, we do not mean primarily the external rites and ceremonies, nor an increased emphasis merely on the solemnity and accuracy with which they are performed. Equally erroneous is the assumption that the liturgy is something with which the priests of the Church alone are concerned, as if the laity, when assisting at divine worship, were to be mere spectators at a sacred pageant. Pius XI states in a pregnant phrase that the liturgy is "the principal organ of the ordinary magisterium of the Church." It is in fact the faith of the Church put into practice by means of official formulas of prayer. The liturgy in its true sense, then, is not merely the official regulation of the external worship of the Church, much less an effort to revive medieval traditions or any other form of antiquarianism, but rather that organized body of prayers and sacred rites which the Church has sanctioned as the expression of the piety and devotion of the Mystical Body of Christ. There is a valid distinction, therefore, between private devotion and public devotion in the Church. The liturgy is a re-enactment of the great mystery of faith. It is essentially the reproduction in, by, and for the Church of the act of our Lord which in His passion and death accomplished our salvation. It is the entire mystery of the cross, inseparably connected with the triumph of the resurrection and the ascension, whereby the grace of salvation is communicated to mankind.

The liturgy presupposes that when the people of God come together for common worship they do so not as individuals, each intent upon his own private prayer or devotion, but for a common purpose and a great social act of divine worship. Not only individually do men owe allegiance to God but collectively as well: as members of human society and particularly as members of that sacred society established by Christ as His kingdom here on earth — His Church. In the new dispensation of grace, the form of worship which has been divinely established for the Christian community is the re-enactment of the Eucharistic Sacrifice, by which Christ as Head of His Mystical Body renews and repeats the great act of redemption. In the Sacrifice of the Mass, therefore, Christ speaks for us to the Father in heaven from the altar, as He did once before from the cross. The Holy Eucharist is the supreme act of worship — being the worship of Christ Himself, rendered to the Father, first, in His own name as Son of God and Son of Man, and then in the name of those who through His grace constitute His Mystical Body. In this sense the Mass belongs to the whole Church — first to Christ the Head, and then to the members of His Church, His Mystical Body. It belongs to the priest, who represents Christ officially, but also to the faithful who through Baptism have been incorporated into Christ. As St. Paul writes in his letter to the Ephesians: "Therefore, you are now no longer strangers and foreigners, but you are citizens with the saints and members of God's household: you are built upon the foundation of the apostles and prophets with Christ Jesus Himself as the chief corner-stone. In Him the whole structure is closely fitted together and grows into a temple holy in the Lord; in Him you too are being built together into a dwelling place for God in the Spirit."

The liturgy, moreover, is not only the supreme act of worship of the entire Church; it is also the bearer of salvation to the members of the Church. The liturgy is in this sense a spiritual highway between heaven and earth, between the Crea-tor and the creature, leading souls to God and bringing God to souls. In the liturgy the fullness of the fruits of redemption is made applicable to the souls of men in the sacraments of the Church, which, together with the Mass, constitute a sort of spiritual solar system. The other sacraments are related to the

Holy Eucharist as the planets to the sun, receiving from it their life and light. The sacraments are not so many separate or parallel channels of grace, independent of one another, but constitute, rather, together with the Eucharist, one unified system of salvation. The liturgy of the sacraments is therefore an essential part of the pastoral ministry, and, in the words of the Supreme Pontiffs, the most significant and formative element in the life of the Christian community.

Not only the sacraments inseparably associated with the Holy Eucharist, but also the divine office as contained in the official breviary, forms an essential part of the sacred liturgy. It is true that the recitation of the divine office is of strict obligation only for priests and certain Religious, but it has its place also in the public worship of the whole Church. If its recitation is not a matter of strict obligation, it is nevertheless highly recommended. There was a time when Vespers or Compline constituted, even here in our own country, an integral part of the Sunday worship in our parish churches. Unfortunately this practice has been allowed to lapse for a variety of reasons. Chief among these reasons is the poor state of instruction of the faithful in this phase of the liturgy. It is to be hoped that with better understanding of the incomparable value of the divine office as a medium of devotion, a well-instructed laity will renew, under the leadership of the priests, a deep interest in this form of prayer.

We look to the priests to lend their warm encouragement and prudent guidance to the members of their parishes who are manifesting a growing interest in the sacred liturgy. In a matter so vitally connected with the very mission of the Church, no priest can be indifferent. He should welcome this manifestation of a renewed interest in religion, and assume his rightful position of leadership in it. The success or failure of a liturgical program in a parish depends in every case on the priests of the parish.

It is highly desirable that our people learn to sing the High Mass as a congregation. As Pius XII has said, the dialogue Mass cannot replace the High Mass, which possesses its own special dignity on account of the impressive character of its ritual and the magnificence of its ceremonies. The Holy Father has exhorted the Bishops to promote congregational singing since it arouses the faith and the piety of the faithful. "Let the full harmonious singing of our people rise to heaven like the bursting of a thunderous sea and let them testify by the melody of their song to the unity of their hearts and minds, as becomes brothers and the children of the same Father." The students of our elementary and high schools have been taught for many years to sing the Mass and the hymns of the liturgy. It is deplorable that they should become mute onlookers at Mass once they leave school.

We likewise urge that our people be taught to participate actively in the Low Mass through the *Missa recitata* or the dialogue Mass, according to the directives of the Holy See. Occasionally hymns should be sung. The singing of the hymns, however, must not become so regular that our people lose the practice of following the Mass with the missal. It is well to remind them that when they do follow the Mass in their missals, it is not necessary that they read every prayer. Such rapid reading often results in a failure to give proper, prayerful attention to any of the prayers.

No program of participation will be successful unless the people have been prepared sufficiently beforehand by a thorough and repeated explanation of the reasons why they should take an active external part in the worship of the Church.

We offer our warmest encouragement to all who seek to bring greater glory to God and to share more deeply in the rich graces of the supernatural life by seeking to participate more intelligently and more fruitfully in the liturgy of the Church.

Part VIII

MAN IN RELATION TO

THE END OF LIFE

"He who believes in Me, even if he die, shall live; and whoever lives and believes in Me, shall never die."

XL

MORS PRETIOSA

DEATH is a fact of human experience as universal as life itself. Our attitude toward death is determined by our attitude toward life. If human life has no origin in divine omnipotence, then death has no meaning. The mystery of death, therefore, can be solved only by unravelling the mystery of life. We must seek and find the answers to the burning questions that have ever haunted the mind of man: What is life? Whence do we come? Why are we here? Whither do we go?

To these all-important questions the agnostic or rationalist answers: "I do not know." Science tells him the answers to many questions. It soars aloft to discover the mystery of the firmament; it plumbs the depths of the earth and the sea to investigate the laws of matter and force; it searches the records of the past in order to trace the pattern of social relationships. But science stands confused and speechless before the mystery of life itself. Its laboratory technique and all its apparatus of scholarship are unable to probe the mystery of human life in such a way as to answer the fundamental questions: Whence do we come? Why are we here? Whither are we going?

What is life? The worldling, who will not lift himself above his sense experience of mere material things, answers: "I do not care." "Life for the moment only" is his motto. "Eat, drink, and be merry, for tomorrow we die."

Can this attitude be rightly described as anything but an attempt to escape reality? There is no honest examination of the evidence in favor of a future life; no serious inquiry into the facts concerning a divine revelation. It is merely an attitude of irresponsibility or an attitude of spiritual inertia. Life for such a one is a riddle, because he is too indifferent to search for its meaning — or perhaps because he is afraid that he may find the answer an inconvenient and disturbing one.

What is life? The man of religion answers with conviction: "It is a gift of God, a trusteeship, a time of probation." Man was created by the Almighty according to His own image and likeness. Life is an endowment of intelligence and will, so that we may know God, serve Him, and be forever happy in our love of Him. St. Paul, in writing to the Romans, states the case briefly and clearly: "For since the creation of the world His invisible attributes are clearly seen . . . , being understood through the things that are made." Our Lord Jesus Christ assures us: "Now this is everlasting life, that they may know Thee, the only true God, and Him whom Thou hast sent, Jesus Christ."

The mystery of life cannot be solved by the sensualist nor by the rationalist, but only by the man of faith. "Faith," says St. Paul, "is the substance of things to be hoped for, the evidence of things that are not seen." Faith is indeed concerned with the invisible, the eternal, the supernatural; but it is not a nostalgic adherence to sentiment, nor an association of childhood fancies. Faith is not an escape from reality or logic. Faith rests on evidence. It is an act of deliberate judgment based upon rational and cogent premises. Faith is not science, nor does it pretend to be. It is not a mathematical demonstration but a conclusion based upon legitimate testimony.

There are two sources whence all knowledge is ultimately derived. One rests on observation or experimental science; the other rests on faith, both human and divine. Each has its own distinctive procedure and follows rigorously the laws of evidence. Science verifies its hypotheses and conclusions by means of renewed experiments. No one can verify by experience the truth of divine creation nor the facts of Christ's birth, death, resurrection, and ascension. History cannot be repeated. These facts can be verified, however, by the testimony of contemporary witnesses. Christ came into this world as a witness to the truth. Being a witness, He demonstrated His credibility, first, by the fulfillment of ancient prophecies, and, secondly, by His godlike command over all the forces of nature through well-attested miracles. The doctrine that He preached and the unexampled beauty and holiness of His life gave cumulative force to the authenticity of His mission. His word bears the seal of divine approval. The testimony which He gave is the key to the mystery of life; it alone conveys an intelligent explanation of death.

A man of faith feels no sense of panic or despair at the approach of death. "He who is just lives by faith," says the Scripture. A man of faith does not wear his religion on his sleeve, nor accommodate his words and actions to mere pious platitudes. He does not hesitate to take a public stand or to declare his convictions when circumstances call for it. He is mindful of the words of our Lord: "Everyone who acknowledges Me before men, I also will acknowledge him before My Father in heaven." A man of faith makes frequent confession of his faith in words, but he makes even more frequent confession of his faith in that which speaks louder than words — namely, action.

Christ came into this world to guarantee us the fulfillment of life's desires. "I came," He says, "that they may have life, and have it more abundantly." It is not a restricted form of life of which Christ speaks, nor happiness diluted with periods of bitterness and strife; not a life circumscribed by time and place, nor subject to the hazards of sickness, insecurity, and death; but a life full and overflowing, without limit or imperfection. Death is the gateway to this life. In the revealed word of God there is a future life with full satisfaction of the intellect in its desire to know the ultimate truth and full satisfaction of the will to possess the plentitude of beauty and goodness. There is for the man of faith an everlasting life made perfect and complete in the beatific vision, wherein we shall see God face to face and know Him even as we are known. Religious enthusiasm, some might say; but, no, this is stark reality, even if it be a truth which is grasped only by those who have laid aside the pride of intellect and see with the vision of supernatural faith.

"I go to prepare a place for you . . . ; that where I am, there you also may be." Only lips divine would dare to speak such words or hold out such hopes. It is a promise given to every man; yet it is a promise which carries with it a condition. To Martha, at the grave of her brother Lazarus, Christ spoke words of consolation: "I am the resurrection and the life; he who believes in Me, even if he die, shall live; and whoever lives and believes in Me, shall never die."

Here, then, is the condition. It is not only faith in the word of Christ, but conformity to His teaching which guarantees the promise, "Whoever lives and believes in Me, shall never die." It is a living faith which Christ requires. He demands the homage of our minds in humble submission to His word, but likewise He demands the homage of our wills in fruitful action according to His commandments. Religion and morality, then, are inseparable. Without clear and definite doctrine there can be no religion. Without faith, good works soon wither on the stem of selfishness.

The solemn ceremonies with which the Church lays to rest the faithful departed constitute an effective lesson for the living, as well as a powerful prayer for the deceased. The great truths of religion are emphasized in the liturgy, reminding us of the immortality of the soul, the resurrection of the body, and life everlasting. The ceremonies are likewise a token of sympathy and a source of comfort for the bereaved. They are, moreover, evidence of the respect and reverence with which the Church regards the human body itself. The body is the instrument of the soul and shares to some extent in that dignity which God conferred on man when He created him to His own image and likeness. The body itself has been sanctified as the temple of the Holy Spirit. It has been cleansed in the waters of Baptism, anointed with holy oil in the Sacrament of Confirmation, and nourished with the heavenly food of the Holy Eucharist.

It is for this reason that the Church bids her ministers pay a tribute of respect to the deceased at the very first moment the body is brought into the House of the Lord. The sacred liturgy puts upon the lips of the priest the words of the psalmist: "Out of the depths I cry to You, O Lord. . . . Let Your ears be attentive to my voice in supplication." As the body is solemnly escorted up the aisle and placed at the foot of the altar, the prayer of supplication, first pronounced by King David, is intoned by the choir: "Have mercy on me, O God, in Your goodness; in the greatness of Your compassion wipe out my offense." Around the casket are placed the lighted candles, indicative of the faith which enlightened the soul during life. At the altar the priest offers the sacrifice of atonement, as Christ offered it at the last supper and on Calvary. All attention is concentrated on the fact that we are members of a sinful race, no matter what our personal merits may be in the sight of God. We all, without exception, stand in need of redemption. It is only through Christ our Saviour that we dare to hope for pardon and for a share in the everlasting glory of eternal life.

But once the sacrifice of atonement has been renewed on the altar, the Church turns her eyes away from the past and fixes her gaze upon the future. There is a significant change in the tone of the liturgy. As the last absolution is pronounced, there is a new note of triumph and rejoicing evident in the final ceremonies. With exultant voice the Church sings her farewell to the faithful departed: "Let the angels carry thee into paradise, and may the martyrs come to welcome thee on thy way, and lead thee into the holy city, Jerusalem."

In spite of the fact that we are familiar with the phenomenon of death from our earliest childhood, it is not until death penetrates our own family circle or the circle of our intimate friends and contemporaries that we realize fully the nature and the force of its visitation. The sorrow and pain which this breaking of the bonds of affection causes us is inescapable, but it can be assuaged by the thought that the soul is immortal and can live forever with God in a world of perfect and enduring happiness. This conviction, this hope, this consolation is not merely a matter of wishful thinking, not merely a desire of continuing our personality beyond the grave, but a sober reality founded upon objective fact and capable of clear and definite demonstration. If we were dependent merely upon our own limited human experience, we might, it is true, be surrounded by doubt and uncertainty, but God has not left us at the mercy of our own feeble intellect or vain imaginings. He has spoken clearly and with authority. He has given us a revelation of hidden truth through the prophets and His Son. "We would not, brethren, have you ignorant," says St. Paul. "concerning those who are asleep, lest you should grieve, even as others who have no hope. For if we believe that Jesus died and rose again, so with Him God will bring those also who have fallen asleep through Jesus. . . . Wherefore, comfort one another with these words."

It is a strange commentary on the blindness and frivolity of this world that it should order its existence for the most part as if this present life were to endure forever, and as if the next life were a mere temporary state. This is a sign of the topsy-turvy attitude of the world. It keeps putting first things last, and last things first. It makes the things of time more important than the things of eternity; attributes to the things of the body greater value than to the things of the soul. If we found practical businessmen disregarding their business information, their data, their graphs and charts in similar manner, we would consider them stupid or slothful. Why is it that men act so differently in matters of spiritual and eternal interests?

The only explanation is that either they do not know the arguments and proof for the credibility of divine faith or they fail utterly to meditate upon its consequences. I think it is safe to say that there is not one person out of five who seriously makes a study of the evidences of religion. A mere cursory examination will not do. Christ still puts the question as forcefully to the present generation as in the days when He walked the earth: "What do you think of the Christ? Whose Son is He?" Christ still warns with awful solemnity: "He who believes and is baptized shall be saved, but he who does not believe shall be condemned." These may seem to be harsh and uncompromising words coming from the gentle Christ, but they cannot be evaded. The plea of ignorance will not avail except for those who had no way of learning the truth.

There are certain questions to which every sincere person, as the years of his earthly life roll on, must give an answer:

Who is Christ? Is He indeed the Son of God?

What did He say of Himself? What proofs did He offer?

Did Christ establish a way of life from which we cannot depart except at the risk of losing our souls?

Did Christ establish one Church to keep alive His teachings and to minister to us in spiritual things?

What right have we to reject Christ's teachings and commandments or to hold ourselves indifferent to what He said and did?

For those of us who have found the right answers to these questions, death holds no terror. If in our lives we have found the truth and have accommodated our lives to it, then with St. Paul we can say: "O death, where is thy victory? O death, where is thy sting?"

A WORD IN CONCLUSION

Archbishop Alter, speaking at the formal celebration of the jubilees of other Bishops and priests, has himself expressed thoughts that might fittingly conclude this volume commemorating his own golden jubilee:

"As we commemorate this jubilee and look back over the record of the past, we are made conscious of the fact that some of us are looking toward the setting sun, and step by step are making our way down the western slopes. *Advesperascit!* 'Stay with us (Lord), for it is getting toward evening, and the day is now far spent.' Even the junior members in our ranks are steadily moving forward to the great reunion in the kingdom of their High Priest. To us all Christ said, 'I go to prepare a place for you . . . ; that where I am, there you also may be.' This is the goal that each priest sets for himself when first he speaks the words: 'Introibo ad altare Dei.' It matters little which road we travel for there are diversities of ministry but the same Lord; there are varieties of workings but the same God who works all in all.

"There is no time when a Bishop is so conscious of his own shortcomings as when he looks back over the years from a vantage point, such as a jubilee celebration. He knows better than anyone else what blessed opportunities have been missed; what things have been left undone; how far short he has fallen of the high ideals which animated him on the day of his consecration. With his fellow priests he shares a sense of privilege and honor which the office of the priesthood confers. With

405

them also he shares a sense of humility and the hope of being united with them some day in the eternal priesthood of our Saviour. We look forward to that final reward, as St. Paul puts it, not as if we had already won the prize, already reached fulfillment. We only press on in hope of winning the mastery, as Christ Jesus has won the mastery over us. No, brethren, we do not claim to have the mastery already, but this at least we do; forgetting what we have left behind, intent on what lies before us, we press on with the goal in view, eager for the prize, God's heavenly summons in Christ Jesus."